AF772103

Handbook of Family Law

Handbook of
Family Law

Lester Wallman
Lawrence J. Schwarz

PRENTICE HALL
Englewood Cliffs, New Jersey 07632

Prentice-Hall International (UK) Limited, *London*
Prentice-Hall of Australia Pty. Limited, *Sydney*
Prentice-Hall Canada, Inc., *Toronto*
Prentice-Hall Hispanoamericana, S.A., *Mexico*
Prentice-Hall of India Private Limited, *New Delhi*
Prentice-Hall of Japan, Inc., *Tokyo*
Simon & Schuster Asia Pte. Ltd., *Singapore*
Editora Prentice-Hall do Brasil, Ltda., *Rio de Janeiro*

© 1989 *by*

PRENTICE-HALL, Inc.

Englewood Cliffs, NJ

All rights reserved. No part of this book may be reproduced in any form or by any means, without permission in writing from the publisher.

10 9 8 7 6 5 4 3 2 1

This publication is designed to provide accurate and authoritative information in regard to the subject matter covered. It is sold with the understanding that the publisher is not engaged in rendering legal, accounting, or other professional service. If legal advice or other expert assistance is required, the services of a competent professional person should be sought.
. . . *From the Declaration of Principles jointly adopted by a Committee of the American Bar Association and a Committee of Publishers and Associations.*

Library of Congress Cataloging-in-Publication Data

Wallman, Lester, 1929-
Handbook of family law / Lester Wallman, Lawrence J. Schwarz.
p. cm.
Includes index.
ISBN 0-13-377946-7
1. Domestic relations—United States. 2. Divorce—Law and Legislation—United States. I. Schwarz, Lawrence J., 1949-
II. Title.
KF505.W35 1989
346.7301'66—dc19 88-34855
[347.306166] CIP

ISBN 0-13-377946-7

PRENTICE HALL
BUSINESS & PROFESSIONAL DIVISION
A division of Simon & Schuster
Englewood Cliffs, New Jersey 07632

Acknowledgments

In preparing this handbook, the legal expertise of several individuals was sought and provided. Our special thanks go to David Pugh, Gerald Gasman, Susan Strawgate, and the late Martin Kramer, without whose help the completion of this guide would not have been possible. Also, the assistance of Judy DeVito in typing this manuscript cannot be forgotten and deserves special mention.

About the Authors

Lester Wallman is an attorney in New York City and is admitted to practice before the State Courts of New York. He obtained an L.L.B. from Brooklyn Law School in 1952 and an L.L.M. from New York University in 1954.

Mr. Wallman is a highly respected expert in the field of family law. *Town and Country Magazine* listed him as one of the best family law practitioners in America, and he was recently cited by Joyce Brothers in her latest best seller, *What Every Woman Ought to Know About Love and Marriage.* He was a member of the special ad hoc committee that wrote the New York State Equitable Distribution Law; former Chairman of the Committee on Legislation, Family Section, New York State Bar Association; former Vice-Chairman of the Committee on Federal Legislation, Family Law Section, American Bar Association; and is a fellow of the American Academy of Matrimonial Lawyers. In addition, Mr. Wallman is a member of the Legislative Policy Committee of the New York State Bar and was a special assistant on Family Law to the Deputy Minority Leader, New York State Assembly.

He has published numerous articles on family law, and his expertise in this field has resulted in his selection as a panelist on several major television network panel shows dealing with matrimonial law topics. In addition, he has been a guest lecturer for the New York State Academy of Trial Lawyers and other local Bar Associations throughout the Eastern Seaboard. Mr. Wallman is currently a partner in the New York City law firm of Wallman and Kramer.

Lawrence J. Schwarz is an attorney in Garden City, New York, and is admitted to practice before the State Courts of New York, the Federal Courts in the 2nd Circuit, and the U.S. Court of Military Appeals. He graduated with a B.A. from Columbia College in 1971 and obtained a J.D. from Notre Dame University School of Law in 1974.

Mr. Schwarz has published several articles and acquired expertise in family law as a director of the Cass County Legal Aid Clinic in Cassopolis, Michigan. Also, as a lawyer in the United States Army he has had extensive need to use his family law knowledge. He is currently an Assistant District Attorney in the Appeals Bureau of the Office of the District Attorney, Nassau County, N.Y.

What This Book Will Do for You

This handbook will enable you to handle quickly and efficiently the myriad of family law problems that your clients present to you. The book provides a step-by-step approach to solving problems associated with the days of courtship, the living-together period, marriage, and divorce. It provides you with the tools—sample contracts, wills, affidavits—that are essential in representing a client effectively. By utilizing this guide, you will be able to devote more time to understanding the client's problems, and less time to handling the *mechanics* of solving them.

The three chapters comprising Part I will enable you to solve the family law problems of the unmarried client. Today, now that formalized homosexual and unmarried heterosexual relationships have become commonplace, it is vital that you consider and address the needs created by these relationships. With Chapter 1 you will be able to breach and solve the legal difficulties encountered by homosexual and heterosexual couples who wish to retain their single status. Chapter 2 explores the legal rights of the unmarried mother re her child. In this regard, new blood tests for determining paternity will be discussed. The final chapter in this part covers premarital legal counseling.

Part II addresses the concerns facing the client during the period of marital bliss. We have provided detailed advice that will enable you to handle effectively adoption proceedings (Chapter 4) and the writing of the client's Will (Chapter 6). Also, counseling tips on the holding of joint property and filing joint tax returns will be discussed. Tax law changes brought about by the 1986 Tax Reform Act will be explained (Chapter 5). Surrogate motherhood will not be handled since it is a rapidly evolving and confusing area which could be the subject of a separate book. It should be noted, however, that since the "Baby M" New Jersey case, surrogate contracts may be enforceable, although the mother that bore the child may be entitled to visitation rights despite contractual provisions to the contrary.

Part III will center on your role as attorney during the early stages of marital disharmony. Chapter 7 will provide you with guidelines for determining whether steps should be taken to rehabilitate the marriage or to dissolve it. In Chapter 8, reconciliation agreements will be explored, and Chapter 9 will focus on the troubled marriage Will.

Part IV is the heart of this handbook. The four chapters in this part deal with, in depth, solutions to the problems engendered during the break-up of the marriage. Detailed guidance will be provided on: how to obtain restraining orders and temporary orders for custody and support; selection of legal alternatives (divorce, annulment, permanent separation); proceedings for separate maintenance; how, when, and where to negotiate the terms of separation; and litigating the divorce, both in the uncontested and the contested setting. We will explain how the 1986 Tax Reform Act affects decisions made during the break-up of the marriage.

In the three chapters of Part V, we delve into post-divorce or separation legal difficulties. We will address the client's potential need to draft a new Will. Additionally, we will explain how to enforce or modify the separation agreement and/or the divorce decree, and which forums to choose in such cases.

The final part, Part VI, will assist you in determining the appropriate compensation to which you are entitled for the services rendered to your client. In this vein, we will provide guidance that will enable you to draft an appropriate retainer agreement. Also, when to use each of the various billing practices—hourly rates, contingency fees, and flat fees—will be discussed.

The 1980s have seen a great increase in the complexity, diversity, and quantity of family law problems. This guide will help you, the modern attorney, to meet the needs engendered by these changes and to function as a competent family law practitioner.

Contents

FORMS, CHECKLISTS AND TABLES

Chapter 1

Chapter 2

Chapter 3

Chapter 4

Chapter 5

Chapter 6

Chapter 7

Chapter 8

Chapter 9

Chapter 11

Chapter 12

Chapter 13

Chapter 14

Chapter 15

Part 1

PRE-MARRIAGE CONCERNS

CHAPTER 1

How to Solve Legal Difficulties Generated by the Unmarried Family Unit

SITUATION

John Jones has for some time vowed that he will never marry. However, he has fallen in love. He now lives with his paramour and hopes to continue his current living arrangements indefinitely. John has come to you, his attorney, for advice as to how he can remain unmarried and yet provide some of the benefits of marriage to his partner.

DETERMINE CLIENT'S DESIRED STATUS

The first task that you must address is the determination of exactly what legal relationship John wishes to attain in regard to his partner. You should formulate a data sheet to help you determine if and what control of any of John's assets will be transferred to his partner. A sample consultation data sheet to help you in this regard follows on the next page.

From your consultation with John, you determine that he is 50 years old, earns $100,000 per year, has a home and rental properties, and has a net worth of $1,500,000. His partner is 30 years old, earns $15,000 per year, has no assets, and owes $10,000 on two college loans. You also determine that John wants to assure the financial security of his partner now, and in the event John should die. John is willing to share some of his assets with his partner, but wishes to retain control over the bulk of his assets.

While John is away on business trips, he wishes to permit his partner to act in his stead. However, he also does not want his partner to have complete discretion in handling his affairs.

CONSULTATION DATA SHEET RE SHARING ASSETS

	Client	Client's Partner
1. Age.		
2. Earned income.		
3. Investment income.		
4. Debt payments.		
5. Real property and value thereof.		
6. Mortgage value of real property and mortgage payment.		
7. Stocks and bonds and value thereof.		
8. Other property and value thereof.		
9. Outstanding loans and loan payments.		
10. Assets willing to share.		
11. Assets willing to transfer at death.		
12. Assets which will be subject to control by other by power of attorney.		

SHARING ASSETS WITH PARTNER

The Disadvantages and Advantages

Before making any arrangements for any transfer of John's assets to his partner, you must make John aware that any transfer of assets is a final transfer. The transfer is irreversible and precludes John from recouping the assets.

However, there is also an advantage. It is important for John to realize that because the transfer of assets deprives John of any ownership claims, he will also avoid the payment of income tax on any income derived from the assets. Considering that the imbalance between John's income and that of his partner places John in a much higher tax bracket, a transfer of income producing assets will result in a lower tax bite to John individually and to the couple as a whole.

Discourage Joint Holdings; Encourage Cash Distributions

In deciding how to transfer assets, all attempts should be made to dissuade John from holding any assets jointly with his partner. If the relationship sours, and the parties decide to go their separate ways, John's partner may not wish to sell the jointly held property. John may then have a long fight before he can realize any of the capital he has invested in the asset.

As to the type of assets that are to be transferred, note that in view of the fact that John wishes to retain control over the bulk of his assets, there is no need for a major transfer. In most situations cash distributions are preferable. Since John does not desire a large transfer of assets you should suggest that he consider making cash distributions.

Stock or real estate distributions are discouraged because such transfers may cause John to realize income taxes on those gains.

If the value of certain personal or real property is large enough, gift tax consequences might result that could be avoided by cash distributions. As of 1986, gifts can be made up to $10,000 in one year without any federal gift tax consequences.

Warning. On the gifts in excess of $10,000 per year, the excess will be applied to the federal unified gift and estate tax credit—which credit is $192,800 beginning 1987, and prevents the imposition of federal tax on a taxable amount up to $600,000—thereby reducing the amount of the credit available at death. Moreover, once the $192,800 unified gift and estate tax is used up, the donor will be required to pay in the year the gift is made the tax imposed in excess of $192,800. For example, a $620,000 gift will result in $1,800 of tax—$10,000 will be excluded, $600,000 will be absorbed by the unified credit, and $10,000 will be taxed at 18% pursuant to 28 USC Sec. 2001.

If John wishes to transfer to his partner a piece of real estate valued at $30,000, it would be difficult to avoid gift tax consequences. On the other hand, John can avoid gift tax consequences by transferring $30,000 in cash, $10,000 each year for three years.

Gifts Other Than Financial

In addition to cash gifts, John can aid his partner financially by giving gifts of: (1) clothing; (2) a car—keeping in mind the $10,000 gift limitation; (3) benefits under a life insurance policy on John's life, with the provision that the proceeds will only pass to his partner if they are living together at the time of John's death; (4) an apartment in a rent controlled or rent stabilized area, by placing his partner's name on the lease. These leases, in certain cities, tend to become very valuable and would provide the partner a place to live if John were to die.

Gifts of real estate will trigger gift tax problems because of the $10,000 per year gift limitation, but John can provide cash payments to enable his partner to acquire interests in real estate wherein gift tax consequences would be eliminated or at least limited.

For example, John would provide his partner with the cash for a down payment on a cooperative apartment, or a condominium. The partner's name would go on the deed in the case of the condominium and the stock certificate and proprietary lease in the case of the cooperative apartment. The partner's name would be on the mortgage and John could furnish cash to his partner for the mortgage payments. In this way, John's gift would be spread over many years and he could take advantage of the $10,000 exclusion each year.

John would not be able to benefit from any income tax deduction relating to the interest and property taxes included in the mortgage payments. Considering that John is in a much higher tax bracket than his partner, John may wish to purchase the property in his name, take advantage of the tax deduction, and bequest the property to his partner in his Will.

If John and his partner were both earning $15,000, the purchase of a cooperative or condominium might be their only asset. Contributions to the down payment and mortgage payments would probably be equal. Although it is usually better to avoid holding property jointly, in this case both should be listed as joint owners of the property and both should be equally liable for the mortgage due to the fact that the property is their only asset and their financial situations are the same.

ASSIGNING RIGHTS AND OBLIGATIONS TO PARTNER BY POWER OF ATTORNEY

John should be extremely cautious in providing a power of attorney to his partner. In the event John's relationship with his partner becomes strained, the partner may unbeknownst to John exercise the powers bestowed upon him/her. John would certainly be ill-advised to execute a general power of attorney—a document which would give John's partner all the powers John possesses over his affairs. Any powers given by John should be extremely specific and limited. For example, as to any real property held by John, he probably should not give his partner the right to sell it or mortgage it, and may only want the partner to have the right to collect rent from it and handle landlord/tenant problems.

Not only should the powers be limited, but the time during which they can be executed should also be severely limited. The types of situations which might generate the need for a special power of attorney are when John is out of town or hospitalized for a long period of time.

The following form will help you formulate a power of attorney for John.

SAMPLE POWER OF ATTORNEY

KNOW ALL MEN BY THESE PRESENTS:

That I, ______________________, have made, constituted and appointed, and by these presents do make, constitute and appoint ______________, whose present address is ________________________________, my true and lawful attorney-in-fact to act as follows, that is to say:

GIVING AND GRANTING unto my said attorney-in-fact full power:

1. DISPOSITION OF PROPERTY. To lease, sell, use, register, insure, transfer, mortgage, maintain, manage, act as my proxy, pledge, exchange or otherwise dispose of or encumber any and all of my property, real, personal, or mixed, and to execute and deliver good and sufficient deeds or other instruments for the lease, conveyance, mortgage, maintenance, or transfer of the same.

2. COLLECTION OF DEBTS. To collect, sue for, compromise or otherwise dispose of any claim, debt, rents, or share in any estate in which I now or hereafter may have an interest.

3. RECOVERING POSSESSION OF PROPERTY. To eject, remove, or relieve tenants or other persons from, and recover possession of any property, real, personal, or mixed, in which I now or hereafter may have an interest.

4. ACQUISITION OF PROPERTY. To buy, receive, lease, accept or otherwise acquire in my name and for my account, property, real, personal, or mixed upon such terms, considerations and conditions as my said attorney-in-fact shall think proper.

5. LITIGATION, REPRESENTATION, AND EMPLOYMENT OF ASSISTANCE. On my behalf and in my name or the name of my attorney, to institute, prosecute, appear in, defend, compromise, arbitrate, settle, or dispose of any legal, equitable, or administrative hearings, actions, suits, attachments, claims, or other proceedings, to which I am or may become a party or in which I have an interest; and to engage, employ, and appoint agents, employees, and counsel upon such terms and conditions and at such compensation as my said attorney shall deem proper in the exercise of the powers herein granted; to dismiss and remove at pleasure any such agents, employees, and counsel as well as any agents, employees, and counsel heretofore or hereafter employed by me or in my behalf.

6. ENDORSING CHECKS AND DEPOSITING MONEY. (a) To deposit in my name and for my account with any bank, banker, trust company, or other financial institution, all monies which may come into (his) (her) hands as such attorney-in-fact and all bills of exchange, drafts, checks, promissory notes and other securities (including, but not limited to, such instruments issued by or drawn on the treasurer, or other fiscal officer or depository of the United States, of any sovereign state or authority, or any political subdivision or instrumentality thereof) for money pay-

able or belonging to me, and for that purpose to sign my name (in the manner provided herein) and indorse the same for deposit or collection, and from time to time to withdraw any and all monies so belonging to me, and for that purpose to draw checks and drafts thereon in my name in the manner provided herein.

(b) To open or close accounts and to receive statements, notices or other documents from any bank or other financial institution concerning any and all accounts or banking transactions in my name or in which I have an interest.

(c) To endorse, cash, and receive the proceeds of any and all checks, certificates of deposit, vouchers, or other orders for money.

7. SAFE DEPOSIT BOXES. To have access for all purposes to any and all safety deposit boxes or vaults rented in my name or in the name of any person or persons and myself, with full power to use the same for safekeeping any property or papers, and to remove therefrom at any time, or from time to time, all or any part of the contents of any such box or vault.

8. TRANSACT BUSINESS. To make, do, and transact business of any lawful kind or nature in my name and to borrow money in my name when deemed necessary to my said attorney-in-fact upon such terms as to my said attorney-in-fact appear proper and to execute such instruments as may be requisite for such purpose.

9. TAX RETURNS. To prepare, execute, and file state and federal income and other tax returns, and to receive from and inspect any documents, returns, files, and opinions maintained by any tax authority.

10. SHIPMENT OF PROPERTY. To take possession and order the removal and shipment of any of my property from or to any warehouse, depot, dock, or other place of storage or safekeeping, and to execute and deliver any release, voucher, receipt, shipping ticket, certificate, or other instrument necessary or convenient for such purpose.

11. AUTOMOBILES. To execute and deliver to the proper persons and authority any and all documents, instruments, and papers necessary to effect proper registration and licensing of any automobile in which I now or may hereafter have an interest, or the sale thereof and transfer of legal title thereto as required by law, and to collect receipt for all monies paid in consideration of such sale and transfer.

12. CHILD CARE. To occupy, use, and expand all or any part of my estate as exists now or is hereafter constituted for the education, health, welfare, and benefit of any and all of my legitimate children, and to otherwise act in loco parentis, including all actions I could take as the natural parent, including authorizing medical care.

13. ADDITIONAL POWERS

FURTHER, I do authorize my aforesaid attorney-in-fact to perform all necessary acts in execution of the aforesaid authorization and generally to do any and all acts on my behalf in any other matter or thing pertaining or belonging to me with the same validity as I could effect if personally present.

AND I HEREBY DECLARE that any act or thing lawfully done hereunder by my said attorney-in-fact shall be binding on myself and my heirs, legal and personal representatives, and assigns:

PROVIDED, however, that all business transacted hereunder for me or for my account shall be transacted in my name, and that all indorsements and instruments executed by my said attorney-in-fact for the purpose of carrying out the foregoing powers shall hear my name followed by that of my said attorney-in-fact and the designation "attorney-in-fact."

FURTHER, this power of attorney shall remain in full force and effect until the occurrence of the first of the following circumstances: (1) my death; (2) the death of my said attorney-in-fact; (3) until the revocation of this power of attorney by me; or (4) until ____________________.

NOTWITHSTANDING my reference to the fact that this power of attorney shall terminate upon my death, I declare that any act or thing lawfully done hereunder by my said attorney-in-fact shall be binding on myself and my heirs, representative and assigns, whether the same shall have been done either before or after my actual death, unless and until reliable notice thereof is received by my said attorney-in-fact.

FURTHER, this power of attorney shall not be affected by my subsequent disability or incompetence.

FURTHER, to induce any third party to act hereunder, I hereby agree that any third party receiving a duly executed copy or facsimile of this instrument may act hereunder, and that revocation or termination hereof shall be ineffective as to such third party unless and until actual notice or knowledge of such revocation shall have been received by such third party, and I for myself and for my heirs, executors, legal representatives, and assigns, hereby agree to indemnify and hold harmless any such third party from and against any and all claims that may arise against such third party by reason of such third party having relied on the provisions of this instrument.

IN WITNESS WHEREOF, I have hereunto signed my name and affixed my seal this ____________ day of ____________, 19____.

________________________ (Seal)

STATE OF COUNTY OF ss.:
On the day of 19 before me personally came to me known and known to me to be the individual described in and who executed the foregoing instrument and he acknowledged to me that he executed the same.

BEQUESTING ASSETS TO PARTNER BY WILL

The easiest method by which John can assure the financial security of his partner is by way of John's Will. He may wish to bequest the bulk of his estate, including his house, to his partner. In writing John's Will for him, it is crucial that a clause be inserted which makes the passing of any property at John's death contingent upon him living with the partner at the time of John's death. A sample Will with such a clause follows.

SAMPLE LIVING-TOGETHER WILL

I, , a resident of , County of and State of , being of sound and disposing mind, do hereby make, publish and declare this to be my Last Will and Testament.

FIRST: I hereby revoke any and all Wills and Codicils heretofore made by me.

SECOND: I direct that all of my just debts, funeral, and testamentary expenses be paid as soon as practicable after my decease from my residuary estate. I direct that all estate, inheritance, succession and transfer taxes and duties, including not only those upon property hereby devised or bequeathed, but also those, if any, imposed or assessed with respect to any other property which for the purposes of the taxes enumerated in this paragraph may be considered or treated as part of my gross estate, shall be a charge upon and payable out of my residuary estate.

THIRD: (A) I give, devise, and bequeath any and all jewelry I may own at the time of my death to my mother, absolutely and free of trust, should she survive me and should she predecease me, then to my son, absolutely and free of trust.

(B) I give, devise, and bequeath any and all household furniture, furnishings, automobiles, personal effects and any other tangible personal property which I may own at the time of my death except for the bequest pursuant to Paragraph "THIRD A", to my son, , should he survive me, or should he fail to survive me, then I give, devise, and bequeath my said personalty in equal shares to the children of my son, who shall survive me, or in default of children, then this bequest shall lapse and be included in the bequest pursuant to Paragraph "FIFTH B" herein.

FOURTH: (A) I give, devise and bequeath the sum of TEN THOUSAND ($10,000.00) DOLLARS absolutely and free of trust to my friend, , should he survive me and should we be living together at the time of my death. Should predecease me or should we not be living together at the time of my death, then this bequest shall lapse and be included in the bequest pursuant to Paragraph "FOURTH B" herein.

(B) I give, devise, and bequeath to my son, , should he survive me, my entire residuary estate, absolutely and free of trust.

Should my son, , not survive me, then this bequest shall lapse and shall be included in the bequest pursuant to Paragraph "FIFTH A" herein.

FIFTH: (A) Should my son, , not survive me and should he leave children surviving me, then I give, devise, and bequeath my entire residuary estate to my Trustees, hereinafter named, IN TRUST NEVERTHELESS, and I direct my Trustees to divide the principal of the trust fund coming into their hands, into as many equal parts as I shall leave grandchildren who shall be living at the date of my death (or should any of my grandchildren have predeceased me but leave issue him or her surviving and surviving me, then such issue should take his or her parent's share in equal parts, per stirpes, and not per capita), to be held in trust all pursuant to the provisions herein, for the benefit of each of said grandchildren (or their issue) as follows:

(1) With respect to each part set apart for a grandchild or his issue: I give, devise, and bequeath such part to my Trustees to invest the same and keep the same invested and to apply so much of the income arising therefrom and so much of the principal of the trust as in the sole and unreviewable discretion of my Trustees may be advisable for the education, maintenance, health and support of the grandchild for whose benefit such trust shall have been created and to accumulate the balance of said net income, if any, until such grandchild shall have attained the age of twenty-one (21) years, at which time all accumulations of income from that portion of the trust due said grandchild shall be paid over to such grandchild, together with one-third (1/3) of the principal remaining in that portion of the trust fund held for said grandchild.

(2) Thereupon I direct my Trustees to continue to invest and keep invested so much of the principal of said trust fund as may be remaining in their hands and to pay the net income arising therefrom quarterly to the grandchild for whose benefit said trust shall have been created until such grandchild shall have attained the age of twenty-five (25) years, at which time I direct that one-half (1/2) of the principal and all of the undistributed income remaining in that part of said trust fund shall be paid over to such grandchild.

During this period the Trustees may apply so much of the principal of the trust and the income arising therefrom as in the sole and unreviewable discretion of the Trustees may be advisable for the education, maintenance, health, and support of that grandchild.

(3) Thereupon, I direct my Trustees to continue to invest and keep invested so much of the principal of said trust fund as may be remaining in their hands and to pay the net income arising therefrom quarterly to the grandchild for whose benefit said trust shall have been created until such grandchild shall have attained the age of twenty-eight (28) years, at which time I direct that all undistributed income from that portion of the trust for said grandchild together with the balance of the principal then remaining in that portion held for said grandchild shall be paid over to such grandchild.

During this period the Trustees may apply so much of the principal of the trust and the income arising therefrom as in the sole and unreviewable discretion of the Trustees may be advisable for the education, maintenance, health, and support of that grandchild.

(4) In the event that the grandchild for whose benefit said trust shall have been created should die before attaining the age of twenty-eight (28) years, then upon the death of such grandchild, the principal of said trust fund as may be re-

maining in the hands of my trustees, together with accrued but unmatured income thereon and accumulations of income, if any, shall continue to be held in trust for the issue of such grandchild surviving such grandchild, per stirpes, pursuant to the provisions of this Paragraph, or in default of such issue, shall be divided equally among my surviving grandchildren, per stirpes, to be added to their corpus then held in trust pursuant to the provisions of this Paragraph.

(5) Upon my youngest grandchild, or his or her issue, if applicable, attaining the age of twenty-eight (28) years, this trust shall terminate and come to an end and shall be distributed, free of trust.

(B) Should my son not survive me and should he not leave children or their issue if applicable surviving me, then in such event, I give, devise and bequeath my entire residuary estate as follows:

(1) In equal shares to my parents , or all to the survivor.
(2) Should both of my parents predecease me, then to my friend, should he survive me and should we be living together at the time of my death.
(3) Should also predecease me or should we not be living together at the time of my death and should my parents have also predeceased me then, I give, devise and bequeath my entire residuary estate as follows:

(a) ONE-SIXTH (1/6) to my aunt and uncle or all to the survivor.
(b) ONE-SIXTH (1/6) to my cousin, .
(c) ONE-SIXTH (1/6) to my cousin, .
(d) ONE-SIXTH (1/6) to my cousin, .
(e) ONE-SIXTH (1/6) to my cousin, .
(f) ONE-SIXTH (1/6) to my cousin, .

Should any of the foregoing not survive me, then his or her bequest, except for the bequest to my aunt and uncle , where both must predecease me, shall lapse and be distributed proportionately to the other beneficiaries pursuant to this Paragraph "FIFTH (B)3" herein.

SIXTH: Upon the termination or change of beneficiary of any trust herein created through the decease, after my decease, of the person entitled to receive the income, there shall be no apportionment to the executor or administrator of such person of any accrued but unmatured income. Said accrued but unmatured income shall, upon the maturity and collection of the several respective items thereof, belong in its entirety to the person or persons entitled to receive the income of the particular trust fund, that is to say, to the remainderman or remaindermen in any case where the principal of the trust shall vest in fee, or to the next beneficiary in any case where the trust shall continue for the benefit of a successive or further beneficiary.

SEVENTH: In the event that any beneficiary of this Will and I or any other person upon whose death such beneficiary shall become entitled to receive either income or principal under this Will shall die in a common disaster or accident or under such circumstances that the order of deaths cannot be established by proof, then I direct that for purposes of this Will such beneficiary shall be deemed to have predeceased me or such other person as the case may be.

EIGHTH: If upon my death any part of my estate shall vest in absolute ownership in a minor, or if at the termination of any of the trusts created by this Will all or any part of any of the trusts created by this Will or if all or any part of the principal of any of the trust funds shall vest in absolute ownership in a minor, I authorize and empower my Trustees or Executors, as the case may be, to continue to hold said principal for the benefit of such minor during his or her legal minority or until the age of twenty-one (21) years, whichever shall be greater, to invest the same and keep the same invested and to collect the income thereof and in the sole and unreviewable discretion of the said Executors or Trustees, as the case may be, either to accumulate the income or pay over the net income arising therefrom to the minor to whom said principal shall belong or to his or her parent or legal guardian, or to the person with whom such minor resides, or to apply said income and such sum or sums out of principal, as in their sole and absolute discretion they deem necessary or advisable to said infant's care, education, maintenance, and support. The authority thus accorded to my Executors or Trustees, as the case may be, shall be construed as a power only and shall not operate to suspend the absolute ownership of such principal by such minor or to prevent the absolute vesting thereof in such minor. The rights, powers, privileges and immunities granted in this my Last Will and Testament to my Executors and/or Trustees shall apply to the administration and investment of any funds held by my Executors or Trustees in accordance with this power, and they shall have the same rights to compensation for so acting as if any such trust had continued and said principal had not vested.

NINTH: (A) I hereby nominate, constitute, and appoint my son   as the Executor of this My Last Will and Testament. Should he either predecease me, fail to qualify, or having qualified, shall for any reason fail to continue to act as such Executor, then I appoint my cousin   and my attorney   , in his place.

(B) I hereby nominate, constitute, and appoint my cousin   and my attorney,   or the survivor of them, as the Co-Trustees of the trust herein created.

(C) I direct that none of the persons named herein as Executor and/or Trustee, original or successor, shall be required to give any bond or other undertaking for the faithful performances of their duties as Executor and/or Trustee, or as successor.

TENTH: I confer upon my Executor and/or Trustees, original or successor, with respect to the management and administration of any property, real or personal, the following discretionary powers, without limitation by reason of specification, and in addition to the powers conferred upon them by statute or by general rules of law:

(1) I authorize and empower my Executor, and/or Trustees to retain and continue any investments which I may own at the time of my death. In the making of new investments I direct that my Executors and/or Trustees shall not be restricted or limited to such legal investments as are provided for the investment of trust funds by any statutes now in force or which may hereafter be enacted, and I specifically authorize my Executors and/or Trustees to invest the assets of my estate and/or the corpus of any trust fund or any part hereof in a discretionary common trust fund, to purchase or acquire in exchange or otherwise real estate, mortgages, stocks, bonds, and securities other than those constituting legal investments for trust funds and to invest and keep invested therein any part of my estate or of the trusts herein created. My Executors and Trustees shall not be held accountable or liable for any loss, depreciation, or damage sustained by reason of the retention, acquisition, or disposition of any investment pursuant to the provisions of this paragraph.

(2) I authorize and empower my Executors and/or Trustees in their discretion and without leave of Court to sell at public or private sale or to lease without public bidding and without restriction or limitation as the length of term (even though for a period longer than authorized by statute or longer than the duration of any trust herein created) or to mortgage or pledge any or all property coming into their hands, whether real or personal or mixed, at such times and upon such terms and conditions as in their judgment they may deem proper, and I authorize and empower them to sign, execute, acknowledge, and deliver any deeds, mortgages, conveyances, leases, and other papers that may be necessary in connection therewith.

(3) I authorize and empower my Executors and/or Trustees in their discretion to purchase property (a) on the foreclosure of any mortgage held by my estate, (b) on which my estate may own a mortgage or mortgages, (c) in which my estate shall have any interest, or any sale in partition, foreclosure or otherwise or (d) which may be sold under any judgment in which my estate may have any interest, and I authorize and empower them to sign, execute, acknowledge, and deliver any deeds, mortgages, conveyances, leases or other papers that may be necessary in connection therewith.

(4) I authorize and empower my Executors and/or Trustees to compromise, settle, or arbitrate any claim or demand in favor of or against my estate.

(5) I authorize and empower my Executors and/or Trustees to vote in person or by proxy upon any and all stocks or other securities held by them; to exercise any rights to subscribe for or to convert into stocks or bonds or other securities of any corporation (whether a going concern or in liquidation or in reorganization or under any other circumstances or conditions whatsoever) for other real or personal property distributed by the same corporation or any other corporation which shall be formed as a reorganization of or in combination, merger or consolidation with the original corporation; to become a party to any plan of reorganization, merger, or consolidation or to become a depositor with and/or give power of attorney to any committee of bondholders or other security holders or creditors formed for the purpose of mutual protection in connection with any plan of corporate financing or reorganization or to represent or enforce the rights of security holders or creditors in connection with any defaults by the corporation or any reorganization or insolvency of the corporation; to accept any new or substituted security of whatever nature in place of the defaulted or previously held security; to make any payments necessary to obtain such new or substituted security, and generally to exercise in respect to any securities held by them the unrestricted rights of a personal owner thereof, in accordance with their best judgment and discretion.

(6) I authorize and empower my Executors and/or Trustees to borrow money, from others or from themselves whether to pay taxes, make subscriptions, exercise options, pay assessments, or to accomplish any other purpose of any nature incidental to the administration of my estate or of any of the trusts herein created, and to mortgage or pledge as security therefor any securities or other property held by them.

(7) So far as I may be legally permitted to do so, I authorize and empower my Executors and/or Trustees to cause any stocks, bonds, or other securities at any time held by them to be in bearer form or to be registered in the name of a nominee or nominees.

(8) I authorize and empower my Executors and/or Trustees to hold and retain so long as to them may seem proper, as part of my estate and trust estate, any real, personal or mixed property, or any interest therein, of which I may die seized or possessed, or to which I may be entitled at the time of my death, notwithstanding that the same may not be of the kind, character, legal, proper, or permissible for the investment of funds or trust funds under the laws of the State of New York, or any other State and without regard to the proportion that any of said property may bear to the entire amount of my estate and trust estate, or of the trusts in which same are held.

(9) I authorize and empower my Executors and/or Trustees to form any corporation, partnership, general or limited, or association, and to sell, convey, exchange, contract, lease, assign, transfer and set over, or otherwise dispose of

to said corporation, partnership or association any or all of my estate, and to accept therefor property, real or personal, stocks, notes, bonds, debentures, mortgages, securities or other evidences of indebtedness from said partnership, corporation or association including the stock of any such corporation, common or preferred, in payment or part payment therefor, and to become directors and officers of any such corporation and with full power and authority on the part of any such corporation and my estate and trust estate to transact any business, including the making of any loans, with or without pledge, mortgage or security between my estate and trust estate and said corporation, with full power and authority on the part of either the corporation or my estate and trust estate to become maker, endorser, guarantor, and surety for each other in respect to any matter whatsoever, and said corporation may be organized under the laws of any State selected by said Executors and/or Trustees with all the powers incident to corporations organized under the laws of such State.

(10) I authorize and empower my Executors and/or Trustees to continue any business of mine and the operation thereof and any interest that I may have either individually or as a partner, stockholder, in any business, firm, enterprise, association, partnership, whether general or limited, company or corporation of whatsoever nature and wherever same may be situated, for so long a time and upon such terms and conditions and in such manner as my said Executors and/or Trustees may deem advisable and beneficial and for the best interest of my estate and trust estate, and for that purpose to retain and permit to be employed therein any capital or investment which shall at my death be employed therein, and generally to act in all matters relating to any such business or interest as herein mentioned as if they owned the same, or were beneficially interested in or entitled to the same.

(11) I authorize and empower my Executors and/or Trustees to carry out any contracts or agreements that I may have entered into with any person or persons, partnership, stockholders or corporation in connection with any such business, interest, partnership, firm, association, or corporation, or affecting or concerning any stock owned or held by me, and to extend and to continue the same or enter into any other agreement or arrangement that they may deem advisable and for the best interest of my estate and trust estate.

(12) I authorize and empower my Executors and/or Trustees to form any firm, partnership, association, company, or corporation with or concerning any business in which I may have any interest, as herein mentioned, and to participate in, consent to, or oppose any plan of liquidation, consolidation, reorganization, merger or similar plan in connection with or concerning the said business or interest with any other business, firm, association, partnership or corporation.

(13) I authorize and empower my Executor and/or Trustees to discontinue, liquidate, dissolve, and dispose of any business, firm, association, partnership, corporation, or any stockholdings or interest that I may have in the same.

(14) I authorize and empower my Executors and/or Trustees to apportion between principal and income all stock dividends and liquidating or extraordinary dividends or distributions. Without limiting the absolute discretion of my fiduciaries, I desire that all such dividends and distributions be allotted to principal except to the extent that my fiduciaries shall determine that they were declared or made in lieu of regular cash dividends or distributions.

(15) I authorize and empower my Executors and/or Trustees at any time and from time to time, to appoint for the time being an agent or attorney to make, execute and deliver any transfer or other instructions, or to do any ministerial act necessary or proper to be done in the administration of my estate.

(16) I authorize and empower my Executors and/or Trustees to employ such attorneys, clerks, agents, accountants, and custodians, and to obtain such investment or other advice, in the transaction of the business of my estate and in the administration of any trust hereunder as my Executors or Trustees, as the case may be, may deem necessary or advisable, and to make such payments and disbursements therefor as they deem reasonable and proper.

(17) Except as otherwise expressly provided in this Will, I authorize and empower my Executors and/or Trustees to pay any pecuniary legacy hereunder, whether in trust or otherwise, and to make any distribution pursuant to this my Will, in whole or in part, in securities or other property owned by me at the time of my decease or thereafter acquired by my Executors or Trustees, subject to the applicable provisions of this Will, which shall fully govern with respect to the bequest therein provided for, and in making such payment or distribution in securities or other property, I direct that valuation placed thereon by my Executors or by my Trustees shall be binding and conclusive on all persons interested in my estate, subject only to the power of a court of competent jurisdiction to pass on such valuation.

(18) My Trustees may at any time and from time to time during the course of the administration of any trust created pursuant to this Will, render an account of their proceedings with respect to such trust to every person who is then of full age and sound mind and who is then currently entitled to be paid the net income of such trust or who then may be entitled in any future contingency to have paid over to him or to her all or any part of the principal of such trust and to every duly appointed guardian of the property of every such person who is not then of full age and who has such a guardian. If the persons to whom such an account is so rendered by my Trustees include both at least one person (or the guardian of one person) who may be entitled in any future contingency to have paid over to him or to her all or any part of the principal, the written approval of such account by all the persons to whom the account is so rendered (including any such guardians) shall be binding and conclusive upon all persons then having or thereafter acquiring or claiming any interest in the subject matter of such account and

shall be a complete discharge to my Trustees with respect to all matters set forth in such account as fully and to the same extent as though such account had been judicially settled and allowed by a judgment or order or decree of a court of competent jurisdiction in an action or proceeding in which all persons so having, acquiring or claiming any interest in the subject matter of such account were duly made parties and were duly represented. The foregoing provisions of this paragraph shall not be deemed to limit the right of my Trustees to have any such account judicially settled despite such written approval.

ELEVENTH: (A) I hereby direct that no disposition charge or encumbrances on any interest in my estate, or on any part thereof, by any beneficiary under this Will by way of anticipation shall be valid or in any way binding upon my Executors or Trustees, and no beneficiary shall have the right to assign, transfer, encumber, or otherwise dispose of such income or principal, or any part thereof until the same shall be paid to such beneficiary by my Executors or by my Trustees, and no income or principal or any part thereof shall be liable to any claim of any creditors of any such beneficiary.

(B) The right of any beneficiary to any payment of income or principal shall be in every case subject to any charges or deduction which my Executors or my Trustees may make against the same under the authority granted to my Executors or to my Trustees by any law or by any provision of this Will.

TWELFTH: The powers and authority hereinbefore granted to my Executors and/or Trustees may be exercised without obligation to or authority from any court or judge, and, to the extent permitted by law, they shall not be liable or responsible for any loss which may be suffered except where the same is due to their dishonest or malicious acts.

THIRTEENTH: The words "child," "children," and "issue," wherever used in this Will, shall include not only the child, children, and issue of the person or persons designated, but also the legally adopted child or children of such person or persons.

FOURTEENTH: Wherever applicable the masculine and feminine genders, and the singular and plural, are used interchangeably in this my Last Will and Testament.

IN WITNESS WHEREOF, I have hereunto set my hand and seal the day of , 19 .

____

The foregoing instrument consisting of pages, including this page, was on the day above signed, sealed, published and declared by , the above-named Testatrix, as and for her Last Will and Testament, in the presence of us and each of us, who at her request, and in her presence and in the presence of each other, have hereunto subscribed our names as attesting witnesses, this day of , 19 . .

________________________ residing at ________________

____

________________________ residing at ________________

____

________________________ residing at ________________

____

HOW TO PROTECT BY CONTRACT CLIENT'S ASSETS FROM HIS OR HER PARTNER

Appropriateness of Contract

Before John continues the relationship with his partner any further, he must enter into a contract with that partner which delineates what occurs to certain property in the event of a breakup. It must be made exceedingly clear to John that having such a contract is a necessity, not a luxury for the following reasons.

Assets Affected by Living Together

In the event John's relationship with his partner terminates and he has not entered into any agreements with the partner, John need only concern himself with the ownership of nontitled items. John must be concerned about the ownership of these items whether or not he acquired them before or after he commenced the relationship with his partner. John need not worry about what has in recent times been referred to as palimony. His partner has no claim for renumeration simply because they are living together. Such a claim can only exist if it is expressed in a written or oral agreement.

A checklist of the types of items, whose ownership might be adversely affected by the failure to delineate ownership in a contract, follows. This checklist will enable you as John's attorney, to determine the actual limits of John's loss of assets in the event his relationship collapses and he does not have a contract.

Checklist of assets affected by living together

1. Hobbies (Stamps, Coins, Antique Collections.)
2. Clothing.
3. Art work.
4. Furniture and other house furnishings.
5. China and silver.
6. Cash.
7. Tools, garden and house.
8. Jewelry.
9. Musical instruments.
10. Cameras, sterios, computers, VCR's, radios, T.V.'S.
11. Sports equipment.

Drafting Contract

In drafting a contract for John, you, as his attorney, should not limit yourself to merely designating the ownership of nontitled items in the event of a separation. You should also address who is responsible for what bills at that juncture. Even though the house shared by John and his partner is owned by John, the fact that the partner is far less financially independent might warrant that John enable the partner to have sole possession of the house for a certain period after the breakup and a payment from John upon the partner's departure from the residence. This payment should include moving expenses, start up expenses at a new residence and perhaps furniture expenses. If the partner is moving into a leased apartment, a payment of two months rent would probably be in order.

The payment could be a certain specified amount if, for example, the partner remains with John for five years. If the relationship lasts longer, the payment should be correspondingly increased. Also, you should address in the contract what assets John wishes to bequest to his partner in the event of John's death. After John executes the contract, he shall execute a Will which bequests the assets to his partner. Finally, if the couple remains together for a certain period of time, i.e., 10 years, perhaps the contract should become null and void.

A sample contract follows that will help you in formulating John's contract:

SAMPLE LIVING-TOGETHER CONTRACT

AGREEMENT, made as of this day of , 19 by and between , residing at , , New York, hereinafter referred to as and , residing at , , hereinafter referred to as .

WITNESSETH:

WHEREAS, the parties hereto, both over the age of twenty-one, contemplate living together in the immediate future. In anticipation thereof, they desire to fix and determine by agreement the rights and claims that will accrue to each of them in the estate and property of the other by reason of such living together, and to fix and determine the rights and claims that will accrue to each of them for maintenance and/or palimony and/or alimony should this living-together arrangement ever be terminated, and to accept the provisions of this arrangement in lieu of and in full discharge, settlement, and satisfaction of all such rights and claims; and

WHEREAS, except as hereinafter provided, has agreed that all of the assets and/or property as presently owned by shall be free of all rights that might acquire by reason of her living together with , except as hereinafter set forth; and

WHEREAS, except as hereinafter provided, has agreed that all of the assets and/or property presently owned by will be free of all rights that might acquire by reason of his living together with ; and

WHEREAS, except as hereinafter provided, each of the parties hereto has agreed to waive any and all rights in the estate of the other, and

WHEREAS, each of the parties hereto has agreed to waive any future rights against the other for payment of any maintenance and/or palimony and/or alimony support in the event of the termination of the living-together arrangement in the future.

NOW, THEREFORE, in consideration of the premises and of the living-together arrangement, and in further consideration of the mutual promises and undertakings hereinafter set forth, the parties hereto agree:

(1) After the parties begin living together, shall separately retain all of his rights in his assets and property which he presently does own and in any and all property which he may acquire in his own name during their living together, and he shall have the absolute and unrestricted rights to dispose of such property free from any claim that may be made by by reason of their living together and with the same effect as if they had not been living together.

Annexed to this Arrangement and made a part hereof as *Schedule "A"* is a list of the approximate Assets as owned by as of 19 .

(2) After the parties begin living together, shall separately retain all of her rights in her assets and property which she presently does own and in any and all property which she may acquire in her own name during their living together and she shall have the absolute and unrestricted right to dispose of such property free from any claim that may be made by by reason of their living together and with the same effect as if they had not been living together.

Annexed to this Agreement and made a part hereof as *Schedule "B"* is a list of the approximate assets as owned by as of 19 .

(3) (A) has agreed that upon execution of this agreement, he will execute a Codicil to his Last Will and Testament, which Codicil to his Last Will and Testament shall be kept in full force and effect during the period the parties are living together and which Codicil to his Last Will and Testament shall provide as follows:

(1) Should the parties be living together for up to ten (10) years at the date of 'S death, then shall provide a specific bequest of Two Hundred and Fifty Thousand ($250,000.00) Dollars to be paid to upon 'S demise, provided that they shall be living together at the time of 'S demise, and provided further that shall survive .

(2) Should the parties be living together for more than ten (10) years at the date of 'S death, then shall provide a specific bequest of Three Hundred and Fifty Thousand ($350,000.00) Dollars to be paid to in lieu of the bequest as provided in 3(A)(1) herein, upon 'S demise, provided that they shall be living together at the time of 'S demise and provided further that shall survive .

(3)(B) It is specifically agreed that shall have the right to make future changes to his Last Will and Testament and/or future Codicils, provided that the bequest to as set forth in Paragraph "(3)(A)" herein shall not be changed nor be altered during their living together, as herein provided.

(3)(C) Except as specifically set forth in Sub-Paragraph "3(A)" herein, hereby waives and releases any and all other rights as she may have, if any, to elect to take against 'S Last Will and Testament, whether heretofore or hereafter made, and/or testamentary substitute as described in the laws of the State of New York and whether the parties are living together and/or married at the date of 'S demise.

Except as specifically set forth in Sub-Paragraph "3(A)" herein, this provision shall constitute a waiver of any and all other rights and of the right of election which has or may have in the Estate of in accordance with the requirements of the Laws of the State of New York, or of the same or similar laws of any jurisdiction which may be applicable.

(4) hereby waives and releases any and all rights as he may have, if any, to elect to take against 'S Last Will and Testament, whether heretofore or hereafter made, and/or testamentary substitute as described in the Laws of the State of New York and whether the parties are living together and/or married at the date of 'S demise.

This provision shall constitute a waiver of any and all rights and of the right of election which has or may have in the Estate of in accordance with the requirements of the Laws of the State of New York, or of the same or similar laws of any jurisdiction which may be applicable.

(5)(A) and do hereby agree, that during the period of their living together, that alone shall pay for any and all costs incurred for maintaining their common residence and for any and all living expenses and costs incurred by them.

All assets acquired or exchanges of assets made during the period of the parties living together, shall be solely paid for and/or be financed by and shall be in 'S name exclusively, unless the parties agree otherwise in writing.

It is specifically understood and agreed that shall not be required to make any payments for the aforesaid.

agrees to provide Blue Cross/Blue Shield and major medical insurance coverage for so long as they are living together.

(5)(B) Any and all debts contracted by both parties prior to their living together shall be the sole responsibility of the party who incurred same.

(6) and do hereby agree that they shall live together wherever both parties mutually agree.

(7)(A) and , each hereby agree that should this living-together arrangement be terminated, at any time, they each hereby waive any and all rights and/or claims, which either may have in the present assets of the other, as presently owned, and/or in any property acquired by the other during the living-together arrangement, except as hereinafter provided.

(7)(B) and hereby waive any and all rights in the said property of the other, should they legally separate and/or be divorced (if applicable), pursuant to the laws of the State of New York, or the same or similar laws of any jurisdiction which may be applicable.

(7)(C) The parties agree that should the living-together arrangement be terminated for any reason whatsoever, no matter if it is the fault of either party, then shall make the following payments to :

(1) Should the parties terminate this living-together arrangement within three (3) years of the date of this agreement, shall pay the sum of One Hundred Fifty Thousand ($150,000.00) Dollars by payment of Fifteen Thousand ($15,000.00) Dollars per year for ten (10) years with interest at the prime rate then pertaining at Citibank, N.A.; the first payment beginning three (3) months after the termination of the living-together arrangement.

(2) Should the parties terminate the living together arrangement more than three (3) months but less than ten (10) years after the date of this arrangement, shall pay the sum of One Hundred Fifty Thousand ($150,000.00) Dollars in one payment, within three (3) months after the termination of the living-together arrangement.

(3) Should the parties terminate the living-together arrangement more than ten (10) years after the date of this agreement, shall pay to the sum of Two Hundred Fifty Thousand ($250,000.00) Dollars in one payment within three (3) months after the termination of the living-together arrangement.

(4) The death of during any of the foregoing periods of living together contained in Paragraph 7(C)(1), (2), or (3) shall be considered a termination of the living-together arrangements and any payments due shall be made to 'S estate.

(7)(D) Should and terminate the living-together arrangement, legally separate and/or be divorced (if applicable), then and in that event, each party shall retain his or her own property brought into the living together arrangement and/or marriage and/or any exchanges of property of equal value and/or any property as acquired by the other during the living-together arrangement and/or marriage (if applicable). Any and all property of and which may be held in joint names, shall be divided equally in the event of a termination of the living-together arrangement, legal separation, and/or divorce (if applicable).

(8)(A) Annexed to this Agreement and made a part hereof as *Schedule "C"* is 'S approximate income for the calendar year ending ,19 .

(8)(B) For good and valuable consideration, hereby acknowledges the fact that she is now fully capable of supporting herself by her sole means and abilities and will continue to be fully capable of supporting herself by her sole means and abilities, in accordance with her accustomed mode of living, reasonable requirements and station of life, and she hereby waives any rights she may have to payments for present and future support and maintenance from , as her husband in the future, and in the event of a termination of the living-together arrangements, separation, or divorce (if applicable) in the future, said hereby waives any rights she may have to payments of palimony, alimony, support, and maintenance from .

(9)(A) Annexed to this Agreement and made a part hereof as *Schedule "D"* is 'S approximate income for the calendar year ending December 31, 19 .

(9)(B) For good and valuable consideration, hereby acknowledges the fact that he is now fully capable of supporting himself by his sole means and abilities and will continue to be fully capable of supporting himself by his sole means and abilities in accordance with his accustomed mode of living, reasonable requirements and station in life, and he hereby waives any rights he may have to payments for present and future support and maintenance from , in the future and in the event of a termination of the living-together arrangements, separation, or divorce (if applicable) in the future, said hereby waives any right he may have to payments for palimony, alimony, support, and maintenance from .

(10) hereby acknowledges that has fully acquainted her with his means and resources; that has ascertained and weighed all of the facts, conditions, and circumstances likely to influence a judgment herein; that all matters have been fully and satisfactorily explained to her; that she has given due consideration to such matters and questions; that she clearly understands and consents to all the provisions hereof; that she had the benefit of the advice of counsel of her own selection; and that she is entering into this agreement freely, voluntarily, and with full knowledge.

(11) hereby acknowledges that has fully acquainted him with her means and resources; that ascertained and weighed all of the facts, conditions and circumstances likely to influence his judgment herein; that all matters embodied herein as well as all questions pertinent hereto have been fully and satisfactorily explained to him; that he has given due consideration to such matters and questions; that he clearly understands and consents to all provisions hereof; that he has had the benefit of the advice of counsel of his own selection; that he is entering into this agreement freely, voluntarily, and with full knowledge.

(12) The consideration of this arrangement is the mutual promises herein contained. If the parties do not commence living together, this agreement shall be in all respects and for all purposes null and void.

(13) This Agreement shall inure to the benefit of and shall be binding and obligatory upon the heirs, personal representatives, administrators, executors, and assignees of the parties hereto.

(14) This instrument contains the entire understandings of the parties and cannot be modified except by written instrument, signed and acknowledged.

(15) If any provision of this Agreement is held invalid, such invalidity shall not affect the other provisions of this Agreement which can be given effect with-

out the invalid provisions and to this end, the provisions of this Agreement are intended to be and shall be deemed severable.

(16) Both parties hereby acknowledge that they have been fully advised by counsel of their own choice who are acting as witnesses hereto.

(17) Should the parties marry, nothing contained in this Agreement shall be construed to prevent either party from instituting any suit, action, or legal proceeding in this or any other jurisdiction for a divorce, separation, or annulment against the other by reason of facts which may heretofore or hereafter occur. In the event that an action, suit, or other legal proceeding for divorce, separation, or annulment shall be instituted at any time by either party against the other, in the State of New York, or in any other jurisdiction, it is agreed that:

(a) Neither of the parties shall cause or request that any provision be inserted in the final judgment or decree of the Court which shall be inconsistent with any of the provisions of this Agreement.

(b) To the extent possible and appropriate, the terms and provisions of this Agreement shall be incorporated by reference into any final judgment or decree obtained in a divorce, separation action, or annulment and shall survive such final judgment or decree.

(c) This Agreement shall in no way and under no circumstances merge in any such judgment or decree of divorce or separation.

(18) Both the legal and practical effect of this Agreement in each and every respect and the financial statements of the parties has been fully explained to both parties by their own counsel, and they both acknowledge that it is a fair Agreement and is not the result of any duress or undue influence exercised by either party upon the other, or by any other person or persons upon either, and they further agree that this Agreement contained the entire understanding of the parties. There are no representations, promises, warranties, covenants, or undertakings other than those expressly set forth herein.

(19) Each of the parties hereto agrees further at any time and from time to time to make, execute, and deliver all instruments necessary to effectuate the provisions of this Agreement. Should either party refuse to make, execute, or deliver such instrument upon due request, then he or she does hereby appoint the other as his or her attorney-in-fact with power to execute such instrument on his or her behalf.

(20) For the purpose of this Agreement, all notices or other communications given or made hereunder shall, until written notice to the contrary, be hand delivered or be sent Certified Mail, Return Receipt Requested to the following addresses, or any other address which either party may subsequently designate in writing, as follows:

To : By mailing or delivering such
notice or communications to:
MR.

And copy to:

ESQ.
ESQS.

To : By mailing or delivering such notice
or communications to:
MS.

And copy to:

(21) All matters affecting the interpretation of this Agreement and the rights of the parties shall be governed by the laws of the State of New York. Each of the parties agrees that the provisions of this Agreement may be enforced in jurisdictions other than New York where either party may reside in the future and that each party hereby agrees to submit himself or herself to said jurisdiction for that purpose.

(22) All the provisions of this Agreement shall be binding upon the respective heirs, next of kin, executors, administrators, and assigns of the parties hereto.

(23) This Agreement shall be executed in quadruplicate, each of which so executed shall be deemed an original and shall constitute one and the same Agreement.

(24) No modification of this Agreement, nor waiver of any provision hereof, right hereunder or condition herein, or release from any obligation imposed hereby, shall be made except by written instrument duly executed by both parties hereto.

IN WITNESS WHEREOF, the said parties hereto have, after consultation with their own counsel relative to the matters herein set forth and agreed upon, having been advised fully and fairly as to all of the facts and circumstances herein set forth, have hereunto set their hands and seals this day of , 19 .

WITNESSED AND APPROVED BY:

For : ______________________________
As Attorney for

For : ______________________________
As Attorney for

____

____

SCHEDULE "A"

Schedule of Approximate Assets
of
as of December 31, 19

SCHEDULE "B"

Assets of as of December 31, 19

SCHEDULE "C"

Schedule of Approximate Income
For Period January 1, 19 -to- December 31, 19

SCHEDULE "D"

Schedule of Approximate Income

of

for Period January 1, 19 -to- December 31, 19

STATE OF NEW YORK)
) ss.:
COUNTY OF)

On this day of , 19 , before me personally came , to me known and known to me to be the individual described in and who executed the foregoing instrument, and he acknowledged to me that he executed the same.

____

Notary Public

STATE OF NEW YORK)
) ss.:
COUNTY OF NEW YORK)

On this day of , 19 , before me personally came , to me known and known to me to be the individual described in and who executed the foregoing instrument, and she acknowledged to me that she executed the same.

____

Notary Public

Enforcement of Contract

In the event John's relationship fails, he should have no difficulty enforcing any contract similar to the above. This is, of course, provided that both John and his partner have been fully represented by counsel during all stages of the contract negotiations and that there has been no overreaching on John's part.

CHAPTER 2

Assistance to the Unmarried Mother

SITUATION

Mary Smith is twenty years old and a secretary earning $15,000. She had been engaged to Harry Jones, a 25-year-old businessman earning $30,000 per year. Several months ago, while she was engaged to Harry and only seeing him, Mary became pregnant. Harry told her that he did not wish to have any children and that he would not marry her unless she had an abortion. Mary decided that she wished to have the child and Harry called off their pending marriage plans.

DETERMINE WHAT CLIENT DESIRES

Since Harry ended his relationship with Mary, there has been no communication between them. Mary has attempted to contact him several times, but has been unsuccessful. Mary wishes to assure the financial security of her unborn child and is not certain that Harry will help her in this regard. She comes to you, her attorney, for advice as to how she can assure that Harry will aid in paying the expenses relating to the birth of her child and the child's upbringing.

FATHER ADMITS PATERNITY

You, as Mary's attorney, should advise her to immediately contact Harry. She should be as pleasant as possible in an attempt to convince him to admit paternity and help support the child. The benefits Mary would obtain as a result of a bargained-for agreement would most likely surpass those obtained after a contested court proceeding. Mary would only obtain minimal support from a court. However, she might be able to convince Harry outside a court proceeding to pay for expenses that would not be otherwise covered in a court order, i.e., the child's college, summer camp, music lessons, etc.

The following is a checklist of the items Mary might request from Harry and will help you determine what aid you should focus on when negotiating with Harry's attorney:

Checklist for Negotiating Child Entitlements for Unmarried Mother

1. Child support, i.e., food, clothing, and health.
2. Limited visitation rights for father.
3. Medical insurance for child.
4. Private lessons, camp, and other fringe benefits for child.
5. Child's college.
6. Life insurance on life of father with mother as beneficiary.
7. Bequests to child in father's Will.
8. Pregnancy expenses, i.e., hospital and doctor bills.
9. Maintenance for mother if she elects to stay home to care for child.
10. Child care expenses of nursery, babysitters, while mother works.

Of course, you should not hope to obtain all of the above items. As will be discussed infra you can only hope to obtain a fraction of these items if Harry refuses to bargain and Mary must seek a court imposed settlement.

Note. Putting aside the pregnancy expenses and child support, which are obviously high priority items, the next priority in the negotiations process should be life insurance and Will bequests. If Harry dies, his support obligations die with him. The only way that Mary can assure that her financial security will not be disrupted by Harry's death is to assure that Harry provides for the child via life insurance and/or his Will.

In order for you to prepare an agreement for Harry to sign regarding his child support obligations, a sample agreement follows.

SAMPLE CHILD SUPPORT AGREEMENT

AGREEMENT made this day of , 19 , between , presently residing at , , State of New York, hereinafter sometimes referred to as the "MOTHER," and , presently residing at , , , State of New York, hereinafter sometimes referred to as the "FATHER."

W I T N E S S E T H

WHEREAS, there is one (1) CHILD of the relationship between the parties, unemancipated and presently under the age of twenty-one (21), namely, , born , 19 , age hereinafter sometimes referred to as the "CHILD"; and

WHEREAS, the parties desire to confirm and make arrangements in connection with the financial support of said child;

NOW, THEREFORE, in consideration of the promises and of the mutual covenants and undertakings herein set forth, the parties covenant and agree as follows:

The FATHER shall pay the MOTHER for the support and maintenance of their CHILD:

A. The sum of and 00/100 ($) DOLLARS per week for 52 consecutive weeks, the first weekly payment to be made to the MOTHER on the first Friday following the execution by both parties of this Agreement.

B. Thereafter, the support payments for the CHILD shall be increased $ per week each year until a maximum payment of $ per week is attained. The FATHER'S maximum liability under this paragraph shall never exceed $ per month.

C. The parties further agree that any week the CHILD is attending a boarding out school, and the MOTHER is not contributing at least one-fourth (1/4) of the tuition, room and board, the FATHER'S obligation for child support under this Paragraph shall be reduced by one-half (1/2) during those weeks the CHILD is attending such boarding out school.

D. Payments for the support of the CHILD shall terminate on the MOTHER'S or FATHER'S death or when the CHILD becomes emancipated as defined below:

(i) Attains the age of twenty-one (21), or if then attending college, until the age of twenty-three (23); or

(ii) Marries; or

(iii) Enters and while a member of the Armed Services or Peace Corps: or

(iv) Becomes employed on a full time basis after the age of eighteen (18); or

(v) Dies, whichever event shall sooner occur.

Both the legal and practical effect of this Agreement in each and every respect and the financial standard of the parties has been fully explained to both parties by their own counsel, and they both acknowledge that it is a fair Agreement and is not the result of any duress or undue influence exercised by either party upon the other, or by any other person or persons upon either, and they further agree that this Agreement contains the entire understanding of the parties. There are no representations, promises, warranties, covenants or undertakings other than those expressly set forth herein.

Each of the parties hereto agrees further at any time and from time to time to make, execute, and deliver all instruments necessary to effectuate the provisions of this Agreement.

For the purpose of this Agreement, all notices or other communication given or made hereunder shall, until written notice to the contrary, be mailed or given directly to the MOTHER and directly to the FATHER at their respective aforementioned addresses.

All matters affecting the Interpretation of this Agreement and the right of the parties shall be governed by the laws of the State of New York.

All the provisions of this Agreement shall be binding upon the respective heirs, next of kin, executors, administrators, and assigns of the parties hereto.

This Agreement shall be executed in triplicate, each of which so executed shall be deemed an original and shall constitute one and the same Agreement.

The failure of either party at any time or from time to time to exercise the rights herein reserved to either party shall not be deemed to constitute a relinquishment of his or her right to exercise the same in the future.

There can and shall be no modification of this Agreement, no waiver of any provision hereof, right hereunder or condition herein, or release from any obligation imposed hereby, except by written instrument duly executed.

If any provision of this Agreement is held to be invalid or unenforceable, all other provisions shall nevertheless continue in full force and effect.

____
Father

____
Mother

IN WITNESS WHEREOF, the said parties hereto have, after consultation with counsel relative to the matters herein set forth and agreed upon, having been advised fully and fairly as to all of the facts and circumstances herein set forth, have hereunto set their hands and seals the day and year first above written.

WITNESSES:

__________________________ __________________________

__________________________ __________________________

STATE OF)
) ss.:
COUNTY OF)

On this day of , 19 , before me personally came , to me known and known to me to be the person described in and who executed the foregoing Agreement and acknowledged that he executed the same.

____
NOTARY PUBLIC

STATE OF)
) ss.:
COUNTY OF)

On this day of , 19 , before me personally came , to me known and known to me to be the person described in and who executed the foregoing Agreement and acknowledged that she executed the same.

____
NOTARY PUBLIC

FATHER DENIES PATERNITY

From Harry's reaction to Mary's birth announcement, it appears that he may refuse to acknowledge that he is the father of the child and may refuse to acknowledge his support obligation. If this is the case Mary will be obliged to commence a filiation proceeding to prove Harry is the father and force him to pay support.

Filiation Proceedings

In most jurisdictions, this is strictly a civil proceeding. The criminal or quasi criminal aspects of the proceeding that were so prevalent in many jurisdictions several years ago, are fading into the past. Indeed, such terms as "bastardy action" are generally in disfavor and the aim is not to punish the father but to assure that he meets his support obligations.

In the filiation proceeding, the burden is on Mary to prove that Harry is the father. She definitely should not initiate an action until after the child is born. The odds against her winning before the birth are great. This is true because blood tests regarding the child would be unavailable until after birth. Also, the man will be more likely close to the date of conception to parade witnesses before the court to establish that he is not the father. These witnesses might, for example, testify that on the date of conception Harry was with them, 1,000 miles away from Mary and, therefore, could not have conceived her child. As we move further and further away from the conception date, any potential witnesses will be less and less likely to remember events that occurred on that date, e.g., that Harry was with them 1,000 miles away from Mary.

Moreover, many judges will not resolve the paternity issue until after the child is born. Thus, proceeding before birth will at the very least be an exercise in futility and may result in the loss of a case that might otherwise be won.

Once the child is born, Mary would commence the filiation proceeding by filing a paternity petition. A sample petition follows.

SAMPLE PATERNITY PETITION

COURT OF THE STATE OF
COUNTY OF

______________________________________ x

In the Matter of the Paternity Petition of

:

:

Petitioner, : PATERNITY PETITION

:

-against- Index No.

, :

:

Respondent.

______________________________________ x

The petition of ____________ alleges and establishes that:

1. Petitioner resides at ____________________.

2. Petitioner engaged in sexual intercourse with the Respondent numerous times. The first sexual encounter with Respondent was on ______________, at ________________, while the last sexual encounter was on __________ __________, at ________________. Petitioner had no sexual relations with anyone except Respondent for the period ________________ to __________ __________. Petitioner and Respondent are not married.

3. Petitioner's sexual relationship with Respondent resulted in Petitioner becoming pregnant.

4. Petitioner gave birth to a child out of wedlock on ________________. Respondent is the father of the child.

5. Respondent orally admitted paternity of the said child to __________ ____________ on ____________________ at ____________________.

6. Respondent has refused to officially acknowledge paternity and has refused to support the said child.

WHEREFORE, Petitioner respectfully requests that this Court issue a summons or warrant that requires Respondent to show cause why this Court should not enter a declaration of paternity, an order of support and any other relief this Court may deem just and proper.

Dated:

____
Petitioner

VERIFICATION

STATE OF NEW YORK)
) ss.:
COUNTY OF ______)

being duly sworn, deposes and says that (s)he is the person who signed the foregoing petition and that it is true to (his) (her) own knowledge, except as to matters therein stated to be alleged on information and belief and as to these matters (s)he believes it to be true.

____
Petitioner

Sworn to before me this
day of , 19

____

Proving Paternity in a Trial

Gathering evidence. The paternity controversy is usually resolved after a hearing by a Judge rather than a jury. In preparing for the hearing, it is extremely important to pinpoint the day of the sexual encounter that caused Mary's pregnancy.

Many courts may require Mary to prove that the child was conceived on a certain day and that Mary had sexual relations with Harry and only Harry on that date. Mary should gather witnesses at the earliest possible moment who can establish these facts. For example, perhaps Mary's friends could testify that Mary was living with Harry during the conception period, spent every night with him during that period, and did not sleep with or even date other men during this period. She should calculate the date of her menstruation which occurred near the date of conception. She should assure that this event did not occur on the estimated date of conception. Harry will attempt to defeat Mary's paternity claim, and may very well do so, by showing that on the estimated date of conception he had no access to Mary, sexual or otherwise, she was having her period or she was having sexual relations with other men.

Aside from evidence relevant to the day of conception, Mary should gather any admissions made by Harry which might link him to the child. Not only should Mary seek direct acknowledgment of paternity, but she should note any conduct by Harry which ties him to the child. For example, the fact that Harry might have accompanied Mary to the doctor while she was pregnant or paid some of the costs of the pregnancy would aid Mary's case.

Important. When Mary obtains the birth certificate for her child, she should be sure that Harry is listed as the father. Otherwise, Harry may be able to successfully argue at the hearing that the birth certificate evidences that Mary concocted the notion of Harry's paternity after the child's birth in order to extort financial assistance from him.

Blood tests. One facet of the filiation proceeding that has changed radically is the use of blood tests. Until recently, blood tests were only admissible at the hearing to prove that the defendant was not the father of the child. They were not admissible to prove paternity. Today by the use of the newly devised HLA (Human Leukocyte Antigen) blood test, paternity can be fairly well pinpointed.

Accordingly, most courts today permit the complainant to utilize blood tests to establish paternity. It is axiomatic that these tests have become an integral, important part of the complainant's case.

Note. The procedure involved in taking the HLA blood test is as follows: First, the trial court should be petitioned by motion for an order requiring that both parties and the child submit to the test. (The form of the motion and order drafted and submitted by you in this regard as Mary's attorney would be the same as any other motion and order. See the sample motion and order in Chapter 14. See Chapter 9 for a sample affidavit of service, a document which must be prepared for every motion made by you.) Then, the court should select a physician to administer the test. The cost of the test should probably be shared equally by both parties. After the physician has taken the required blood samples and analyzed them, the physician should submit the results to the court.

Support and visitation. If, after reviewing the evidence obtained at the hearing pertinent to paternity, the court rules that paternity has been established, the next step is the resolution of the defendant's support obligation and visitation rights. Some courts may permit the parties at this juncture to bargain amongst themselves to attempt to resolve these issues. Other courts may proceed to conduct another hearing wherein the court resolves these issues.

From a court imposed settlement the most that Mary can hope to obtain is the payment of bills relative to the pregnancy re doctor and hospitalization bills, and child support payments. The support ordered will be consonant with the mother's life style. If she is accustomed to the life style enjoyed by those in the higher economic strata of society, she will obtain more than if she is not. The court may include in the support decree an obligation that Harry provide for the medical needs of the child. The court will most likely not include in the support payments the cost of child care for Mary while she works or maintenance and support for her so that she can remain at home with the child.

To enable you to quickly see what items should be contemplated in a filiation proceeding, the following checklist is provided which summarizes the considerations discussed above.

Checklist for Filiation Proceedings

1. Establish date of conception.
2. Find witnesses who can prove sexual relations between your client and defendant on conception date.
3. Secure defendant admissions.
4. Determine menstrual cycle dates of client near conception date.
5. Place defendant's name on child's birth certificate.

6. Secure blood tests.
7. Determine client's income and social status.
8. Establish defendant's income.
9. Calculate pregnancy expenses.
10. Formulate further medical expense needs of child.

A sample court order re paternity and child support follows. This order will prove helpful in summarizing the court's decision in order form.

SAMPLE COURT ORDER RE PATERNITY

State of New York, held in and
for the County of _______, at,
New York, on ________, 19__.

PRESENT
Hon. ____________
Judge

In the Matter of the Paternity Petition of	:	ORDER OF FILIATION
,	:	Index No.
Petitioner,	:	
-against-	:	
,	:	
Respondent.	:	

NOTICE: YOUR WILLFUL FAILURE TO OBEY THIS ORDER MAY, AFTER COURT HEARING, RESULT IN YOUR COMMITMENT TO JAIL FOR A TERM NOT TO EXCEED SIX MONTHS, FOR CONTEMPT OF COURT.

The Petitioner herein, ______________, has filed a petition alleging that ______________ is the father of ______________ , a (male) (female) child, born out of wedlock to Petitioner on ______________.

This Court ordered Respondent to show cause why a declaration of paternity, order of support, and other just relief should not be made.

NOW, after hearing evidence submitted by both sides as to the facts and circumstances involved in this case, and Respondent, denied of all the allegations made in the petition, it is:

ADJUDGED and DECREED that Respondent is the father of ____________ ; ____________ and it is further

ORDERED, ADJUDGED, AND DECREED that Respondent, after notice of this order, pay $___ each week, beginning on ______________ to ______________, as Trustee, until ______________ attains the age of 21, for ______________ support and education; and it is further

ORDERED, ADJUDGED, AND DECREED that the Respondent pay $___ to Petitioner for the expenses incurred by Petitioner during her pregnancy and recovery from her pregnancy, and for the expenses incurred by Petitioner for the support and education of the child from the date of the child's birth on ____________, to the date of the entry of this order; and it is further

ORDERED, ADJUDGED, AND DECREED that Respondent pay to ____________, Petitioner's attorney, the sum of $_____, for attorney's fees relating to this proceeding; and it is further

ORDERED, ADJUDGED, AND DECREED that Respondent report to the Support Collection Unit at ____________, any changes in his address, or employment; and it is further

ORDERED, ADJUDGED, AND DECREED, that pursuant to Article 4, Section 471 of the N.Y. Family Court Act, Respondent provide the Clerk of this Court with a written undertaking, in the amount of $_____, for ___ months, with sufficient surety approved by this Court that Respondent will abide by this Court's order for support.

Dated ________________________

ENTER

____

CHAPTER 3

Counseling the Client on Marriage Rights and Obligations

SITUATION

Gregory Jones, a 35-year-old teacher who earns $45,000 a year and has $60,000 in assets, plans to marry. His bride to be—Melanie Smith—is a 25-year-old teacher who earns $22,000 a year and has no assets. This is Melanie's first marriage. Gregory has been previously married. That marriage ended 10 years ago in an ugly divorce, where Gregory was forced to part with most of the assets he had acquired at that point in his life. Gregory currently makes no alimony payment to his first wife. However, he does pay child support for a 12-year-old boy born during that marriage. Gregory does not foresee any problems with his upcoming marriage.

DETERMINE WHAT CLIENT DESIRES

Gregory comes to you for advice on how to favorably resolve his situation. He wants to assure the following: (1) in the event his upcoming marriage fails, he does not face the same financial hardships faced after the breakup of his first marriage, and (2) if he should die while they are married he wants Melanie to be financially secure. He also desires advice as to (1) if it would be appropriate to give Melanie a power of attorney, and (2) the possible tax consequences of marriage.

EFFECT OF MARRIAGE ON PROPERTY AND ASSETS

Perhaps the most important advice you can give Gregory pertains to what effect his marriage will have on his assets. The answer to this query depends on whether, in the event of the breakup of his marriage, Gregory resides in a common law, community property, or equitable distribution state.

In a common law state, all assets in his name will be his, all assets in Melanie's name will be hers, and any assets in both names will be 50% his and 50% hers. This applies whether the assets have been acquired before or after the marriage.

In a community property or equitable distribution state the crucial query pertains to a determination of what constitutes marital property. In a community property state there will be, upon a breakup of a marriage, a 50–50 distribution of marital assets. In an equitable distribution state there will be, upon a breakup of a marriage, an equitable distribution of marital property. This equitable distribution may depend on such factors as how long the couple has been married, the liquidity of marital property, what income each spouse earns or, in the case of a non-working spouse, what income the spouse would have earned if not married, and housing needs of the spouse taking custody of the children. The chart below depicts whether a particular state is a common law, community property, or equitable distribution state.

CATEGORIES OF PROPERTY DISTRIBUTION

State	Common law distribution	Community property distribution	Equitable distribution
Alabama			X
Alaska			X
Arizona		X	
Arkansas			X
California		X	
Colorado			X
Connecticut			X
Delaware			X
District of Columbia			X
Florida			X
Georgia			X
Hawaii			X
Idaho		X	

CATEGORIES OF PROPERTY DISTRIBUTION

State	Common law distribution	Community property distribution	Equitable distribution
Illinois			X
Indiana			X
Iowa			X
Kansas			X
Kentucky			X
Louisiana		X	
Maine			X
Maryland			X
Massachusetts			X
Michigan			X
Minnesota			X
Mississippi	X		
Missouri			X
Montana			X
Nebraska			X
Nevada		X	
New Hampshire			X
New Jersey			X
New Mexico		X	
New York			X
North Carolina			X
North Dakota			X
Ohio			X
Oklahoma			X
Oregon			X
Pennsylvania			X
Rhode Island			X
South Carolina			X
South Dakota			X
Tennessee			X
Texas		X	
Utah			X
Vermont			X
Virginia	X		
Washington		X	
West Virginia	X		
Wisconsin			X
Wyoming			X

The minority rule is that marital property constitutes all assets acquired before or during the marriage. This minority rule is in force in, for example, Illinois, Iowa, Kansas, Massachusetts, Montana, Washington, Vermont, and Wyoming. Generally, however, most states deem marital property to be only that property acquired after the marriage—and any property acquired before the marriage will be treated as separate property. Further, in those jurisdictions that treat pre-marital property as separate property, the general rule is that gifts and inheritance acquired after the marriage will also be treated as separate property. (Delaware and New Jersey are among those states that would follow the minority rule, i.e. all property acquired post-marriage is marital property.) Some states take the view that the post-marriage gifts and inheritance are always separate property, and will never be shared with the other spouse. These states include Colorado, District of Columbia, Idaho, Illinois, Kentucky, Maine, Missouri, Nevada, New York, and Pennsylvania. Other states take the view that gifts and inheritances are generally treated as separate property, but may, when justice dictates, be included in the property to be shared with the other spouse. These states include Alabama, Arkansas, Minnesota, and New Mexico. It should be noted that most states that treat post-marriage gifts and inheritances as separate property would include gifts from one spouse to another in this category. However, in New York, for example, post-marriage gifts from one spouse to another are treated as marital property.

Warning. Generally, income from assets acquired before marriage will be treated as separate property if maintained in a separate account. However, if the income is placed in a joint account it becomes marital property. This same rationale applies to increases in the value of bonds and certificates of deposit acquired pre-marriage. If these items remain in the name of the spouse that purchased them, they will remain separate property. If they are ever placed in both names, they will become marital property.

Exception to the General Rule. Increases in the value of pre-marriage assets remain separate property if they are passive assets. However, as to assets that are active e.g. husband's business, a large increase in the value during the marriage may be deemed a marital asset and subject to distribution. Almost every jurisdiction will determine that in those cases where there has been a tremendous appreciation in the value of a particular pre-marriage asset due to active participation by either spouse, the appreciation in value will be treated as a marital asset subject to distribution.

TAX CONSEQUENCES OF MARRIAGE

Gregory should be aware that when he marries, his income tax liability will not remain the same. If Melanie did not work and Gregory was the only income earner, his income tax liability would be much less. This would result because Gregory and Melanie could file a joint return, a benefit they could not utilize outside marriage. However, since Gregory and Melanie both work, their combined tax liability may be greater or smaller, depending on their respective incomes. This occurs because single taxpayers are taxed differently from married taxpayers. Most likely, once Gregory is married, he and Melanie will elect to file a joint return rather than separate returns. A separate married return will most likely result in higher tax consequences than a joint return.

Specifically addressing Gregory and Melanie's case, assume that Gregory's $45,000 income is reduced by deductions to $36,800 and Melanie's $22,000 income is reduced by deductions to $16,950 and that none of the deductions are for medical expenses or miscellaneous deductions. Let us further assume that their income was earned in 1988, where the personal exemption is $1,950. If Gregory and Melanie were single, after taking into account their personal exemptions, Gregory would have a taxable income of $34,850 and a tax bill of $7,438; while Melanie would have a taxable income of $15,000 and a tax bill of $2,250. If Gregory and Melanie were married and filed a joint return, after taking into account their personal exemptions they would have a taxable income of $49,850 and a tax bill of $10,091. If they were married and filed separate returns, after taking into account their personal exemptions, Gregory would have a taxable income of $34,850 and a tax bill of $7,824.50, while Melanie would have a taxable income of $15,000 and a tax bill of $2,266.50. Thus, in Gregory and Melanie's specific case, they would have a greater total tax bill on their combined income if they married than if they remained single. However, once they are married their total tax bill on their combined income would be the same whether they filed jointly or separately.

Important. Inserted on the next page, for your aid in determining personal income tax liabilities for your clients is a chart which depicts income tax brackets in 1988 for single, married filing jointly, and married filing separately taxpayers.

Note. It should be noted that after 1988, the tax rate brackets will be adjusted to reflect changes in the rate of inflation.

TAX BRACKETS FOR 1988

Type of taxpayer	% Of taxable income to be paid	On taxable income which exceeds
Single	15	0
	28	$ 17,850
	33	$ 43.140
	38	$ 89,560*
Married Filing Jointly	15	0
	28	$ 29,750
	33	$ 71.900
	38	$149,250*
Married Filing Separately	15	0
	28	$ 14,875
	33	$ 35.950
	38	$113,300*

*In 1988 the 33% bracket is increased by $10,920 for each personal exemption you claim. For example if you are married filing jointly and you claim two exemptions, you will be taxed at the 33% rate until $171,090, not $149,250. After 1988, the $10,920 figure will be adjusted annually to compensate for changes in the personal exemption. Changes in the personal exemption will be tied to changes in the inflation rate.

One area of tax liability in which Gregory will have greater flexibility after marriage is the federal gift tax. Once married, Gregory can make unlimited gifts to Melanie without tax consequences. Prior to marriage, at least into 1987, Gregory could only make gifts to Melanie up to $10,000 a year without federal gift tax consequences. Moreover, once married, Gregory and Melanie can possibly combine their federal gift tax exemptions so as to avoid tax consequences on gifts up to $20,000 to another individual.

NEED FOR A POWER OF ATTORNEY IN A MARRIAGE

You should give Gregory the same advice that you gave your client that was living unmarried with his partner. That is, tell him to:

1. avoid a general power of attorney;
2. provide a special power of attorney in limited circumstances (e.g., when Gregory is out of town or hospitalized for a long period of time); and

3. make the special power of attorney specific and limited as to the powers granted and the time period during which it is effective.

It must be remembered that Gregory's marriage is just beginning. While Gregory and his spouse-to-be may have good intentions, Gregory can not be certain that the marriage will last or that he can totally trust his wife. Once Gregory is married for a significant period of time—say, five years—it may be appropriate to consider passing more extensive powers via a power of attorney from Gregory to Melanie.

NEED FOR A WILL OR NEW WILL AFTER MARRIAGE

There is no doubt that, once married, Gregory should rewrite his existing Will, or write a Will. If Gregory dies intestate, his assets will be distributed according to the laws of the state where he resides at death. Particularly if he has children at his death, he may not be satisfied with the state plan for distribution of his assets. Moreover, he may wish to establish a trust fund for Melanie's benefit at his death and the state will not set up such a fund if he dies intestate. If Gregory has an existing Will, there is even more reason for writing a Will now. Without a new Will, Gregory's assets shall be distributed in accordance with the provisions outlined in his pre-marriage Will. He may not have provided for Melanie at all in that Will. If he did, he probably has not adequately provided for her needs in the event of his death.

NEED FOR COUNSELING TO HANDLE PERSONAL MATTERS

Before embarking on his new marriage, Gregory should determine how certain personal matters will be resolved so as to minimize early marriage conflicts. In regard to Gregory's finances, you should advise him to consider whether he will have separate checking and savings accounts, or joint accounts with his wife. Gregory must be made aware that by placing assets in joint names, he will limit his claim to these assets as separate assets in the event of a divorce.

You should also discuss with Gregory whether he and Melanie will jointly pay their bills or whether he will pay certain bills and Melanie will pay certain bills. The bills for which Gregory becomes personally liable, he must personally pay even if he is no longer married to Melanie. Melanie will incur the same burden as to bills for which she accepts responsibility.

As to bills for which they incur joint responsibility, they will ultimately be equally liable for payment of the bill.

Next, Gregory should consider who will have and use which credit cards and which name or names will appear on the cards. The person whose name appears on the card will probably be responsible for debts incurred under it. If both names appear on the card, Gregory and Melanie will probably be equally responsible for debts incurred under it.

Additionally, Gregory should consider who will pay the security deposit on the apartment rented by him and Melanie, or who will pay the downpayment on a house bought by them. The person who pays the security deposit may have a claim to the apartment if it becomes a co-op or condominium even if such person is not designated on the lease. If both Melanie and Gregory share equally in paying the security deposit, they may both have a right to the apartment in the event of conversion. As to the down payment on the house, the person who pays such will have no greater or lesser ownership rights because he or she paid the down payment. Ownership is determined by viewing which person or persons appear on the deed. If one person appears on the deed, that person solely owns the house. If both Gregory and Melanie appear on the deed, they own the house jointly.

Gregory should avoid any hard and fast rules in regard to the above, as such a course of conduct will create more friction than it will solve. However, Gregory can limit friction by having a general plan as to how these matters should be resolved.

Child Support Advice

You should also provide advice regarding Gregory's support payments to his child from a prior marriage. Gregory probably should be totally responsible for the payments. If Melanie had a child from a prior marriage, and particularly if child support for this child would have continued after her marriage to Gregory, she should be totally responsible for the bills incurred by the child. Of course, Gregory may have considered adopting Melanie's child, in which case he should share in the expenses of the child's upbringing.

Life Insurance Benefits

Perhaps Gregory wishes Melanie to be a total or partial beneficiary on an insurance policy taken out on his life. If so, it should be decided who will pay the premiums on the policy and whether term or ordinary life insurance will be procured.

Note. Who pays the premiums may be an important factor in determining whether the proceeds of the life insurance are included in Gregory's estate upon his death and thereby subject to estate tax. Gregory's estate would include the proceeds of insurance on his life if: (1) his estate receives the proceeds; (2) Melanie receives the proceeds for the benefit of his estate; or (3) although the proceeds are not received by or for the benefit of his estate, he possessed incidents of ownership in the insurance policy. If Gregory is paying the premiums on the policy, he may have incidents of ownership in the policy which will cause the proceeds to be included in his estate. If Melanie is paying the premiums where Gregory does not have any incidents of ownership in the policy, and the proceeds are not received by or for the benefit of his estate, none of the proceeds of the policy will be included in his gross estate.

ANTENUPTIAL AGREEMENTS

Appropriateness of Agreement

Antenuptial agreements are not necessarily for everyone. The young couple embarking on their first marriage need not have one. However, where one party to the marriage has acquired considerable wealth prior to the marriage, an antenuptial agreement would be in order. Further, where one of the parties has been previously married, an antenuptial agreement is in order. This is particularly true where there are children from the first marriage whose inheritance rights will be affected by their mother's or father's second marriage.

Moreover, through the use of an antenuptial agreement, a client with children who plans to marry can not only protect his children's inheritance rights, but the client might obtain the children's approval of the marriage when such would not otherwise be forthcoming. For example, assume that you have a wealthy male client with adult children who has decided to marry a young woman. The children may not approve of the marriage because they believe the young bride-to-be is after their father's money. When they see that she has entered into an antenuptial agreement which leaves much of their inheritance rights intact, they may give their blessings.

In light of the above discussions, you should advise Gregory to enter into an antenuptial agreement with Melanie.

Drafting Antenuptial Agreement

Before you begin negotiations for and drafting of an antenuptial agreement for Gregory, it is important that you understand that Gregory and Melanie are attempting to reach an accord. They wish to marry and there is no need to seek out the other party's jugular vein. Compromises should be sought. If compromises cannot be obtained, perhaps the couple should think of canceling their marriage plans.

Issues to address in antenuptial agreement.

(1) *Determine and incorporate into the agreement the minimum amount of assets Gregory wishes to bequest to Melanie in the event of his death.* This is your first and foremost task. After executing the agreement, Gregory shall execute a Will which bequests the amount in question to Melanie. He should also insert in the antenuptial agreement a clause which specifies that if he wishes to change the Will and provide more to Melanie, he may do so.

(2) *Arrange in the agreement for the present transfer of assets.* In other words, you should determine what assets will be in Gregory's name after the marriage, what assets will be in Melanie's name, and what assets will be held jointly.

(3) *Determine responsibility for and payment of bills in the event of a breakup of the marriage.* In this regard, differentiation should be made between bills for necessaries and bills for luxuries. Since Gregory has a higher income than Melanie, he should pay bills for necessaries. As to luxuries, the party that incurs the bill should pay for it.

(4) *Ascertain who will obtain the use of the house or the apartment in the event of a breakup.*

(5) *If the apartment is rented, determine who will receive the security deposit after the breakup.*

(6) *If the apartment is to become a co-op or a condominium, ascertain who will have the right to buy it after the breakup.*

(7) *If the living quarters are owned by Gregory and/or Melanie, determine whether the house or apartment will be sold and how the proceeds of the sale will be divided after the breakup.*

(8) *Ascertain the ownership at divorce of personal effects.* These effects might be furniture, artwork, rugs, etc.

(9) *Determine the distribution or partial distribution at divorce of all other assets.* These assets, e.g., bonds, real estate, etc., should probably be valued as of the time a separation agreement is written or when the case proceeds to trial. A differentiation should be made between items or assets acquired prior to or during the marriage.

(10) *Determine whether and to whom alimony or maintenance payments should be made.* Possibly, alimony to a particular spouse should be waived entirely if that spouse earns a certain income. Or, the amount of alimony should be dependent upon the duration of the marriage. For example, alimony should only be provided if the marriage lasts five years. If the marriage lasts 10 years, a larger alimony payment should be provided.

(11) *Specify in the agreement whether Gregory will be responsible for Melanie's legal fees at divorce or vice versa.* If either spouse is earning a certain amount at this time, he or she should probably pay his or her own legal fees.

(12) *Ascertain if the antenuptial agreement should have a limited duration.* For example, if Gregory and Melanie are married after 10 years, the agreement will become null and void.

(13) *Determine who will incur the legal costs of drafting the antenuptial agreement.*

A checklist follows which summarizes the foregoing and will enable you to quickly determine what should be included in an antenuptial agreement.

Checklist for Drafting Antenuptial Agreement

1. Assets to be bequeathed
2. Present transfer of assets
3. Payment of bills at divorce
4. Use of living quarters at divorce
5. Obtaining security deposit at divorce
6. Apartment conversion to co-op, condominium; right to buy at divorce
7. Sale of house at divorce and distribution of proceeds
8. Ownership of personal effects at divorce
9. Ownership and valuation of other assets at divorce
10. Alimony/maintenance expenses
11. Payment of divorce legal fees
12. Duration of antenuptial agreement
13. Payment of legal fees re agreement

A sample antenuptial agreement follows which will enable you to quickly and efficiently draft an agreement for Gregory.

SAMPLE ANTENUPTIAL AGREEMENT

AGREEMENT, made as of this day of 19 , by and between , residing at , , hereinafter referred to as , and , residing at , herein-after referred to as .

W I T N E S S E T H:

WHEREAS, the parties hereto, both over the age of 21, residents of the State of New York, do presently contemplate marriage in the immediate future. In anticipation thereof, they desire to fix and determine by Antenuptial Agreement, the rights and claims that will accrue to each of them in the property of the other and in the estate of the other by reason of such marriage, and to fix and determine the rights and claims that will accrue to each of them for property division, maintenance and/or alimony should this marriage ever be terminated by divorce, separation or annulment, and to accept the provisions of this Agreement in lieu of and in full discharge, settlement, and satisfaction of all rights and claims; and

WHEREAS, has agreed that all of the assets and/or property as owned by as of the date of the marriage, as detailed in Schedule "A" annexed hereto, shall be free of all rights that might acquire by reason of his marriage to , or any subsequent divorce, except as hereinafter set forth; and

WHEREAS, has agreed that all of the assets and/or property as owned by as of the date of the marriage, as detailed in Exhibit "B" annexed hereto, shall be free of all rights that might acquire by reason of her marriage to , or any subsequent divorce, except as hereinafter set forth; and

WHEREAS, each of the parties has agreed that any and all "Income" arising during the marriage, and any and all property acquired by either of the parties during the marriage, including "Separate Property," shall be deemed as owned exclusively by the party earning the income and by the party so acquiring title to the property; and

WHEREAS, "Separate Property" of the parties is defined pursuant to Paragraph "FIRST," "SECOND," and "EIGHTH A and B," respectively herein, and

WHEREAS, "Marital Property" is defined pursuant to Paragraph "FIRST" herein, and

WHEREAS, each of the parties hereto has agreed to waive any future rights against the other for payment of any maintenance and/or alimony, support, or similar or comparable payments in the event of a divorce, separation, or annulment in the future;

WHEREAS, each of the parties hereto has agreed to waive any and all rights in each other's respective estates, except as herein provided;

NOW, THEREFORE, in consideration of the premises and of the marriage, and in further consideration of the mutual promises and undertakings hereinafter set forth, the parties hereto agree as follows:

FIRST: Except for any provisions to the contrary as may be set forth in this Agreement, after the marriage, and in the event of any subsequent divorce, separation or annulment of the marriage, shall separately retain all of her rights in her present assets and property which she presently owns (an approximate list of such assets as of 19 is set forth in Schedule "A" herein and which schedule may not include accrued assets and/or future interests presently unknown to her), and also in any and all property which she may inherit during her marriage to , and also in any assets and property which she may acquire prior to the date of the marriage, and she shall have the absolute and unrestricted right to dispose of such property free from any claim that may be made by by reason of their marriage and/or otherwise and with the same effect as if no marriage had been consummated between them. Such property shall be deemed "Separate Property" as defined in amended Section 236 of the New York Domestic Relations Law, which took effect July 19, 1980, also known as the New York Equitable Distribution Law, and shall include any and all appreciation in the value of such "Separate Property" regardless of the contribution, either direct or indirect by to such appreciation. "Marital Property" wherever used in this Agreement shall be deemed as all property acquired during the marriage which is not otherwise specifically defined as "Separate Property" in this Agreement.

SECOND: Except for any provisions to the contrary as may be set forth in this Agreement, after the marriage, and in the event of any subsequent divorce, separation, or annulment of the marriage, shall separately retain all of his rights in his present assets and property which he presently owns (an approximate list of such assets as of is set forth in Schedule "B" herein and which Schedule may not include accrued assets and/or future interests presently unknown to him), and also in any and all property which he may inherit during his marriage to , and also in any assets and property which he may acquire prior to the date of the marriage, and he shall have the absolute and unrestricted right to dispose of such property free from any claim that may be made by by reason of their marriage and/or otherwise and with the same effect as if no marriage had been consummated between them. Such property shall be deemed "Separate Property" as defined in amended Section 236 of the New York Domestic Relations Law, which took effect July 19, 1980, also known as the New York Equitable Distribution Law, and shall include any and all appreciation in the value of such "Separate Property" regardless of the contribution, either direct or indirect by to such appreciation.

THIRD: (A) The parties warrant and represent that the Schedules "A" and "B" annexed to and made a part of this Agreement represent the present approximate assets, property and liabilities of the respective parties hereto as of the dates as set forth in the Schedules annexed hereto and made a part thereof. Should either party inadvertently fail to list and include presently owned assets and property in his or her respective Schedule, then such assets and property shall also be deemed as "Separate Property" hereunder should said party be able to establish his or her respective ownership existed prior to the date of this Agreement.

(B) It is further understood and agreed that "Separate Property" of each party shall include any and all assets and property which may have been or which may be separately acquired prior to the date of the marriage by and between the parties hereto, including all income earned therein and any appreciation in value.

FOURTH: The parties agree that all liabilities presently existing as detailed on Exhibits "A-1 and B-1" annexed hereto, and/or which may be incurred by either party prior to the date of the marriage or during the marriage, and which were incurred in   name alone or in   name alone, shall remain as an individual liability of the party so incurring the liability and at no time hereafter will the other party have any responsibility to pay liabilities so incurred by the other prior to the marriage, and the parties shall hold each other harmless and indemnified in this connection. All reasonable liabilities incurred by   during the marriage, which are consented to by   , shall be deemed a joint responsibility for which   shall be solely liable to pay.

FIFTH: The parties agree that in the event of any audits of all future filed tax returns, each party respectively shall be responsible to pay any assessments, penalties and interest charges which are attributable to his or her failure to declare income or due to his or her taking improper deductions which may arise for that period.

SIXTH: (A) The parties agree that should   liquidate, sell, encumber, exchange, and/or otherwise transfer any of her "Separate Property" or her assets as contained in Schedule "A" herein, during the period of the marriage, then and in that event,   acknowledges and agrees that such liquidation, sale, encumbrance, exchange, and/or transfer shall be solely decided by   .   shall have the absolute right to dispose of the proceeds from any such transaction in any manner she may wish, or to replace such liquidated and/or substituted asset with a new asset of her choice, whether or not such new asset is productive of income; however, any income derived during the marriage from any such new asset shall be owned by   . The new or replacement assets shall continue as her "Separate Property." Any and all taxes arising from any such transaction described in this Paragraph "SIXTH" (A) or otherwise as to her "Separate Property" shall be the sole responsibility of   .

(B) The parties agree that should liquidate, sell, encumber, exchange, and/or otherwise transfer any of his "Separate Property" or his assets as contained in Schedule "B" herein, during the period of the marriage, then and in the event, acknowledges and agrees that such liquidation, sale, encumbrance, exchange, and/or transfer shall be solely decided by . shall have the absolute right to dispose of the proceeds from any such transaction in any manner he may wish, or to replace such liquidated and/or substituted asset with a new asset of his choice, whether or not such new asset is productive of income; however, any income derived during the marriage from any such new asset shall be owned exclusively by . The new or replacement assets shall continue as his "Separate Property." Any and all taxes arising from any such transaction described in this Paragraph "SIXTH" (B) or otherwise as to his "Separate Property" shall be the sole responsibility of .

SEVENTH: A. The parties herewith agree that in the event of "divorce," the apartment and lease governing their residency at , or any other apartment which is presently held in the name of and shall be assigned by and to solely and exclusively and alone shall be responsible to pay all future rental and/or liabilities connected with the occupancy of said apartment. In the event of divorce the parties agree that shall immediately vacate said apartment and she shall give sole and exclusive occupany of same, and shall be entitled to retain as his own the security deposit paid on said apartment. For the purpose of this paragraph the term "divorce" shall be defined as such time as either party serves the other with a summons for divorce, separation, or annulment.

B. The parties agree that all furniture and furnishings presently in their apartment at shall be deemed as owned solely and exclusively by and in the event of a "divorce" as hereinabove defined he shall retain same as his own.

C. The parties further agree that all furniture and furnishings accrued during the marriage, in the event of a "divorce" (as hereinafter defined) shall be divided equally between them with the exception of any and all beer steins, valuable paintings, and boat models, which items shall be deemed as owned solely and exclusively by .

D. The parties further agree that should the building at , (or any other apartment which may be rented by the parties hereto as their residence) adopt a cooperative or condominium plan, then and in such event, shall have the exclusive right to purchase the apartment and shall be solely responsible to make all payments for same.

E. The parties agree that they will file joint income tax returns during the marriage, but shall be responsible to pay on a *pro rata* basis, all income taxes which may be assessed on income earned by him or on income earned on assets held in his name solely and exclusively while shall be responsible for all income taxes which may be assessed on income earned by her or on income earned on assets held in her name solely and exclusively.

EIGHTH: A. The parties agree that any and all "income" which is received during the marriage, whether arising from the assets listed on Schedules "A," or from substituted or replacement assets as described in Paragraph "SIXTH A" above, and any and all assets acquired with or by the use of such income by shall be deemed as owned solely by and shall be deemed during the marriage or at the time of a separation, divorce, or annulment, as her "Separate Property," as defined in amended Section 236 of the Domestic Relations Law, which took effect July 19, 1980 (also known as the Equitable Distribution Law) and shall belong to only.

B. The parties agree that any and all "income" which is received during the marriage, whether arising from the assets listed on Schedule "B," or from substituted or replacement assets as described in Paragraph "SIXTH B" above. and any and all assets acquired with or by the use of such income by shall be deemed as owned solely by and shall be deemed as his "Separate Property," during the marriage or at the time of a separation, divorce, or annulment as defined in amended Section 236 of the Domestic Relations Law, which took effect July 19, 1980, (also known as the Equitable Distribution Law) and shall belong to only.

NINTH: A. The parties agree that for a period of two (2) years commencing from the date of the marriage, or in the event either party commences an action for divorce, separation, or annulment against the other at any time during the marriage, then does hereby waive, release, and relinquish any and all rights against or against her Estate, which he might otherwise have as a surviving spouse, whether any such rights may arise as a result of said marriage or otherwise, and whether claim is heretofore or hereinafter made, pursuant to the provisions of the Estates, Powers, and Trusts Laws of the State of New York or pursuant to such law as may be amended, or pursuant to the statutes and common law now or hereafter in effect in any jurisdiction, in the property and estate of including but not limited to a distributive share in the event of intestacy, the right of election to take against the Will, the right of election to take against testamentary substitutes, homestead rights, the right to act as Administrator or Executor or other fiduciary, dower, curtesy, widower's allowances, equitable distribution, and community property.

This provision shall constitute a waiver of any and all rights and of the right of election which has or may have in the Estate of , in accordance with the requirements of Section 5-1.1(f) of the Estates, Powers and Trusts Law of the State of New York, as said law may be amended, or of the same or similar law of any jurisdiction which may be applicable.

B. The parties agree that for a period of two (2) years commencing from the date of the marriage, or in the event either party commences an action for divorce, separation, or annulment against the other at any time during the marriage, then does hereby waive, release, and relinquish any and all rights against or against his Estate, which she might otherwise have as a surviving spouse, whether any such rights may arise as a result of said marriage or otherwise and whether claim is heretofore or hereinafter made, pursuant to the provisions of the Estates, Powers, and Trusts Laws of the State of New York or pursuant to such law as may be amended, or pursuant to the statutes and common law now or hereafter in effect in any jurisdiction, in the property and estate of including but not limited to a distributive share in the event of intestacy, the right of election to take against the Will, the right of election to take against testamentary substitutes, homestead rights, the right to act as Administrator or Executor or other fiduciary, dower, curtesy, widow's allowances, equitable distribution, and community property.

This provision shall constitute a waiver of any and all rights and of the right of election which has or may have in the Estate of , in accordance with the requirements of Section 5-1.1(f) of the Estates, Powers and Trusts Law of the State of New York, as said law may be amended, or of the same or similar law of any jurisdiction which may be applicable.

TENTH: A. (1) Should and separate or be divorced or the marriage be annulled in the future, then and in any such events, shall retain as his own:

(a) all of his "Separate Property"

(b) any and all property and assets which he has an interest in or are held in his name, including all property and assets acquired in his name during the marriage.

(c) all "Marital Property" which is held in his name or he has an interest in.

(2) Should and separate or be divorced or the marriage be annulled in the future, then and in any of such events, shall retain as her own:

(a) all of her "Separate Property"

(b) any and all property which she has an interest in or are held in her name, including all property and assets acquired in her name during the marriage;

(c) all "Marital Property" which is held in her name or she has an interest in.

(3) Should and separate or be divorced or the marriage be annulled in the future, then and in any of such events shall be solely responsible to pay all legal fees he incurs for his legal representation in such proceedings and shall be solely responsible to pay all legal fees she incurs for her legal representation in

such proceedings. Legal fees for the purpose of this paragraph shall include any and all fees to be paid including fees for expert witnesses.

B. Except as specifically set forth in this Agreement, and hereby waive any and all rights in the said "Separate Property" or "Marital Property" of the other, should they separate, be divorced, or the marriage be annulled whether pursuant to the Equitable Distribution Law of the State of New York, as said law may be amended, or pursuant to the terms and provisions of any same or similar law of any jurisdiction which may then be applicable.

C. The parties agree that any property and assets wherein title is held in both names at the date an action for divorce, separation or annulment is initiated, including any and all appreciation as earned or accrued thereon, shall be deemed as marital property and shall be divided equally between them.

D. For good and valid consideration, hereby acknowledges the fact that he is now fully capable of supporting himself by his sole means and abilities and will continue to be fully capable of supporting himself by his sole means and abilities, in accordance with his accustomed mode of living, reasonable requirements and station in life, and he hereby waives any and all rights he may have to payments for present and future support and maintenance from as his wife in the future, and in the event of a separation, divorce, or annulment in the future, does hereby waive any rights which he may have to payments of alimony, support, maintenance, and/or otherwise from

E. does hereby acknowledge that has acquainted him fully with respect to her present approximate income and earnings, as set forth in Schedule "A", annexed to and made a part hereof, and with her present approximate assets and property, as set forth in Schedule "A" annexed hereto. has ascertained and weighed all of the facts, conditions, and circumstances likely to influence his judgment herein. All matters embodied herein as well as all questions pertinent hereto have been fully and satisfactorily explained to him. He has given due consideration to such matters and questions. He clearly understands and consents to all of the provisions hereof. He has had the benefit of the advice of counsel of his own selection and he is entering into this Agreement freely, voluntarily, and with full knowledge.

F. For good and valid consideration, hereby acknowledges the fact that she is now fully capable of supporting herself by her sole means and abilities and will continue to be fully capable of supporting herself by her sole means and abilities, in accordance with her accustomed mode of living, reasonable requirements and station in life, and she hereby waives any and all rights she may have to payments for present and future support and maintenance from as her husband in the future, and in the event of a separation, divorce, or annulment in the future, does hereby waive any rights which she may have to payments of alimony, support, maintenance, and/or otherwise from .

G. does hereby acknowledge that has acquainted her fully with respect to his present approximate income and earnings, as set forth in Schedule "B", annexed to and made a part hereof, and with his present approximate assets and property, as set forth in Schedule "B" annexed hereto. has ascertained and weighed all of the facts, conditions, and circumstances likely to influence her judgment herein. All matters embodied herein as well as all questions pertinent hereto have been fully and satisfactorily explained to her. She has given due consideration to such matters and questions. She clearly understands and consents to all of the provisions hereof. She has had the benefit of the advice of counsel of her own selection and she is entering into this Agreement freely, voluntarily, and with full knowledge.

H. The parties further agree that at such time as a divorce, separation, or annulment proceeding may be initiated by either party against the other, then each party will sign all documents necessary to effectuate the transfer to the other party of all of such other party's interests in the "Separate Property" or "Marital Property" or "Joint Property" as provided for herein.

I. The parties further agree that each of them shall pay his or her own respective share of any and all capital gains taxes and/or any and all other taxes or assessments which might accrue or arise from such transfer or exchange of such assets between the spouses resulting from divorce, separation, or annulment.

J. The parties acknowledge the fact that each party has been furnished with all information requested by the other and that each has had the opportunity to make full and complete examination of the other's income, property, assets, and financial affairs.

TWELFTH: The consideration of this Agreement is the mutual promises herein contained and the marriage about to be solemnized.

THIRTEENTH: and acknowledge that each of them has executed this Agreement of his or her own volition, free from any persuasion, influence, fraud, or duress on the part of the other or any person whomsoever and that each of them has been duly represented by his or her independent respective counsel and attorneys of his or her own choice before executing this Agreement. represents that she has been represented and advised by , of , and represents that he has been represented and advised by , New York.

FOURTEENTH: Nothing contained in this Agreement shall be construed to prevent either party from instituting any suit, action, or other legal proceeding in this or any other jurisdiction for a divorce, separation, or annulment against the other by reason of facts which may heretofore or hereafter occur. In the event that an action, suit, or other legal proceeding for divorce, separation, or annulment shall be instituted at any time by either party against the other, in the State of New York, or in any other jurisdiction, it is agreed that:

(A) Neither of the parties shall cause or request that any provision be inserted in the final judgment or decree of the Court which shall be inconsistent with any of the provisions of this Agreement.

(B) To the extent possible and appropriate, the terms and provisions of this Agreement shall be incorporated by reference into any final judgment or decree obtained in a divorce, separation action, or annulment and shall survive such final judgment or decree.

(C) This Agreement shall in no way and under no circumstances merge in any such judgment or decree of divorce or separation.

FIFTEENTH: Both the legal and practical effects of this Agreement in each and every respect and the financial standards of the parties has been fully explained to both parties by their own counsel, and they both acknowledge that it is a fair Agreement and is not the result of any duress or undue influence exercised by either party upon the other, or by any other person or persons upon either, and they further agree that this Agreement contains the entire understanding of the parties. There are no representations, promises, warranties, covenants, or undertakings other than those expressly set forth herein.

SIXTEENTH: Each of the parties hereto agrees further at any time and from time to time to make, execute, and deliver any and all instruments or documents necessary to effectuate the provisions and intent of this Agreement. Should either party refuse to make, execute, or deliver such instrument or document upon due request, then he or she does hereby appoint the other as his or her attorney-in-fact with power to execute such instrument on his or her behalf.

SEVENTEENTH: For the purpose of this Agreement, all notices or other communications given or made hereunder shall, until written notice to the contrary, be hand delivered or be sent by Certified Mail, Return Receipt Requested, to the following addresses or to any other address which either party may subsequently designate in writing, as follows:

To :By mailing or delivering such
notice or communications to:

To :By mailing or delivering such
notice or communications to:

EIGHTEENTH: All matters affecting the interpretation of this Agreement and the rights of the parties shall be governed by the laws of the State of New York.

Each of the parties agree that the provisions of this Agreement may be enforced in jurisdictions other than New York where either party may reside in the future and that each party hereby agrees to submit himself or herself to said jurisdiction for that purpose.

NINETEENTH: All the provisions of this Agreement shall be binding upon the respective heirs, next of kin, executors, administrators, and assigns of the parties hereto.

TWENTIETH: This Agreement shall be executed in quadruplicate, each of which so executed shall be deemed an original and shall constitute one and the same Agreement.

TWENTY-FIRST: The failure of either party at any time or from time to time to exercise the rights herein reserved to either party shall not be deemed to constitute a waiver of his or her right to exercise the same in the future.

TWENTY-SECOND: No modification of this Agreement, nor waiver of any provision hereof, right hereunder or condition herein, or release from any obligation imposed hereby, shall be made except by written instrument duly executed by both parties hereto.

TWENTY-THIRD: If any provision of this Agreement is held to be invalid or unenforceable, all other provisions shall nevertheless continue in full force and effect.

IN WITNESS WHEREOF, the said parties hereto, after consultation with their own counsel relative to the matters herein set forth and agreed upon, having been advised fully and fairly as to all of the facts and circumstances herein set forth, have hereunto set their hands and seals this day of , 19 .

WITNESSETH:

____________________ ____________________

Witness for

____________________ ____________________

Witness for

Approved By:

____

As Attorneys for

Approved By:

____
As Attorney for

SCHEDULE "A"

STATEMENT OF APPROXIMATE INCOME & ASSETS AS OF JULY 1, 19

INCOME

ASSETS

____

SCHEDULE "A-1"

STATEMENT OF LIABILITIES AS OF , 19

____

SCHEDULE "B"

STATEMENT OF APPROXIMATE INCOME AND ASSETS AS OF , 19

INCOME

ASSETS

____

SCHEDULE "B-1"

STATEMENT OF LIABILITIES AS OF 19

____

STATE OF NEW YORK)
) ss.:
COUNTY OF NEW YORK)

On this day of , 19 , before me personally came , to me known and known to me to be the individual described in and who executed the foregoing instrument, and she acknowledged to me that she executed the same.

____
NOTARY PUBLIC

STATE OF NEW YORK)
) ss.:
COUNTY OF NEW YORK)

On this day of , 19 , before me personally came , to me known and known to me to be the individual described in and who executed the foregoing instrument, and he acknowledged to me that he executed the same.

____

NOTARY PUBLIC

Legal Validity of Agreement

In the recent past, most states felt that antenuptial agreements were void except insofar as they outlined the rights of the parties in the event of death. Agreements that determined the rights of the parties in the event of a divorce were deemed to be against public policy and not binding. Today, most jurisdictions permit agreements that not only outline estate rights but that outline marital breakup rights. However, no jurisdiction has as yet permitted the parties to an antenuptial agreement to determine, in the event of a divorce, the relationship they will have with the children who are subsequently born during their marriage. This is probably true since prior to the birth of the children, there is absolutely no way to ascertain what relationship will be in the best interest of a particular child.

To assure that an antenuptial agreement is not declared void by the courts, you must make certain that there is no overreaching. For example, an agreement that would give everything to your client and nothing to your client's spouse in the event the marriage breaks down, will be struck down. Moreover, you should not have your client enter into an antenuptial agreement unless his spouse has an attorney. That attorney should not merely look at the agreement and give approval. Rather, negotiations must take place, and that attorney should be intimately involved in the negotiations. Additionally, your client must make complete representations in the agreement as to current and expected future assets, liabilities, and income if the agreement is to withstand legal attack. In this regard, it is insufficient for your client to state that he is worth X dollars. He must give a detailed accounting of each asset, liability, and source of income. In short, it is crucial to a court reviewing an antenuptial agreement that both parties knew exactly what they were doing, that negotiations took place between attorneys, that the agreement is fair, without duress, fraud, or misrepresentation, and that the assets, liabilities, and income of the parties are disclosed in detail.

Part 2

HOW TO HANDLE LEGAL CONSIDERATIONS DURING MARITAL BLISS

CHAPTER 4

Adoption Proceedings

SITUATION

Steve and Joan Jones are, respectively, 35 and 34 years old, and have been married for ten years. They are unable to have children and desire to adopt a child through an adoption agency.

DETERMINE WHAT CLIENT DESIRES

They have come to you, their attorney, for advice concerning what steps they must follow to finalize an adoption.

AGENCY ADOPTIONS

You should inform Steve and Joan that most adoption agencies, before they will grant adoptive parents approval to adopt, will require that the potentially adoptive parents undergo a preliminary home study. In this study, the home environment of the prospective parents is investigated. Their reasons for choosing to adopt are explored, their educational background and financial status are investigated, and the health and ages of the prospective parents and other household matters will be noted. Further, an investigation will probably be conducted to determine if Steve and Joan have a record of child abuse or neglect.

The Physical Custody Period

After the agency has granted Steve and Joan approval to adopt, when a child is available for adoption, it will be placed in their physical, but not legal, custody. This period of physical custody will last for several months. For example, in New York, the period is a minimum of six months. During this physical custody period, the adoption agency will retain legal custody of the child. The agency would have previously obtained legal custody of the child and consent to place the child for adoption from the natural mother or natural parents.

One of the reasons for the physical custody period is so that the interaction between prospective adoptive parents and child can be viewed to determine if the prospective parents will be fit parents. During that physical custody period, the prospective adoptive parents can make day-to-day decisions as to the general health, education, and welfare requirements of the child. However, for extremely important decisions regarding the child, the prospective adoptive parents must obtain agency approval. For example, the prospective adoptive parents must obtain agency approval if the child is to undergo a serious operation, or if they wish to take the child out of the country.

Filing the Petition to Adopt

After the physical custody period begins, Steve and Joan can petition to the appropriate court to adopt the child. Only the local court that has jurisdiction over adoptions can finalize the adoption (usually the Surrogates and/or Family Courts). Steve and Joan will initiate the adoption proceeding in this Court by filing a petition for adoption. They can file this petition at any time after they have physical custody of the child, but the adoption cannot be approved and/or finalized until after the initial physical custody period is complete.

Generally, attached to and made a part of the petition for adoption are certain documents which must also be completed. One of these may be a confidential affidavit which requires disclosure of the prospective adoptive parents' educational level, employment, financial status, state of health, living quarters, and other children.

Other documents that may have to be filed with the adoption petition are: (1) the natural mother's or natural parents' consent to adopt, (2) any agreement the prospective parents have consummated with the adoption agency, (3) the original birth certificate and ongoing medical records of the child, (4) the agency home study report, and (5) the results of any investigation conducted regarding the child abuse or neglect history of the prospective parents. All of the documents will be given to you, as the attorney for Joan and Steve, by the agency. The agency would have prepared the home study report, and obtained any data regarding child abuse or neglect by Steve and Joan. Also, the agency would have (1) obtained from the natural parents their consent to adopt; (2) obtained from the town where the child was born a copy of the child's original birth certificate; and (3) obtained from the natural parents the name of the hospital where the child was born, the doctors who cared for the child since birth, and all medical records pertaining to the child.

Aside from these filing requirements, you may be required to file an attorney's affidavit detailing, among other things, what expenses have been incurred and have been paid in connection with the adoption and the manner in which contact was made between the attorney and the adoptive parents. In New York for example, such an affidavit is required and a copy must be filed with the New York State Office of Court Administration. One of the purposes of this form is to attempt to prevent the illicit acquisition of children.

Agency Expenses to be Paid by Adoptive Parents

In regard to the expenses paid in an agency adoption (aside from legal expenses), Steve and Joan will pay the agency a fee which will help cover the expenses incurred by the agency on the child's or natural mother's behalf up until the time Steve and Joan assume physical custody of the child. In particular, this fee will help cover medical expenses at birth and thereafter, clothing, shelter, and food for the child. Once Steve and Joan have physical custody of the child, they will pay all expenses relating to the child.

Follow-up Study

After all necessary documents have been filed for the adoption, the Court will probably conduct a follow-up study, unless the agency has conducted one. In the study, an analysis will be made as to how the child is adapting to the prospective adoptive parents and vice versa.

Court Approval of Adoption

When the Law Department of the court has reviewed the results of this study and all the filed documents, and insured that all legal requirements have been met, the adoption will be approved if that is in the best interest of the child. A date will be set for the prospective parents to appear before the court and obtain the final order of adoption. Usually, this is a *pro forma* proceeding without a hearing. A copy of the order of adoption will probably be sent to the Department of Health in the state where the adoption proceeding is taking place with new birth certificate information for the child. The original birth certificate will remain in the court file, and will remain confidential.

In order to guide you in handling Joan and Steve's adoption proceedings, a sample petition for and order of adoption in the agency setting follows.

SAMPLE AGENCY PETITION FOR AND ORDER OF ADOPTION

SURROGATE'S COURT, COUNTY

---x

In the Matter of the Adoption by	:	
	:	Petition for Adoption
of a minor (under) (over) the age of fourteen years,* having the first name of	:	(Agency)
	:	
whose full name is contained in the Schedule annexed to the Petition herein.	:	

---x

To THE HONORABLE
JUDGE OF THE
SURROGATE'S COURT OF
THE COUNTY OF

The petitioners show to this Court:

1. (a) The name and place of residence of the petitioning proposed adoptive mother are:

   NAME:

   ADDRESS:

   COUNTY:

   She is of full age, born on

   She is (unmarried) (married to and they are living together as husband and wife).

   Her occupation is

   and her approximate annual income is $

*For the child over a certain age, e.g. 14 in New York, his or her consent may be crucial to the success of the adoption proceeding. See section "Adoption of Step Child," infra.

(b) The name and place of residence of the petitioning proposed adoptive father are:

NAME:

ADDRESS:

COUNTY:

He is of full age, born on

He is (unmarried) (married to and they are living together as husband and wife).

His occupation is

and his approximate annual income is $

2. That your petitioners desirous of adopting as their own child a (male) (female) minor child born on the day of , 19 .

And upon information and belief, there will be annexed to this petition a schedule containing all the facts as required by Section 112 (3) of the Domestic Relations Law of New York concerning said child, verified by a duly constituted official of .

3. That the religious faith of said minor child is ; that the religious faith of the parents of said child as petitioners are informed and verily believe, is ; that the religious faith of petitioners is

4. That petitioners have not paid or given any compensation or thing of value, directly or indirectly to any person or to any agency, association, corporation, institution, society, or other organization for receiving the above-named child, except

medical fees paid to
in the amount of

hospital fees paid to
in the amount of

5. That the family residing with petitioners consists of

6. That said minor child has resided continuously with petitioners since

7. That the occupations of your petitioners are

8. That your petitioners obtained custody of the minor child in the following manner:

9. That said minor child has no property or means of support, except

10. That on information and belief said minor child has general or testamentary guardian

11. That there are no persons other than those herein mentioned interested in this proceeding, to the best of your petitioners' information and belief, except

12. The petitioners request the Clerk of the Court to transmit the certificate of birth to the Department of Health having jurisdiction of the birth record.
13. That no previous application has been made to any court or judge for the relief sought or if so made, the disposition of it and a statement as to whether the minor child has been previously adopted,

WHEREFORE, your petitioners pray for an order allowing and approving the adoption of said by your petitioners and directing that the said shall henceforth be regarded and treated in all respects as the child of your petitioners . and , and be known and called by the name of .

____

____

____

STATE OF)
) ss.:
COUNTY OF)

and

the above named petitioners, being duly sworn, depose and say, that they have read the foregoing petition subscribed by and know the contents thereof, and that the same is true to their own knowledge, except as to matters therein stated to be alleged on information and belief, and as to those matters they believe it to be true.

Subscribed and sworn to before me

this day of

19

____

____

Notary Public

(Seal)

ORDERED that ____________ is hereby designated to investigate the within application and submit a written report in accordance with Section 116. N.Y. D.R.L, Subdivision 3.

Dated:

____
Judge of the Surrogate's Court

Name, post office
address, and telephone
number of Attorney for
Petitioners:

Supporting Documents:

Consent
Agreement of Adoption
Marriage Record of Petitioner(s) (Certified Copy)
Birth Certificate of Adoptive Child (Certified Copy)

Affidavits: 1.
2.
3.

Other Documents: (List)

ORDER OF ADOPTION

At a Surrogate's Court, held in and for the County of at the County Court House, at in said County on the day of , 19

PRESENT:

HON.

Judge of the Surrogate's Court

---x

In the Matter of the Adoption by	:	ORDER OF ADOPTION (AGENCY)
of an adoptive child having the first name of	:	
	:	
whose full name is contained in the Schedule annexed to the Petition herein.	:	

---x

On the petition of and , his wife, adults, duly verified before me the day of , 19 , and the affidavit of , Attorney at Law, duly sworn to, and the above-named parties having severally appeared before me together with , a minor, and said parties constituting all of the parties required to appear before me pursuant to the provisions of an Act relating to the Domestic Relations Law, constituting Chapter Fourteen of the Consolidated Laws of New York, as amended, and said parties having been examined by me, as required by said law, and said parties having presented to me an instrument containing substantially the consents required by said law, an agreement on the part of the adoptive parents to adopt and treat the minor as their own lawful child, and a statement of the date and place of birth of the minor to be adopted, as nearly as the same can be ascertained, the religious faith of the parent of the minor, the manner in which the adoptive parent obtained the minor, and said instrument having been duly signed, sealed, and acknowledged as required by law by each person whose consent is necessary to the adoption;* and having been specifically designated by me to make an investigation to verify the truth of the allegations set forth in the petition, the instrument or agreement of adoption and other papers in this proceeding and such other

*If citation has issued, recite facts relative thereto. If no citation has issued, make no insertion.

facts relating to the said minor, , and to the adoptive parents, as would give me full knowledge as to the desirability of approving said adoption, and the said investigator, having made his (her) report in writing, and the same having been filed in this court; and said investigator having reported that the facts and conditions as set forth in the petition, the instrument or agreement of adoption and other papers in this proceeding are true and are fairly stated, and further reporting that in his (her) opinion the adoption of the said minor, , as prayed for in the petition herein would be for the best interests of said minor; And it appearing to my satisfaction that the moral and temporal interests of the minor, , will be promoted by granting the petition of said and , his wife, and allowing and approving the proposed adoption; and it appearing to my satisfaction that there is no reasonable objection to the change of name proposed,

NOW, ON MOTION OF , attorney for the petitioners herein, it is

ORDERED that the petition of and for the adoption of , a minor, born on the day of , 19 , in , be and the same is hereby granted and that such adoption and the agreement therefor submitted upon this application be and the same hereby are in all respects allowed and approved, and it is

FURTHER, ORDERED that the minor, shall be henceforth regarded and treated in all respects as the child of said and , his wife, and will be known and called by the name of .

____

Judge of the Surrogate's Court

PRIVATE ADOPTIONS

Steve and Joan may not be able to adopt a child of their choosing through an agency adoption. This is true because in recent years the supply of children to be adopted has decreased while the demand has increased. Also, the scrutiny of an agency may be greater or lesser than by a natural parent. If Steve and Joan are unsuccessful in their bid for an agency adoption, you may suggest that they attempt to adopt a child privately. However, certain states do not allow private placement adoptions at all, [i.e., Connecticut, Delaware, Georgia, Massachusetts, Michigan, Minnesota, North Dakota, Rhode Island, and Virginia]. Other states greatly restrict private adoptions [i.e. Montana, Nebraska, New Jersey, and Wisconsin]. Local law should be investigated.

You, as the attorney for Steve and Joan, should not become involved in the process of locating an adoptable child. You should merely provide advice to Steve and Joan as to how they can locate a child to adopt. For example, you might suggest that they place an advertisement in the newspaper, although some newspapers will not print this type of advertising.

Once Steve and Joan have focused on a particular child for adoption, you should enter the picture to handle the adoption proceedings. You should assure that the natural mother or parents are represented by counsel during all stages of the proceedings, keeping in mind that the adoptive parents may have to bear this added expense. What you do not want is a claim by the natural parents at some point in the future that they were unduly pressured to permit the adoption of their child.

Procedures for Private vs. Agency Adoptions

In most jurisdictions, the procedures for consummating a private placement adoption are essentially the same as those for an agency adoption. The prospective adoptive parents will obtain merely physical custody for a certain period of time, will file a petition for adoption in the court having jurisdiction over such matters, and will become adoptive parents pursuant to an order of the court. However, there are some slight variations in procedure and certain responsibilities that were handled by the agency must now be handled by you as attorney for Steve and Joan.

Differences between agency and private adoptions

(1) *Responsibility for Expenses.* For example, while the agency handled all expenses prior to the prospective adoptive parents having physical custody of the child, Steve and Joan will be negotiating with the natural

parents to determine who will pay for what expenses. If the child is not yet born, Steve and Joan may very well bear the responsibility for all expenses relating to the child's birth. This might include both the natural mother's and child's medical expenses, the natural mother's maternity clothing, and a temporary residence for her while she is pregnant.

(2) *Obtaining Consent.* Next, while in the agency adoption the agency obtains the consent to adopt from the natural mother, or parents, in the private placement adoption, you, as Steve and Joan's attorney, must obtain this consent by working with the natural parents' attorney. If both natural parents can be identified and their locations are known, consent to adopt must be given by both of them. If only the natural mother is known, a petition for the termination of the father's parental rights should be filed in a court with jurisdiction over the father. The natural father's parental rights need not be terminated before Steve and Joan obtain physical custody of the child. However, before the adoption can be finalized by the court, the consent of both natural parents or the consent of one and the termination of the rights of the other, must be obtained. Finally, while in the agency adoption situation most jurisdictions will accept the consent to adopt if given to the adoption agency, in the private adoption situation the consent will probably have to be given in court. The rules surrounding the natural parents' consent vary from jurisdiction to jurisdiction and the consent should be checked carefully for its validity, i.e. time limitations, revocability, and witnesses.

(3) *Care of Child During the Physical Custody Period.* Another facet of the private placement adoption that is different from the agency adoption pertains to the care of the child during the physical custody period. While in the agency adoption proceeding, the agency retains a certain amount of control over decisions pertaining to the child, (e.g. serious operations), in the private placement adoption proceeding Steve and Joan can negotiate with the natural mother or parents in an attempt to obtain full temporary control over decisions pertaining to the child. They may want the natural mother or parents to execute a power of attorney giving them full decision making powers over the health, welfare, and educational needs of the child. The sample power of attorney included in Chapter 1, will help you formulate the necessary power of attorney.

(4) *Arrangement of the Home Study.* Also in the private placement adoption, the adoptive parents usually arrange for the home study themselves because there is no agency to arrange it for them. If the adoptive parents don't arrange for the home study, the court will arrange for it.

To enable you to handle Joan and Steve's nonagency adoption, a sample petition for and order of adoption follows. Also, a sample consent to adopt authorization and a sample petition and order for the termination of parental rights is annexed. These samples will help you terminate the rights of the natural parents of the child and avoid the possibility of facing a nonconsenting natural parent or parents at the time Joan and Steve are in a position to finalize the adoption proceedings.

SAMPLE NONAGENCY PETITION FOR AND ORDER OF ADOPTION

SURROGATE'S COURT
______________________________x

In the matter of the adoption
of

a minor (over) (under) the age of
fourteen years,*

by
______________________________x

Petition for Adoption
(Private Placement)

To: THE HONORABLE
JUDGE OF THE
SURROGATE'S COURT OF
THE COUNTY OF

The petitioners show to this Court

1. (a) The name and place of residence of the petitioning proposed adoptive mother are:
   NAME:
   ADDRESS:
   COUNTY:
   She is of full age, born on
   She is (unmarried) (married to and they are living together as husband and wife).
   Her occupation is
   and her approximate annual income is $

*For the child over a certain age, e.g. 14 in New York, his or her consent may be crucial to the success of the adoption proceeding. See section "Adoption of Step Child", infra.

(b) The name and place of residence of the petitioning proposed adoptive father are:

NAME:

ADDRESS:

COUNTY:

He is of full age, born on

He is (unmarried) (married to and they are living together as husband and wife).

His occupation is

and his approximate annual income is $

2. That your petitioner desirous of adopting as own child a minor child born on the day of , 19

3. That the religious faith of said minor child is ; that the religious faith of the parents of said child, as petitioners are informed and verily believe is ; that the religious faith of petitioners is

4. That petitioners have not paid or given any compensation or thing of value, directly or indirectly to any person or to any agency, association, corporation, institution, society or other organization for receiving the above-named child, except

medical fees paid to
in the amount of

hospital fees paid to
on the amount of

5. That the family residing with petitioners consists of

6. That said minor child has resided continuously with petitioner since

7. That the occupations of your petitioners are

8. That the parents of said minor child

9. That your petitioners obtained custody of the minor child in the following manner:

10. That said minor child has no property or means of support, except

11. That on information and belief said minor child has general or testamentary guardian

12. That there are no persons other than those herein mentioned interested in this proceeding, to the best of your petitioners' information and belief, except

13. The petitioners request the Clerk of the Court to transmit the certificate of birth to the Department of Health having jurisdiction of the birth record.
14. That no previous application has been made to any court or judge for the relief sought or if so made, the disposition of it and a statement as to whether the minor child has been previously adopted,

WHEREFORE, your petitioners pray for an order allowing and approving the adoption of said by your petitioners and directing that the said shall henceforth be regarded and treated in all respects as the child of your petitioners and , and be known and called by the name of .

____

____

____

STATE OF)
) ss.:
COUNTY OF)

and

the above named petitioner being duly sworn, depose and say, that they have read the foregoing petition subscribed by and know the contents thereof, and that the same is true to their own knowledge, except as to matters therein stated to be alleged on information and belief, and as to those matters they believe it to be true.

Subscribed and sworn to before me

this day of

19

____

____

Notary Public

(Seal)

ORDERED that ______________ is hereby designated to investigate the within application and submit a written report in accordance with Section 116. N.Y. D.R.L, Subdivision 3.

Dated:

____
Judge of the Surrogate's Court

Name, post office
address, and telephone
number of Attorney for
Petitioners:

Supporting Documents:

Consent
Agreement of Adoption
Marriage Record of Petitioner(s) (Certified Copy)
Birth Certificate of Adoptive Child (Certified Copy)

Affidavits: 1.
2.
3.

Other Documents: (List)

ORDER OF ADOPTION

At a Surrogate's Court held in and for the County of at the Courthouse at in said County on the day of , 19 .

PRESENT:

HON.
Judge of the Surrogate's Court

In the matter of the adoption
of
a minor over/under the age of
fourteen years
by

ORDER OF
ADOPTION
(Private Placement)

On the petition of and , his wife, adults, duly verified before me the day of , 19 , and the affidavit of , Attorney at Law, duly sworn to, and the above-named parties having severally appeared before me together with , a minor, and said parties constituting all of the parties required to appear before me pursuant to the provisions of an Act relating to the Domestic Relations Law, constituting Chapter Fourteen of the Consolidated Laws of New York, as amended, and said parties having been examined by me, as required by said law, and said parties having presented to me an instrument containing substantially the consents required by said law, an agreement on the part of the adoptive parents to adopt and treat the minor as their own lawful child, and a statement of the date and place of birth of the minor to be adopted as nearly as the same can be ascertained, the religious faith of the parents of the minor, the manner in which the adoptive parents obtained the minor, and said instrument having been duly signed, sealed and acknowledged as required by law by each person whose consent is necessary to the adoption;* and have been specifically designated by me to make an investigation to verify the truth of the allegations set forth in the petition, the instrument or agreement of adoption and other papers in this proceeding and such other facts relating to the said minor, , and to the adoptive parents, as would give me full knowledge as to the desirability of approving said adoption, and the said investigator, having made his (her) report in writing and the same having been filed in this court; and said investigator having reported that the facts and conditions as set forth in the petition, the instrument or agreement of adoption and other

*If citation has issued, recite facts relative thereto. If no citation has issued, make no insertion.

papers in this proceeding are true and are fairly stated, and further reporting that in his (her) opinion the adoption of the said minor, , as prayed for in the petition herein would be for the best interests of said minor;

And it appearing to my satisfaction that the moral and temporal interests of the minor, , will be promoted by granting the petition of said and , his wife, and allowing and approving the proposed adoption; and it appearing to my satisfaction that there is no reasonable objection to the change of name proposed.

NOW, ON MOTION OF , attorney for the petitioner herein, it is

ORDERED that the petition of and , his wife, for the adoption of , a minor, born on the day of , 19 , in be and the same is hereby granted and that such adoption and the agreement therefore submitted upon this application be and the same hereby are in all respects allowed and approved, and it is

FURTHER ORDERED that the minor, , shall be henceforth regarded and treated in all respects as the child of said and , his wife and be known and called by the name of

Judge of the Surrogate's Court

SAMPLE CONSENT FOR ADOPTION

SURROGATE'S COURT: COUNTY OF
———————————————————— x

In the Matter of the Adoption of

Adoptive Child

a minor over (under) the age of fourteen years.
———————————————————— x

IN COURT CONSENT TO ADOPTION

(Private Placement)

File No. __________

1. I, ______________________, reside at ______________________, and acknowledge that I am the natural parent of ______________________.

2. That my child, ______________________, was born on ______________________ at ______________________.

3. I hereby consent to the adoption of my child, ______________________, by ______________________, who reside at ______________________.

4. I am advised that the adoptive parent(s) will commence adoption proceedings in the Surrogate's Court of ______________________ County, located at ______________________.

5. I fully understand that upon my signing of this Consent to the adoption of my child, ______________________, by ______________________, before a Judge of the Surrogate's Court, my Consent shall be for all times FINAL AND IRREVOCABLE, and no action or proceeding may be brought by me to revoke this Consent or for the return of the custody of my child to me.

6. By signing this Consent I also acknowledge that I have received a copy of this Consent.

Dated:

______________________ ______________________

Attorney Natural Parent(s)

ACKNOWLEDGEMENT

STATE OF)
) ss.:
COUNTY OF)

On this day of 19 , before me personally appeared , known to me and to me known to be the person described in and who executed the foregoing affidavit and verification and he/she severally acknowledged that he/she executed the same.

Judge of the Surrogate's Court
of the State of
for the County of

SAMPLE PETITION AND ORDER FOR TERMINATION OF PARENTAL RIGHTS

IN THE SUPERIOR COURT OF

STATE OF

STATE OF

____

Petitioner,

ADOPTION DOCKET
NO. __________ __________

EX PARTE: BABY

____

Petition for Termination of Parental Rights

COMES NOW Petitioner, , and shows this Court the following:

1. Petitioner is a private child-placing agency, licensed by the State of , Department of Human Resources and having its principal office in the County of .
2. Baby is a minor child born on the day of , in the State of .
3. The natural mother of the child has surrendered to the Petitioner all parental rights to . This surrender was executed on the day of , and complied in all respects with the requirements of .
4. Attached hereto as Exhibits are the following:
   (a) The Mother's Surrender of Parental Rights (Exhibit "A");
   (b) The Mother's Acknowledgement of Surrender of Parental Rights (Exhibit "B");
   (c) The Affidavit of Agency Representative regarding Mother's Surrender of Parental Rights (Exhibit "C"); and
   (d) The Mother's Affidavit Regarding Putative Father (Exhibit "D").
5. The Mother's Affidavit Regarding the Putative Father (Exhibit "D") states the following:
   (a) The identity of the putative father of the child is unknown;
   (b) The location of the putative father of the child is unknown;
   (c) The putative father has not lived with the child;

(d) The putative father has not contributed to the support of the child;
(e) The putative father has not provided support for the mother of the child, including medical care, either during her pregnancy or during her hospitalization for the birth of the child; and,
(f) The putative father has made no attempt to legitimize the child.

6. Contemporaneously with the filing of this Petition, the Agency will cause to be published in the appropriate newspaper the notice required by in the form of the notice attached hereto and incorporated herein as Exhibit "E". Agency will hereafter file with the Court proof of publication of said notice.
7. Petitioner has complied with all the requirements of , and is in lawful custody of for the purpose of placing said child for adoption.

WHEREFORE, Petitioner prays a hearing be held on the matter within twenty (20) days as provided by law and that it be ORDERED that all parental rights, if any, the natural father of may have to said child be terminated, and that it be further ORDERED that Petitioner, is the lawful custodian of .

This day of .

Respectfully submitted,

____
Attorney for Petitioner

VERIFICATION

IN THE SUPERIOR COURT OF

______________________________X

Adoption Docket
Petitioner,

No.

EX PARTE: BABY __________
______________________________X

STATE OF
COUNTY OF

Personally appeared before the undersigned officer duly authorized to administer oaths, who upon being duly sworn states and deposes that the facts set forth in the within and foregoing Petition are true and correct to the best of his/her information and belief.

____

SWORN TO AND SUBSCRIBED BEFORE
ME THIS DAY OF

____

NOTARY PUBLIC

Exhibit A

SURRENDER OF PARENTAL RIGHTS FINAL RELEASE FOR ADOPTION

Notice to Parent or Guardian

This is an important legal document and by signing it you are surrendering all your rights, title, and claim to the child named herein, so as to facilitate the child's placement for adoption. You are to receive a copy of this document and as explained below have the right to withdraw your surrender within ten (10) days* from the date you sign it.

____

I, the undersigned, being solicitous that my (male) (female) child, born on _________________________ and now (days) (weeks) (months) (years) old, should receive the benefits and advantages of a good home, to the end that (he) (she) may be fitted for the requirements of life, consent to this surrender.

*Check local statute for applicable time limit.

I, the undersigned ______________________ of the aforesaid child do hereby surrender said child to ______________________ and promise not to interfere in the management of said child in any respect whatever, and in consideration of the benefits guaranteed by ______________________ in thus providing for said child, I do relinquish all rights, title and claim to the child named herein it being my wish, intent, and purpose to relinquish absolutely all parental control over said child.

Furthermore, I hereby agree that said ______________________ may seek for said child a legal adoption by such person or persons as may be chosen by said ______________________ or its authorized agents without further notice to me. I do, furthermore, expressly waive any other notice or service in any of the legal proceedings for the adoption of said child.

Furthermore, I hereby certify that I have received a copy of this document and that I understand I may only withdraw this surrender by giving written notice, deliver in person or by registered or certified mail, to ______________________, within ten (10) days* from the date hereof; and I understand that it may not be withdrawn thereafter.

Furthermore, I hereby certify that I have not been subjected to any duress or undue pressure in the execution of this surrender document, and do so freely and voluntarily.

Furthermore, I understand that under the provisions of ______________ is required to conduct an investigation and render a report to the court in connection with the legal proceedings for the legal adoption of said child and I hereby agree to cooperate fully with said agency in the conduct of its investigations.

Witness my hand and seal this ____________
day of , 19 .

____
Parent or Guardian

____
Unofficial Witness

Sworn and subscribed before me, this
__________ day of ____________, 19 .

____
Notary Public

*Check local statute for applicable time limit.

Exhibit B

ACKNOWLEDGEMENT OF SURRENDER OF PARENTAL RIGHTS

By execution of this paragraph, the undersigned expressly acknowledges: (1) that I have read the accompanying SURRENDER OF PARENTAL RIGHTS/FINAL RELEASE FOR ADOPTION of my minor child, born ____________, 19 , a (female) (male); (2) that I understand that this is a full, final and complete surrender, release and termination of all my rights to said child; (3) that I have the unconditional right to revoke said surrender by giving written notice, delivered in person or by registered or certified mail, to not later than ten (10) days* from the date of the surrender and that after such ten-day period I shall have no right to revoke the surrender; (4) that I have read the accompanying surrender and received a copy thereof; (5) that any and all questions regarding the effect of said surrender and its provisions have been satisfactorily explained to me; (6) that I have been afforded an opportunity to consult with counsel of my choice prior to execution of the surrender; and (7) that the surrender of my rights has been knowingly, intentionally, freely, and voluntarily made by me.

Witness my hand and seal this ________________________ day of ________________________, 19 .

____
Parent or Guardian

Sworn and subscribed before me, this ____________ day of ____________, 19 .

____
Notary Public

*Check local statute for applicable time limit.

Exhibit C

AFFIDAVIT OF AGENCY REPRESENTATIVE

STATE OF

COUNTY OF ____________

Personally appeared before me, the undersigned officer duly authorized to administer oaths, __________________________, who, after having been sworn, deposes and says as follows: That I am employed by ____________ ____________. I am of the age of majority and have personal knowledge of the facts stated herein.

Prior to the execution of the accompanying SURRENDER OF PARENTAL RIGHTS/FINAL RELEASE FOR ADOPTION by __________________________, (hereinafter referred to as "parent"), releasing and surrendering all of (his) (her) rights in and to a (male) (female) minor child born __________________________, I reviewed with and explained to the parent all of the provisions of the surrender, and particularly the provisions which provide that said surrender is a full surrender of all parental rights.

Based on my review and explanation to said parent, it is my opinion that the parent knowingly, intentionally, freely, and voluntarily executed the surrender of parental rights.

____

Agency Representative

Sworn and subscribed before me this ________ day of ________ , 19

____

Notary Public

Exhibit D

MOTHER'S AFFIDAVIT REGARDING PUTATIVE FATHER

Notice to Mother:

This is an important legal document which deals with your child's right to have the biological father's rights properly terminated. You have the right not to disclose the name and address of the father of your child; however, should you decline to provide such information, understand that you may be required to appear in court to explain your refusal or your name may be used in connection with the publication of notice to the putative father. Understand that you are providing this affidavit under oath and that the information provided will be held in strict confidence and will be used only in connection with the adoption of your child.

STATE OF

COUNTY OF

Personally appeared before me, the undersigned officer duly authorized to administer oaths , who after having been sworn, deposes and says as follows:

That my name is

That I am the mother of a (male) (female) child born . That I am years of age, having been born on

That I have personal knowledge of the facts stated herein.

That my marital status is (check the status and complete the appropriate information):

( ) single, never having been married. ( ) separated but not legally divorced; the name of my spouse is and his last known address is ; we have been separated since . ( ) divorced; the name of my previous spouse is ; his last known address is ; divorce granted in the State of on . ( ) legally married; the name of my spouse is we were married in the State of on ; and his last known address is ( ) married through common-law marriage relationship; the name of my spouse is ; and his address is ; the date and place our relationship began is . ( ) widowed; the name of my deceased spouse is his date and place of death was .

That the name of the biological father of my child and his last known address is .

That the biological father of my child (strike the inappropriate phrase): (has) (has not) lived with the child; (has) (has not) contributed to its support; (has) (has not) provided for my support (including medical care) during my pregnancy or hospitalization for the birth of the child; and (has) (has not) made any attempt to legitimize such child.

That I have neither received nor been promised any direct financial assistance from in connection with my pregnancy, the birth of my child, and its placement for adoption. I have received direct financial assistance in connection with my pregnancy, the birth of my child, and its placement for adoption in the form of reimbursement for directly related expenses in the amount of (if none, state so) $____ from

(state name and relationship)

In addition, I have been informed by that certain payments to providers of medical services and products have been made on my behalf in connection with my pregnancy, the birth of my child, and its placement for adoption, and that these payments are as set forth on Exhibit D-1 attached hereto.

Signed

Sworn and subscribed before me, in person this day of , 19 .

____

Notary Public

Exhibit D-1

The following is a statement of expenses incurred and to be incurred by on my behalf in connection with my pregnancy and the birth of my child and the placement of my child for adoption:

Hospital	$
Obstetrician	$
Pediatrician	$
Prescriptions	$
Living expenses	$
Photocopies	$
Foster care/baby	$

Exhibit E

NOTICE OF PETITION FOR PLACEMENT FOR ADOPTION

Case No.____________

TO: Putative Father of

BORN:

YOU ARE HEREBY NOTIFIED that the mother of has surrendered her parental rights with respect to said child to as agent for the adoptive parents for placement for adoption, and that said agency has filed a Petition for Termination in the Superior Court of . All parental rights you may have with respect to said child will be lost, and you will receive neither notice of nor be entitled to object to the adoption of this child unless, within thirty (30) days of receipt of this notice, you file (1) a petition to legitimate this child pursuant to Section of the and (2) such notice of the filing of the petition to legitimate with the Superior Court of and you must make known such other objections as you may have to the adoption of said child within thirty (30) days of receipt of this notice.

WITNESS the Honorable
Judge of the Superior Court of
this day of 19 .

____

RULE NISI

IN THE SUPERIOR COURT OF

______________________________x

:

Petitioner, : ADOPTION DOCKET

EX PARTE: BABY ____________ :

NO. ____________

______________________________x

The within and foregoing Petition to Terminate Parental Rights of being presented regarding the child named therein,

It is considered, ordered and adjudged by the Court that said application be set down and made returnable before me in Chambers, at o'clock m. on the day of 19 . In the meantime, let service be made by publication upon the party named therein whose consent or notice may be required. Let notice also be given by publication to any unknown parties who may have an interest in this matter and be entitled to notice.

This the day of .

JUDGE, SUPERIOR COURT OF

ORDER TERMINATING PARENTAL RIGHTS

IN THE SUPERIOR COURT OF
STATE OF

x

Petitioner, : ADOPTION DOCKET

: NO. ___________

EX PARTE: BABY ___________ :

x

Petitioner, having moved this Court to terminate the parental rights of the natural mother and natural father of , a minor child born on the day of and it appearing to the Court that upon consideration of the Affidavits presented that the natural mother of said child has voluntarily surrendered all parental rights in and to said child to and that the biological father of said child is unknown; that reasonable effort has been made to identify the putative father without success; and that the biological father has not lived with the child or contributed to its support for the biological mother including medical care either during the pregnancy or during her hospitalization for the birth of the child; and it further appearing to the Court that Petitioner has complied in all respects with the requirements of law for obtaining the surrender of parental rights to the putative father of said child, IT IS HEREBY ORDERED AS FOLLOWS:

1.

All parental rights, if any, of the natural mother and putative father in and to are hereby terminated; and

2.

is the lawful custodian of for the purpose of placing said child for adoption.

SO ORDERED, this day of , 19 .

JUDGE, Superior Court of
County

ADOPTION OF STEPCHILD

Assuming arguendo that Joan brought to the marriage with Steve a child from a previous marriage and that Steve wishes to adopt that child, the adoption pleadings and procedures required are essentially the same as in the non stepchild situation. However, it is axiomatic that there would be no need for a power of attorney to handle the child's needs since Joan would have legal custody of the child.

The greatest concern in stepchild adoptions pertains to consent to adopt authorizations. In any adoption, if the child has attained a certain age, his or her consent to adoption must be obtained unless the child is mentally ill or retarded. In New York State the age is 14. (In drafting a written consent to adopt document for the child's signature, use as a guide the "Sample Consent for Adoption" form attached supra in this chapter.) Further, if the natural father's whereabouts are known, he must be contacted and his consent to adoption must be obtained. If the natural father refuses to consent, the adoption can proceed only if it can be shown that the natural father has totally disregarded his financial and other personal responsibilities to the child, and abandoned the child. It is extremely difficult to terminate an unwilling natural parent's parental rights if he or she is providing any child support or has shown any other interest in the child.

INTERSTATE ADOPTIONS

Significantly, an adoption involves interstate considerations if the child was born in one state and the adoption proceedings are in another state. If the child was conceived in state "X," born in State "Y," and the adoption proceedings are in state "Y," there are no interstate considerations.

There are a few states which do not allow children born in their state to be adopted in another state. However, most states permit interstate adoptions. For those states that are signatories to the Interstate Compact Act, additional requirements of the Interstate Compact Unit, located in the state where the child was born, must be met. For example, the Interstate Compact Unit may require that the adoptive parents keep the unit appraised of all action taken in regard to the adoption in the other state.

ATTORNEYS FEES

Most jurisdictions reasonably limit the extent of the fees paid or to be paid by adoptive parents to their attorney, any local counsel which may be needed, and other fees paid in connection with the adoption.

LEGAL EFFECT OF ADOPTION

An order of adoption terminates any rights the natural parents previously had with respect to the child and vice versa. Through the adoption process a new lineage results and a child possesses the same status he would have had if he was born to the adoptive parents. For example, once adopted, the child has the right to be supported by the adoptive parents and the right to inherit from and through them.

REVOKING CONSENT TO ADOPT

Once the natural mother or parents have consented to the adoption of their child, they have a certain time period—usually specified by state statute—during which they can automatically revoke their consent to adopt. For example, the time period may be 10–30 days. After the applicable time period has elapsed, consent to adopt can only be withdrawn by legal proceedings to show that the consent was obtained by fraud, duress, or misrepresentation.

Checklist for Adoptions

In order to help you pinpoint what concerns must be addressed in handling an adoption proceeding, the following checklist is provided:

1. Agency fee in agency adoption.
2. Agreement of Adoption.
3. Payments to natural mother for her and child's birth expenses in private placement adoption.
4. Agency or privately retained home study.
5. Consent from agency during physical custody period for child's medical operation, travel abroad, and other important decisions regarding the child.
6. Consent to adopt from natural mother or parents and/or petition and order for termination of parental rights.
7. Power of attorney re child from natural mother or parents in private placement adoptions.
8. Possible consent to adopt from child if child has attained certain age.
9. Petition for and order of adoption.
10. Confidential affidavit, child's original birth certificate and medical records, and child abuse and neglect investigation report (re prospective parents) to be submitted with adoption petition.

11. Attorney's affidavit re adoption expenses.
12. File documents required under Interstate Compact Act in interstate adoptions.
13. Attorney fees.

CHAPTER 5

Helping Client Determine Whether to Function as One or Two Legal Entities

SITUATION

Bob and Susan Jones are 50 and 45 years old respectively. They have been married for twenty-five years and their two children are working adults. Both Bob and Susan work. Bob earns $80,000 per year while Susan earns $20,000 per year. Bob and Susan jointly own a $300,000 house. Further, Bob separately holds assets worth $800,000 while Susan holds assets worth $75,000.

Medical Bills

This year Susan has had large medical bills—most of which are not covered by insurance—and she expects to continue to have large medical expenses during the next few years.

Assets

A $48,000 asset owned by Bob for three years, has lost half its value this year. Predictions are that this asset will continue to lose value and Bob intends to sell it immediately to minimize his loss. However, some of Bob's other assets are expected to greatly appreciate in value in the next few years.

Investments

Bob plans to make some risky investments in the future. If these investments go sour, creditors will undoubtedly come after Bob's personal assets. Finally, Bob has been quite liberal in interpreting certain tax deductions and runs a great risk that his present and future tax returns will be questioned.

DETERMINE WHAT CLIENT DESIRES

Bob has always filed joint returns with Susan. In light of his questionable tax deductions, he asks you for advice as to whether Susan will be liable for any penalty imposed for an underestimation of tax. He also queries you as to whether a joint, rather than separate, return will in his present circumstances result in the least amount of federal income tax. Further, he desires advice as to whether he can protect his assets from potential creditors by transferring them into either their joint name or to Susan's name. Finally, he wonders what tax consequences will result from a transfer of assets to Susan or a transfer to their joint name.

FILING JOINT OR SEPARATE TAX RETURNS

Tax Advantages of Joint Filing

As mentioned in Chapter Three, generally the married couple derives tax advantages by filing a joint return. This is particularly true since the child and dependent care credit is only available to a couple that files joint returns. Also, as the combined income of the couple becomes higher, and the disparity between the couple's income becomes greater, the tax advantage of filing jointly becomes greater and greater. For example, utilizing the tax tables that are in effect beginning in 1988, (see table in Chapter Three), if Bob and Susan had a taxable income of $30,000 each, their tax would be the same if they filed jointly or separately. However, if Bob's taxable income is $80,000 and Susan's is $10,000, their total tax bill would be substantially higher if they filed separate tax returns. If Bob's taxable income were $90,000 and Susan's was $0, the disparity would be even greater.

Burden of Separate Filing

Besides the tax advantage of joint filing, joint filing is preferable from an administrative standpoint. By filing a joint return, the couple is not required to undergo the extra burden of filing another return. Also, the couple need not undergo the extra burden of separating their accounts so as to determine who has what income, and who has what expenses.

Tax Advantages of Separate Filing

There are occasions where it is more beneficial for the married couple to file separate returns. This might occur when both spouses work and one has a high income while the other has a much lower income, and the spouse with the lower income has large medical expenses and miscellaneous deductions. This is true because beginning in 1987 medical expenses can only be claimed for amounts in excess of 7.5% of adjustable gross income and miscellaneous deductions can only be claimed for amounts in excess of 2% of adjusted gross income. The lower the adjusted gross income, the greater the amount of medical expenses and miscellaneous deductions that can be deducted. Of course, the benefit of the deduction may be less for the spouse with the lower income since that spouse may be in a lower tax bracket than the spouse would have been if he or she had filed jointly. Each situation must be separately evaluated to determine whether the benefits of filing a joint tax return—including the fact that the medical and miscellaneous deductions may be taken against income in a higher tax bracket—outweigh the benefits of filing separate tax returns—including the benefit of matching medical and miscellaneous expenses against a lower adjusted gross income.

Example illustrating a situation where separate returns should be filed. Assume that Bob's adjusted gross income is $50,000 while Susan's adjusted gross income is $20,000. Further assume that Bob has $10,000 in itemized deductions other than medical and miscellaneous and Susan has $3,750 in medical expenses, $1,000 in miscellaneous expenses, and $2,000 in other itemized deductions. Finally assume that they are filing a return for 1988 where the personal exemption is $1,950. If Bob and Susan were filing a joint return, their adjusted gross income would be $70,000 and they would not be able to deduct any of their medical and miscellaneous expenses. After deducting their $12,000 in other itemized expenses and deducting $1,950 for their personal exemptions, they would have a taxable income of $54,100 and a tax of $11,281. If Bob and Susan filed separate returns, the result would be as follows: Bob's $50,000 adjusted gross income would be reduced by his $10,000 itemized deductions and $1,950 personal exemption to arrive at a taxable income of $38,050. On this taxable income he would pay a tax of $8,720. Susan's $20,000 adjusted gross income would be reduced by her $1,950 personal exemption, $2,250 deductible medical expenses ($1,500 of expenses cannot be deducted), $800 miscellaneous expenses ($400 cannot be deducted), and $2,000 other itemized expenses to arrive at a taxable income of $13,200. On this taxable income she would pay a tax of $1,980. Thus, if Bob and Susan file jointly they will pay a tax of $11,281 while if they file separately they will pay a total tax of $10,700.

Capital Gains and Losses

In Bob's case, another factor that may make filing separate returns advantageous relates to capital gains and losses. [The 1986 Tax Reform Law deletes the difference that previously existed between long-term and short-term capital gains and losses.] In many situations it is worthwhile taxwise, to attempt to match any capital gains realized against capital losses realized. If Bob's capital loss is realized this year, and his capital gain is to be realized in future years, it may not be possible to match much, if any, of his capital losses against his capital gains if joint tax returns are filed. This occurs because in the joint return situation—where, beginning in 1987, 100% of the long term capital loss will be deducted and applied against joint income—a $3,000 loss deduction will be taken this year and the capital loss carry-over will be deducted in succeeding years. In Bob's case, he will utilize all his loss in eight years—assuming he has no capital gains—since he will deduct $3,000 each year. However, if Bob and Susan file separately, the capital loss will only be realized against Bob's income and he will only take a $1,500 loss deduction on this and succeeding years. Thus, it will take sixteen rather than eight years for him to utilize all of his losses. Accordingly, if for example he realizes a $20,000 long-term capital gain in eight years, he would not have any capital loss to apply against it if he filed jointly with Susan. However, if he filed separately he would have $12,000 of capital loss carry-over to apply against his $20,000 long-term capital gains and would reduce his capital gains for that year to $8,000.

Questionable Tax Practices

Considering that Bob is taking some questionable tax deductions, Susan should seriously consider filing a separate tax return. Generally speaking, husbands and wives are jointly and severally liable for all tax due. Thus, should Bob's deductions be disallowed by the IRS at a later date, and should additional tax and penalties be imposed, Susan may be held liable for these amounts.

Innocent spouse doctrine. There is an exception to this general rule. Under the innocent spouse doctrine, a spouse might be relieved of liability if certain conditions are met. First, the underpayment of tax must be substantial. Second, the underpayment must be due to grossly erroneous items attributable to the other spouse. An example of a grossly erroneous item might be the taking of a deduction for which there is absolutely no basis. Third, the innocent spouse can not know or have reason to know of the other person's underpayment of tax. Fourth, equity must dictate that the innocent spouse not be held liable.

In order to avoid the burdens imposed by the innocent spouse doctrine, Susan could simply file her return separately. Deductions on Bob's return, and any tax difficulties that might ensue would solely be directed toward him.

Comparison of joint and separate returns

In order to help you determine whether you should advise Bob and Susan to file jointly or separately, the following chart, which lists the significant reasons for choosing one alternative over the other, will prove helpful.

JOINT V. SEPARATE RETURNS

Joint favored	Separate favored
1. One spouse earns all income or disparity in income earned by spouses.	1. Disparity in income of spouse with lower income earner having substantial medical and miscellaneous expenses.
2. Child and dependent care credit claimed.	2. Spouse with large capital loss in current year wishes to postpone recapture of capital loss as long as possible.
3. Burden of filing two tax returns and keeping wife and husband's accounts separate.	3. One spouse taking questionable deduction.

HOLDING PROPERTY JOINTLY OR SEPARATELY

Potential or Actual Liens

If Bob had any liens currently pending against him, he could not insulate his property from being used to satisfy these liens by transferring the property out of his sole name. Simply put, an individual will not be permitted to defraud creditors by transferring assets out of his name.

Transfer of assets. However, in Bob's case, since there are no actual liens pending and there is only the potential for liens in the future, he may be able to safely transfer assets out of his sole ownership without any repercussions. Transfer of assets by individuals that are made well in advance of the imposition of any liens on the individual, will survive any challenge to the propriety of the transfer.

If Bob decides to make any transfers of his assets to protect them from potential creditors, he would be best advised to transfer them into Susan's sole name. If they are held solely by Bob, they are subject to liens by Bob's creditors. Also, if they are held jointly, at the very least a lien can be placed against Bob's one-half (1/2) share of the assets. Moreover, although some jurisdictions will preclude the forceable sale of a jointly held asset in the situation where a lien has been placed on the asset by a creditor of one of the asset owners, other jurisdictions will permit such a forceable sale.

Note. In making a transfer of his assets to Susan, Bob should be made aware that in so doing, he may be relinquishing any claims he has to the asset. In particular, in the event of a divorce, Susan may be entitled to sole possession of the asset whereas if Bob had not transferred the asset he might be entitled to sole possession of it. There is an exception to this general rule. If Bob can show that he transferred a particular asset to Susan only to avoid potential liens and taxes, the courts may hold that he never intended to transfer ownership to her and that she was merely holding the asset in constructive trust for him. If Bob's constructive trust argument succeeds, his claim to the asset will be the same as it was before the transfer to Susan.

Tax Consequences

For income tax purposes it is axiomatic that if you derive income from a certain asset, you are responsible for the tax due on that income. Thus, if Bob transfers an asset he owns separately into joint name, Susan will be responsible for the tax on one-half (1/2) the income generated by the asset since she will be deemed to own one-half (1/2) of the asset. Likewise, if Bob transfers a particular asset into Susan's sole name, she will be responsible for all the tax due on the income generated by the asset. If Bob and Susan are filing a joint return such transfer will have no income tax consequences. However, if they are filing separate returns, there will most likely be income tax consequences. Considering that Bob's tax rate is much higher than Susan's, if they are filing separate returns, the income tax consequences may be favorable.

The transfer of assets from Bob will also have tax consequences at his death. For example, let us presume that Bob owns a $100,000 asset which has a $50,000 basis. If Bob dies tomorrow and his Will bequeaths this asset to Susan, she will obtain the asset and it will have a stepped-up basis of $100,000. However, if Bob had placed the asset in joint name prior to death, Susan would upon his death obtain the asset with a $75,000 basis. Bob's one-half (1/2) or $50,000 share would pass to Susan with a stepped-up basis of $50,000, and Susan would retain the $25,000 basis on her one-half (1/2) share of the asset. Additionally, had Bob transferred the asset prior to his death to Susan's sole name, his death would have no effect on the basis of the property and Susan would retain the $50,000 basis.

Assuming Bob has bequeathed all of his assets to Susan, and Susan has done likewise, the federal estate tax consequences upon the death of Bob or Susan would be the same—i.e., no federal tax—whether certain assets are owned separately, by either Bob or Susan, or jointly. This occurs because there is an unlimited estate tax marital deduction. For example, upon Bob's death, if Susan solely owned all the assets, there would be no estate tax consequences since nothing would pass through Bob's estate. If, upon Bob's death, Bob solely owned all the assets, the result would be the same. Although all the assets would pass through Bob's estate, the marital deduction would preclude tax consequences.

Just as no federal estate tax is levied on death transfers from one spouse to another, no federal gift tax is levied on lifetime transfers from one spouse to another. Thus, Bob can make unlimited lifetime gifts to Susan and vice versa without any federal gift tax consequences.

CHAPTER 6

How to Write a Will for the Client

WRITING A WILL IN THE CASE OF CHILDLESS MARRIAGE

Situation

Tom Jones is 60 years old and his wife, Maria, is 59. They do not have children. Tom and Maria jointly own a house valued at $400,000. Tom separately owns assets valued at $700,000. The same is true for Maria. Both Tom and Maria have worked their entire lives and are each able to understand and handle their finances.

Determine What Client Desires

Neither Tom nor Maria has ever written a Will. They realize that, since the house is jointly owned, there is no need for a Will to pass their one-half (½) share of the house to the other spouse at death. Maria comes to you, her attorney, for advice as to the writing of a Will for her and Tom which will cover the $700,000 in assets that each of them owns separately. Maria wishes to bequeath all of her assets to her spouse and Tom wishes to do the same. However, there exists certain relatives to whom they wish to bequeath their assets after their death. They want their assets to flow to these relatives with as little tax consequences as possible.

Will Provisions

If Maria and Tom were not concerned about the tax consequences to their respective estates after they both die, they would probably be best advised to write Wills in which Tom would simply bequeath his assets to Maria and Maria would simply bequeath her assets to Tom. Their assets, including the jointly held real estate, would then flow to whomever they wish to obtain the property after the death of the surviving spouse. The federal marital deduction would preclude any tax consequences vis-a-vis the transfer to Tom upon Maria's death or the transfer to Maria upon Tom's death. There would be no need to set up a trust for the other spouse since each is able to understand and handle his or her financial affairs.

Setting up a trust. Since Maria and Tom are concerned about tax consequences after their death, a different approach should be taken. In their respective Wills, they should set up a trust—whose principal would not be included in the estate of the income beneficiary of the trust—that takes advantage of the maximum credit allowed under the federal unified gift and estate tax credit. For example, beginning in 1987 the credit is $192,800. This would preclude tax on amounts up to $600,000. Thus, the trust set up in Tom's and Maria's Wills should be $600,000 in 1987.

The beneficiary of the trust—be it Tom or Maria—should obtain the income generated by the trust during his or her lifetime. Moreover, the trustee should be permitted to invade the principal of the trust for expenses that relate to the beneficiaries' health and welfare expenses.

The trust would of course only come into effect for the surviving spouse. Also, for the spouse that dies last, his or her property will never flow into a trust but will flow directly to the relative or relatives who are to receive the assets after the death of both spouses. And, upon the death of the second spouse, what remains in the trust fund will flow to a particular named relative or relatives.

Applying the above principles to Tom and Maria's case, and assuming arguendo that Tom predeceased Maria in 1987, the following tax consequences would result: (1) Upon Tom's death, $600,000 would flow to the trust for the benefit of Maria; (2) his remaining $100,000 in assets would flow directly to Maria as would his $200,000 share of the $400,000 house; (3) the funds in the trust would not be taxed due to the unified gift and estate tax credit; (4) the other assets would not be taxed due to the marital deduction; (5) upon Maria's death—in 1987—her $900,000 in assets, plus the $300,000 in assets bequeathed from Tom, plus the $600,000 trust would flow to the particular named relative or relatives;

(6) the $600,000 trust fund, since it does not flow through Maria's estate, will not be a part of her taxable estate; (7) of the remaining $1.2 million in assets, only $600,000 will be subject to tax since the unified gift and estate tax credit will preclude the imposition of tax on the first $600,000 in assets; and (8) thus, by setting up the trust, Maria's death would result in the imposition of tax on $600,000 in assets rather than $1.2 million in assets.

A sample Will which will enable you to draft a Will for both Tom and/or Maria follows.

SAMPLE WILL WITH UNIFIED CREDIT TRUST AND BALANCE OUTRIGHT TO WIFE

I, _______________, a resident of the City, County, and State of _______________, being of sound and disposing mind, do hereby make, publish, and declare this to be my Last Will and Testament.

FIRST: I hereby revoke any and all Wills and Codicils heretofore made by me.

SECOND: I direct that all of my just debts, funeral and testamentary expenses be paid as soon as practicable after my decease, and that such debts, funeral and testamentary expenses and all administration expenses and all estate, inheritance, succession, and transfer taxes and duties, including not only those upon property hereby devised or bequeathed, but also those, if any, imposed or assessed with respect to the proceeds of life insurance, and those, if any, imposed or assessed at or upon or by reason of my death with respect to any other property which for the purposes of the taxes enumerated in this paragraph may be considered or treated as part of my gross estate, shall be a charge upon and payable out of the property not qualifying for the marital deduction hereunder and are to be specifically charged against the Unified Tax Credit portion of my Estate.

THIRD: I give, devise, and bequeath any and all household furniture, furnishings, automobiles, jewelry, personal effects, and any other tangible personal property which I may own at the time of my death to my wife, _______________, absolutely and free of trust, should she survive me. Should my wife fail to survive me, then I give, devise, and bequeath all said personalty and personal effects to my brother and sister, in equal shares, absolutely and free of trust.

FOURTH: (A) Should my wife, _______________, survive me, then I give, devise, and bequeath a sum equal to the exemption equivalent of the Unified Tax Credit, as of the date of my death less administration expenses and taxes pursuant to Paragraph "SECOND" herein to my Trustees, hereinafter named, IN TRUST NEVERTHELESS, to invest the same and to keep the same invested, to collect the income thereof and to pay over and distribute the net income arising therefrom to my wife, _______________, during her lifetime. I expressly direct that all the income from the corpus of this trust shall be paid to my wife at least quarterly.

(B) I hereby authorize and empower my Trustees to pay out of the principal of the trust fund created under this Paragraph "FOURTH" so much of the principal from time to time in whole or in part to my wife, _______________, as they in their sole and unreviewable discretion may determine for the health, comfort, and welfare of my said wife or such sums may be applied for her health, comfort, and welfare.

(C) Upon the death of my said wife, I direct my Trustees to distribute the principal of the trust fund remaining in their hands and all undistributed income, absolutely and free of trust to my brother and sister, in equal shares.

FIFTH: I give, devise and bequeath to my wife, ______, should she survive me, absolutely and free of trust, all of the rest, residue and remainder of my estate. Only assets (or their proceeds) which would qualify for the marital deduction shall be used in making payment of this bequest. In determining the assets to be distributed pursuant to this bequest, my Executors shall distribute assets, including cash, fairly representative of appreciation or depreciation in the value of all property available for distribution.

Should my wife, ______, predecease me, then this bequest shall lapse and shall be included in my residuary estate pursuant to Paragraph "SIXTH" herein.

SIXTH: Should my wife, ______, not survive me, then I give, devise, and bequeath my entire residuary estate in equal shares, absolutely and free of trust, to my brother and sister.

SEVENTH: Upon the termination or change of beneficiary of any trust herein created through the decease, after my decease, of the person entitled to receive the income, there shall be no apportionment to the Executor or Administrator of such person of any accrued but unmatured income. Said accrued but unmatured income shall, upon the maturity and collection of the several respective items thereof, belong in its entirety to the person or persons entitled to receive the income of the particular trust fund, that is to say, to the remainderman or remaindermen in any case where the principal of the trust shall vest in fee, or to the next beneficiary in any case where the trust shall continue for the benefit of a successive or further beneficiary.

EIGHTH: In the event that my wife, ______, and I should die in a common disaster or accident or under such circumstances that the order of deaths cannot be established by proof, then I direct that for purposes of this Will, my said Wife shall be presumed to have survived me. In the event that any other beneficiary of this Will and I or any other person upon whose death such beneficiary shall become entitled to receive either income or principal under this Will shall die in a common disaster or accident or under such circumstances that the order of deaths cannot be established by proof, then I direct that for purposes of this Will such beneficiary shall be deemed to have predeceased me or such other person as the case may be.

NINTH: If upon my death any part of my estate shall vest in absolute ownership in a minor, or if at the termination of any of the trusts created by this Will all or any part of any of the trusts created by this Will or if all or any part of the principal of any of the trust funds shall vest in absolute ownership in a minor, I authorize and empower my Trustees or Executors, as the case may be, to continue to hold said principal for the benefit of such minor during his or her legal minority or until the age of twenty-one (21) years, whichever shall be greater, to invest the same and keep the same invested and to collect the income thereof and in the sole and unreviewable discretion of the said Executors or Trustees, as the case may be, either to accumulate the income or pay over the net income arising therefrom to the minor to whom said principal shall belong or to his or her parent or legal guardian, or to the person with whom such minor resides, or to apply said income and such sum or sums out of principal, as in their sole and absolute discretion they deem necessary or advisable to said infant's care, education, maintenance, and support. The authority thus accorded to my Executors or Trustees, as the case may be, shall be construed as a power only and shall not operate to suspend the absolute ownership of such principal by such minor or to prevent the absolute vesting thereof in such minor. The rights, powers, privileges, and immunities granted in this my Last Will and Testament to my Executors and/or Trustees shall apply to the administration and investment of any funds held by my Executors or Trustees in accordance with this power, and they shall have the same rights to compensation for so acting as if any such trust had continued and said principal had not vested.

TENTH: I hereby nominate, constitute, and appoint my wife, , and my attorney, , as the Co-Executors of my Last Will and Testament and as the Co-Trustees of the Trusts herein established. Should predecease me, fail to qualify as such Co-Executor, and/or Co-Trustee or having qualified, shall for any reason fail to continue to act as such Co-Executor and/or Co-Trustee, then I hereby nominate, constitute and appoint my attorney, , as Co-Executor and/or Co-Trustee in his place.

(B) I direct that none of the persons named herein as Executor and/or Trustee, original or successor, shall be required to give any bond or other undertaking for the faithful performance of their duties as Executor, and/or Trustee, or as successor.

ELEVENTH: I confer upon my Executors and/or Trustees, original or successor, with respect to the management and administration of any property, real or personal, the following discretionary powers, without limitation by reason of specification, and in addition to the powers conferred upon them by statute or by general rules of law:

(1) I authorize and empower my Executors and/or Trustees to retain and continue any investments which I may own at the time of my death. In the making of new investments I direct that my Executors and/or Trustees shall not be restricted or limited to such legal investments as are provided for the investment of trust funds by any statutes now in force or which may hereafter be enacted, and I specifically authorize my Executors and/or Trustees to invest the assets of my estate and/or the corpus of any trust fund or any part hereof in a discretionary common trust fund, to purchase or acquire in exchange or otherwise real estate, mortgages, stocks, bonds, and securities other than those constituting legal investments for trust funds and to invest and keep invested therein any part of my

estate or of the trusts herein created. In any case, my fiduciaries shall make investments as would be acquired by prudent men of discretion and intelligence in such matters who are seeking a reasonable income and preservation of capital.

(2) I authorize and empower my Executors and/or Trustees in their discretion and without leave of Court to sell at public or private sale or to lease without public bidding and without restriction or limitation as the length of term (even though for a period longer than authorized by statute or longer than the duration of any trust herein created) or to mortgage or pledge any or all property coming into their hands, whether real or personal or mixed, at such times and upon such terms and conditions as in their judgment they may deem proper, and I authorize and empower them to sign, execute, acknowledge, and deliver any deeds, mortgages, conveyances, leases, and other papers that may be necessary in connection therewith.

(3) I authorize and empower my Executors and/or Trustees in their discretion to purchase property (a) on the foreclosure of any mortgage held by my estate, (b) on which my estate may own a mortgage or mortgages, (c) in which my estate shall have any interest, or any sale in partition, foreclosure, or otherwise or (d) which may be sold under any judgment in which my estate may have any interest, and I authorize and empower them to sign, execute, acknowledge, and deliver any deeds, mortgages, conveyances, leases, or other papers that may be necessary in connection therewith.

(4) I authorize and empower my Executors and/or Trustees to compromise, settle, or arbitrate any claim or demand in favor of or against my estate.

(5) I authorize and empower my Executors to join with my wife in executing and filing a joint Income Tax Return and agree with her as to the shares or proportions of the tax shown thereon which are to be paid respectively by my estate and by her. My Executors shall not be held accountable or liable for any error of judgment as to the filing of a separate or a joint return or as to the apportionment of the tax on a joint return.

(6) I authorize and empower my Executors and/or Trustees to vote in person or by proxy upon any and all stocks or other securities held by them; to exercise any rights to subscribe for or to convert into stocks or bonds or other securities of any corporation (whether a going concern or in liquidation or in reorganization or under any other circumstances or conditions whatsoever) for other real or personal property distributed by the same corporation or any other corporation which shall be formed as a reorganization of or in combination, merger or consolidation with the original corporation; to become a party to any plan of reorganization, merger or consolidation or to become a depositor with and/or give power of attorney to any committee of bondholders or other security holders or creditors formed for the purpose of mutual protection in connection with any plan of corporate financing or reorganization or to represent or enforce the rights of security

holders or creditors in connection with any defaults by the corporation or any reorganization or insolvency of the corporation; to accept any new or substituted security of whatever nature in place of the defaulted or previously held security; to make any payments necessary to obtain such new or substituted security, and generally to exercise in respect to any securities held by them the unrestricted rights of a personal owner thereof, in accordance with their best judgment and discretion.

(7) I authorize and empower my Executors and/or Trustees to borrow money, from others or from themselves whether to pay taxes, make subscriptions, exercise options, pay assessments, or to accomplish any other purpose of any nature incidental to the administration of my estate or of any of the trusts herein created, and to mortgage or pledge as security therefor any securities or other property held by them.

(8) So far as I may be legally permitted to do so, I authorize and empower my Executors and/or Trustees to cause any stocks, bonds, or other securities at any time held by them to be in bearer form or to be registered in the name of a nominee or nominees.

(9) I authorize and empower my Executors and/or Trustees to hold and retain so long as to them may seem proper, as part of my estate and trust estate, any real, personal, or mixed property, or any interest therein, of which I may die seized or possessed, or to which I may be entitled at the time of my death, notwithstanding that the same may not be of the kind, character, legal, proper, or permissable for the investment of funds or trust funds under the laws of the State of New York, or any other State and without regard to the proportion that any of said property may bear to the entire amount of my estate and trust estate, or of the trusts in which same are held.

(10) I authorize and empower my Executors and/or Trustees to form any corporation, partnership, general or limited, or association, and to sell, convey, exchange, contract, lease, assign, transfer and set over, or otherwise dispose of to said corporation, partnership, or association any or all of my estate, and to accept therefor property, real or personal, stocks, notes, bonds, debentures, mortgages, securities, or other evidences of indebtedness from said partnership, corporation, or association including the stock of any such corporation, common or preferred, in payment or part payment therefor, and to become directors and officers of any such corporation and with full power and authority on the part of any such corporation and my estate and trust estate to transact any business, including the making of any loans, with or without pledge, mortgage, or security between my estate and trust estate and said corporation, with full power and authority on the part of either the corporation or my estate and trust estate to become maker, endorser, guarantor, and surety for each other in respect to any

matter whatsoever, and said corporation may be organized under the laws of any State selected by said Executors and/or Trustees with all the powers incident to corporations organized under the laws of such State.

(11) I authorize and empower my Executors and/or Trustees to continue any business of mine and the operation thereof and any interest that I may have either individually or as a partner, stockholder in any business, firm, enterprise, association, partnership, whether general or limited, company or corporation of whatsoever nature and wherever same may be situated, for so long a time and upon such terms and conditions and in such manner as my said Executors and/or Trustees may deem advisable and beneficial and for the best interest of my estate and trust estate, and for that purpose to retain and permit to be employed therein any capital or investment which shall at my death be employed therein, and generally to act in all matters relating to any such business or interest as herein mentioned as if they owned the same, or were beneficially interested in or entitled to the same.

(12) I authorize and empower my Executors and/or Trustees to carry out any contracts or agreements that I may have entered into with any person or persons, partnership, stockholders, or corporation in connection with any such business, interest, partnership, firm, association, or corporation, or affecting or concerning any stock owned or held by me, and to extend and to continue the same or enter into any other agreement or arrangement that they may deem advisable and for the best interest of my estate and trust estate.

(13) I authorize and empower my Executors and/or Trustees to form any firm, partnership, association, company, or corporation with or concerning any business in which I may have any interest, as herein mentioned, and to participate in, consent to, or oppose any plan of liquidation, consolidation, reorganization, merger, or similar plan in connection with or concerning the said business or interest with any other business, firm, association, partnership, or corporation.

(14) I authorize and empower my Executors and/or Trustees to discontinue, liquidate, dissolve, and dispose of any business, firm, association, partnership, corporation, or any stockholdings or interest that I may have in the same.

(15) I authorize and empower my Executors and/or Trustees to apportion between principal and income all stock dividends and liquidating or extraordinary dividends or distributions. Without limiting the absolute discretion of my fiduciaries, I desire that all such dividends and distributions be allotted to principal except to the extent that my fiduciaries shall determine that they were declared or made in lieu of regular cash dividends or distributions.

(16) I authorize and empower my Executors and/or Trustees at any time and from time to time, to appoint for the time being an agent or attorney to make, execute, and deliver any transfer or other instructions, or to do any ministerial act

necessary or proper to be done in the administration of my estate, it being my present wish and desire that   be the attorneys for my estate and trust established herein.

(17) I authorize and empower my Executors and/or Trustees to employ such attorneys, clerks, agents, accountants, and custodians, and to obtain such investment or other advice, in the transaction of the business of my estate and in the administration of any trust hereunder as my Executors or Trustees, as the case may be, may deem necessary or advisable, and to make such payments and disbursements therefor as they deem reasonable and proper.

(18) Except as otherwise expressly provided in this Will, I authorize and empower my Executors and/or Trustees to pay any pecuniary legacy hereunder, whether in trust or otherwise, and to make any distribution pursuant to this my Will, in whole or in part, in securities or other property owned by me at the time of my decease or thereafter acquired by my Executors or Trustees, subject to the applicable provisions of this Will, which shall fully govern with respect to the bequest therein provided for, and in making such payment or distribution in securities or other property, I direct that valuation placed thereon by my Executors or by my Trustees shall be binding and conclusive on all persons interested in my estate, subject only to the power of a court of competent jurisdiction to pass on such valuation.

(19) My Trustees may at any time and from time to time during the course of the administration of any trust created pursuant to this Will, render an account of their proceedings with respect to such trust to every person who is then of full age and sound mind and who is then currently entitled to be paid the net income of such trust or who then may be entitled in any future contingency to have paid over to him or to her all or any part of the principal of such trust and to every duly appointed guardian of the property of every such person who is not then of full age and who has such a guardian. If the persons to whom such an account is so rendered by my Trustees include both at least one person (or the guardian of one person) who may be entitled in any future contingency to have paid over to him or to her all or any part of the principal, the written approval of such account by all the persons to whom the account is so rendered (including any such guardians) shall be binding and conclusive upon all persons then having or thereafter acquiring or claiming any interest in the subject matter of such account and shall be a complete discharge to my Trustees with respect to all matters set forth in such account as fully and to the same extent as though such account had been judicially settled and allowed by a judgment or order or decree of a court of competent jurisdiction in an action or proceeding in which all persons so having, acquiring, or claiming any interest in the subject matter of such account were duly made parties and were duly represented. The foregoing provisions of this para-

graph shall not be deemed to limit the right of my Trustees to have any such account judicially settled despite such written approval.

TWELFTH: (A) I hereby direct that no disposition charge or encumbrances on any interest in my estate, or on any part thereof, by any beneficiary under this Will by way of anticipation shall be valid or in any way binding upon my Executors or Trustees, and no beneficiary shall have the right to assign, transfer, encumber, or otherwise dispose of such income or principal, or any part thereof until the same shall be paid to such beneficiary by my Executors or by my Trustees, and no income or principal or any part thereof shall be liable to any claim of any creditors of any such beneficiary.

(B) The right of any beneficiary to any payment of income or principal shall be in every case subject to any charges or deduction which my Executors or my Trustees may make against the same under the authority granted to my Executors or to my Trustees by any law or by any provision of this Will.

THIRTEENTH: The powers and authority hereinbefore granted to my Executors and/or Trustees may be exercised without obligation to or authority from any court or judge, and, to the extent permitted by law, they shall not be liable or responsible for any loss which may be suffered except where the same is due to their dishonest or malicious acts.

FOURTEENTH: The words "child," "children," and "issue," wherever used in this Will, shall include not only the child, children, and issue of the person or persons designated, but also the legally adopted child or children of such person or persons.

FIFTEENTH: Wherever applicable the masculine and feminine genders, and the singular and plural, are used interchangeably in this my Last Will and Testament.

IN WITNESS WHEREOF, I have hereunto set my hand and seal the day of , 19 .

____

The foregoing instrument consisting of ( ) pages, including this page, was on the day above signed, sealed, published, and declared by , the above-named Testator, as and for his Last Will and Testament, in the presence of us and each of us, who at his request, and in his presence and in the presence of each other, have hereunto subscribed our names as attesting witnesses, this day of , 19 .

______________________ residing at ______________________

____

______________________ residing at ______________________

____

______________________ residing at ______________________

____

WRITING A WILL IN THE CASE OF MARRIAGE WITH CHILDREN

Situation

Mike Jones, age 45, is married to Pam Jones, age 40. They have two children, a boy age 10, and a girl age 6. Mike has always been the sole income earner in the household and has handled all household finances. Mike and Pam do not own a house, but rather rent an apartment. Pam and Mike hold no assets jointly and Pam has no assets in her name. Mike has $700,000 in assets in his name.

Currently, Mike and Pam have Wills in which Mike bequeaths all his assets to Pam and Pam bequeaths all her assets to Mike. If Pam does not survive Mike, Mike has bequeathed his assets to a trust fund set up for the benefit of their children and grandchildren. Pam has a similar provision in her Will in the event Mike does not survive her. All of the assets of any trust fund established will be fully distributed to the children or grandchildren by the time they attain 30 years of age.

Determine What Client Desires

Mike is worried about Pam's ability to handle the family finances in the event he should die. He also wishes to assure that when his assets eventually flow to the children, there will be as few tax consequences as possible. Mike comes to you, his attorney, for advice as to how he should alter his Will to reflect these concerns.

Will Provisions

Setting up a unified credit trust. In drafting Mike's Will, you should include a unified credit trust which takes advantage of the maximum credit available. If the trust was created in 1987, it should consist of $600,000 in assets. By creating this trust, you will avoid tax on the assets when Mike dies. You will also prevent the assets from being included in Pam's estate when she dies, thereby insulating the assets from tax consequences upon her death.

A separate trust. Further, considering that Mike does not feel secure in regard to Pam's ability to handle the family finances, you should assure that Mike bequeaths any assets remaining after the unified credit trust has been established to another separate trust. Someone other than Pam will then manage all of Mike's assets after his death.

In setting up the separate trust, you want to assure that the assets that flow into it qualify for the marital deduction. Otherwise, tax will be imposed on these assets at Mike's death since he has already utilized the maximum credit available under the federal unified gift and estate tax credit in setting up the unified credit trust. In the past, normally Pam would have had to have a general power of appointment during her lifetime over this separate trust and at her death over the trust property in order for Mike to take advantage of the marital deduction. However, now she need not possess a general power of appointment. You can construct a qualified terminable interest property trust in Mike's Will. Such a trust would effectively give Pam no power over the trust during her lifetime and at her death. Mike's executor can elect to qualify the property in the trust as terminable interest property so that Mike's estate can take advantage of the marital deduction. The value of the property will be included in Pam's estate upon her death and the value will be calculated at her death.

A trust for children. Also, in Mike's Will, you should set up a trust for the children and possible grandchildren in the event Pam predeceases Mike. While they are minors, the children certainly cannot manage the assets properly. Moreover, perhaps the trust should continue past the point where the children attain majority. Even though the children are no longer minors they may not be able to handle financial responsibilities and may pointlessly dissipate the assets in the trust if distributed to them. If one of Mike's children or grandchildren is mentally defective, you should probably continue the trust for the life of that child or grandchild.

The income generated by the trust should accumulate in the trust until the children or grandchildren concerned attain majority. However, the trustee should be permitted to invade the accumulated income and/or principal of the trust for the health, education, or welfare of the beneficiaries of the trust. When a particular child or grandchild reaches majority, for example, any accumulated income that remains for that particular beneficiary should be distributed to him or her along with a certain percentage of the principal. Each year thereafter accumulations in income for that year should be distributed until a certain point in time when all the assets that remain in the trust for that particular beneficiary should be distributed. In drafting the trust, you should assure that no beneficiary of the trust can assign to another individual his or her expectancy to money in the trust. It has become a common occurrence for children who are beneficiaries of trusts to assign such an expectancy at a fraction of its value so they can acquire assets now rather than wait until they are entitled to certain assets under the terms of the trust.

To aid you in constructing Mike's Will, a sample Will follows which contains a unified tax credit trust, a qualified terminable interest property trust, and a trust for the children and/or grandchildren. Also, in the event you do not wish to utilize a qualified terminable interest property trust for Mike, a sample marital trust containing a power of appointment is annexed.

SAMPLE WILL WITH UNIFIED CREDIT TRUST, QUALIFIED TERMINABLE INTEREST PROPERTY TRUST, AND TRUST FOR CHILDREN

I, , a resident of the City, County, and State of , being of sound and disposing mind, do hereby make, publish, and declare this to be my Last Will and Testament.

FIRST: I hereby revoke any and all Wills and Codicils heretofore made by me.

SECOND: I direct that all of my just debts, funeral and testamentary expenses be paid as soon as practicable after my decease, and that such debts, funeral and testamentary expenses and all administration expenses and all estate, inheritance, succession and transfer taxes and duties, including not only those upon property hereby devised or bequeathed, but also those, if any, imposed or assessed with respect to the proceeds of life insurance, and those, if any, imposed or assessed at or upon or by reason of my death with respect to any other property which for the purposes of the taxes enumerated in this paragraph may be considered or treated as part of my gross estate, shall be a charge upon and payable out of the property not qualifying for the marital deduction hereunder and are to be specifically charged against the Unified Tax Credit portion of my Estate.

THIRD: I give, devise, and bequeath any and all household furniture, furnishings, automobiles, jewelry, personal effects, and any other tangible personal property which I may own at the time of my death, to my wife, , absolutely and free of trust, should she survive me. Should my wife fail to survive me, then I give, devise, and bequeath all said personalty and personal effects to my children, in equal shares, absolutely and free of trust.

FOURTH: (A) Should my wife, , survive me, then I give, devise and bequeath a sum equal to the exemption equivalent of the Unified Tax Credit, as of the date of my death less administration expenses and taxes pursuant to Paragraph "SECOND" herein to my Trustees, hereinafter named, IN TRUST NEVERTHELESS, to invest the same and to keep the same invested, to collect the income thereof and to pay over and distribute the net income arising therefrom to my wife, , during her lifetime. I expressly direct that all the income from the corpus of this trust shall be paid to my wife at least quarterly.

(B) I hereby authorize and empower my Trustees to pay out of the principal of the trust fund created under this Paragraph "FOURTH" so much of the principal from time to time in whole or in part to my wife, , as they in their sole and unreviewable discretion may determine for the health, comfort, and welfare of my said wife or such sums may be applied for her health, comfort, and welfare.

(C) Upon the death of my said wife, I direct my Trustees to divide the principal of the trust fund remaining in their hands and all undistributed income, into as many equal parts as I shall leave children who shall be living at the date of the death of my wife, (or should any of my children have predeceased my wife but leave issue him or her surviving and surviving my wife, then such issue should take his or her parent's share in equal parts, per stirpes, and not per capita, to be held in trust all pursuant to the provisions herein) to be separately held and disposed of in a single trust fund, if possible, for the benefit of each of said children (or their issue) as follows:

(1) With respect to each part set apart for a child or his issue: I give, devise, and bequeath such part to my Trustees to invest the same and keep the same invested and to apply so much of the income arising therefrom and so much of the principal of the trust as in the sole and unreviewable discretion of my Trustees may be advisable for the education, maintenance, health, and support of the child for whose benefit such trust shall have been created and to accumulate the balance of said net income, if any, until such child shall have attained the age of twenty-three (23) years, at which time all accumulations of income from that portion of the trust for said child shall be paid over to such child, together with one-quarter (1/4) of the principal remaining in that portion of the trust fund held for said child.

(2) Thereupon I direct my Trustees to continue to invest and keep invested so much of the principal of said trust fund as may be remaining in their hands and to pay the net income arising therefrom quarterly to the child for whose benefit said trust shall have been created until such child shall have attained the age of twenty-seven (27) years, at which time I direct that all undistributed income from that portion of the trust for said child together with one-third (1/3) of the principal then remaining in that portion of the trust fund held for said child shall be paid over to such child.

During this period the Trustees may apply so much of the principal of the trust and the income arising therefrom as in the sole and unreviewable discretion of the Trustees may be advisable for the education, maintenance, health, and support of that child.

(3) Thereupon I direct my Trustees to continue to invest and keep invested so much of the principal of said trust fund as may be remaining in their hands and to pay the net income arising therefrom quarterly to the child for whose benefit said trust shall have been created until such child shall have attained the age of thirty-two (32) years, at which time I direct that all undistributed income from that portion of the trust for said child together with the balance of the principal then remaining in that portion held for said child shall be paid over to such child.

During this period the Trustees may apply so much of the principal of the trust and the income arising therefrom as in the sole and unreviewable discretion of the Trustees may be advisable for the education, maintenance, health, and support of that child.

(4) In the event that the child for whose benefit said trust shall have been created should die before attaining the age of thirty-two (32) years, then upon the

death of such child, the principal of said trust fund as may be remaining in the hands of my Trustees, together with accrued but unmatured income thereon and accumulations of income, if any, shall continue to be held in trust for the issue of such child surviving such child, per stirpes, pursuant to the provisions of this Paragraph, or in default of such issue, shall be divided equally among my surviving children, per stirpes, to be added to their corpus then held in trust pursuant to the provisions of this Paragraph.

(5) Upon my youngest child, or his or her issue, if applicable, attaining the age of thirty-two (32) years, this trust shall terminate and come to an end and shall be fully distributed, free of trust.

FIFTH: (A) Should my wife, , survive me, then I give, devise, and bequeath the entire balance and residue of my Estate to my Trustees, hereinafter named, to hold IN TRUST NEVERTHELESS, to invest the same and keep the same invested, to collect the income thereof and to pay over and distribute the net income arising therefrom to my wife, , during her lifetime. I expressly direct that all of the income from the corpus of this Trust shall be paid to my wife at least quarterly.

(B) I hereby authorize and empower my Trustees to pay out of the principal of the trust fund created under this Paragraph " " so much of the principal from time to time in whole or in part to my wife, , as they in their sole and unreviewable discretion may determine for the health, comfort, and welfare of my said wife or such sums may be applied for her proper support, maintenance, health, or comfort.

(C) Upon the death of my wife, , my Trustees shall divide the balance of the principal and undistributed income of the trust remaining, into as many equal parts as I shall leave children who shall be living at the date of my wife's death, (or should any of the children have predeceased me but leave issue him or her surviving and surviving my wife, then such issue should take his or her parent's share in equal parts, per stirpes, and not per capita, to be held in trust all pursuant to the provisions herein) to be separately held and disposed of in a single trust fund, if possible, for the benefit of each of said children (or their issue) as follows:

(1) With respect to each part set apart for a child or his issue: I give, devise, and bequeath such part to my Trustees to invest the same and keep the same invested and to apply so much of the income arising therefrom and so much of the principal of the trust as in the sole and unreviewable discretion of my Trustees may be advisable for the education, maintenance, health, and support of the child for whose benefit such trust shall have been created and to accumulate the balance of said net income, if any, until such child shall have attained the age of twenty-three (23) years, at which time all accumulations of income from that portion of the trust for said child shall be paid over to such child, together with one-quarter (1/4) of the principal remaining in that portion of the trust fund held for said child.

(2) Thereupon I direct my Trustees to continue to invest and keep invested so much of the principal of said trust fund as may be remaining in their hands and to pay the net income arising therefrom quarterly to the child for whose benefit said trust shall have been created until such child shall have attained the age of twenty-seven (27) years, at which time I direct that all undistributed income from that portion of the trust for said child together with one-third (1/3) of the principal then remaining in that portion of the trust fund held for said child shall be paid over to such child.

During this period the Trustees may apply so much of the principal of the trust and the income arising therefrom as in the sole and unreviewable discretion of the Trustees may be advisable for the education, maintenance, health, and support of that child.

(3) Thereupon I direct my Trustees to continue to invest and keep invested so much of the principal of said trust fund as may be remaining in their hands and to pay the net income arising therefrom quarterly to the child for whose benefit said trust shall have been created until such child shall have attained the age of thirty-two (32) years, at which time I direct that all undistributed income from that portion of the trust for said child together with the balance of the principal then remaining in that portion held for said child shall be paid over to such child.

During this period the Trustees may apply so much of the principal of the trust and the income arising therefrom as in the sole and unreviewable discretion of the Trustees may be advisable for the education, maintenance, health, and support of that child.

(4) In the event that the child for whose benefit said trust shall have been created should die before attaining the age of thirty-two (32) years, then upon the death of such child, the principal of said trust fund as may be remaining in the hands of my Trustees, together with accrued but unmatured income thereon and accumulations of income, if any, shall continue to be held in trust for the issue of such child surviving such child, per stirpes, pursuant to the provisions of this Paragraph, or in default of such issue, shall be divided equally among my surviving children, per stirpes, to be added to their corpus then held in trust pursuant to the provisions of this Paragraph.

(5) Upon my youngest child, or his or her issue, if applicable, attaining the age of thirty-two (32) years, this trust shall terminate and come to an end and shall be fully distributed, free of trust.

(D) I authorize my Executors in their sole discretion, to elect that all of the property passing under this trust be treated as qualified Terminable Interest Property under Section 2056 (b) (7) of the Internal Revenue Code of 1954, as amended, or any corresponding provision of any subsequent Federal Tax Law (herein called the "Code") for the purposes of qualifying for the Marital Deduction allowable in determining the Federal estate tax upon my estate. The determination of my Executors with respect to the exercise of such an election shall be conclusive upon all affected parties.

SIXTH: Should my wife, , not survive me, then I give, devise, and bequeath my entire residuary estate to my Trustees, hereinafter named, IN TRUST NEVERTHELESS, and I direct my Trustees to divide the principal of the trust fund coming into their hands, into as many equal parts as I shall leave children who shall be living at the date of my death, (or should any of my children have predeceased me but leave issue him or her surviving and surviving my wife, then such issue should take his or her parent's share in equal parts, per stirpes, and not per capita), to be held in trust all pursuant to the provisions herein, for the benefit of each of said children (or their issue) as follows:

(1) With respect to each part set apart for a child or his issue: I give, devise, and bequeath such part to my Trustees to invest the same invested and to apply so much of the income arising therefrom and so much of the principal of the trust as in the sole and unreviewable discretion of my Trustees may be advisable for the education, maintenance, health, and support of the child for whose benefit such trust shall have been created and to accumulate the balance of said net income, if any, until such child shall have attained the age of twenty-one (21) years, at which time all accumulations of income from that portion of the trust due said child shall be paid over to such child, together with one-third (1/3) of the principal remaining in that portion of the trust fund held for said child.

(2) Thereupon I direct my Trustees to continue to invest and keep invested so much of the principal of said trust fund as may be remaining in their hands and to pay the net income arising therefrom quarterly to the child for whose benefit said trust shall have been created until such child shall have attained the age of twenty-five (25) years, at which time I direct that all undistributed income from that portion of the trust for said child together with one-half (1/2) of the balance of the principal then remaining in that portion held for said child shall be paid over to such child.

During this period the Trustees may apply so much of the principal of the trust and the income arising therefrom as in the sole and unreviewable discretion of the Trustees may be advisable for the education, maintenance, health, and support of that child.

(3) Thereupon I direct my Trustees to continue to invest and keep invested so much of the principal of said trust fund as may be remaining in their hands and to pay the net income arising therefrom quarterly to the child for whose benefit said trust shall have been created until such child shall have attained the age of twenty-eight (28) years, at which time I direct all undistributed income from that portion of the trust for said child together with the balance of the principal then remaining in that portion held for said child shall be paid over to such child.

During this period the Trustees may apply so much of the principal of the trust and the income arising therefrom as in the sole and unreviewable discretion of the Trustees may be advisable for the education, maintenance, health, and support of that child.

(4) In the event that the child for whose benefit said trust shall have been created should die before attaining the age of twenty-eight (28) years, then upon the death of such child, the principal of said trust fund as may be remaining in the hands of my Trustees, together with accrued but unmatured income thereon and accumulations of income, if any, shall continue to be held in trust for the issue of such child surviving such child, per stirpes, pursuant to the provisions of this Paragraph, or in default of such issue, shall be divided equally among my surviving children, per stirpes, to be added to their corpus then held in trust pursuant to the provisions of this Paragraph, providing such issue are alive at the time of my death, otherwise such issue shall receive their share outright, but subject to the powers in trust provisions of Paragraph "NINTH."

(5) Upon my youngest child, attaining the age of twenty-eight (28) years, this trust shall terminate and come to an end and shall be fully distributed, free of trust.

SEVENTH: Upon the termination or change of beneficiary of any trust herein created through the decease, after my decease, of the person entitled to receive the income, there shall be no apportionment to the executor or administrator of such person of any accrued but unmatured income. Said accrued but unmatured income shall, upon the maturity and collection of the several respective items thereof, belong in its entirety to the person or persons entitled to receive the income of the particular trust fund, that is to say, to the remainderman or remaindermen in any case where the principal of the trust shall vest in fee, or to the next beneficiary in any case where the trust shall continue for the benefit of a successive or further beneficiary.

EIGHTH: In the event that my wife, , and I should die in a common disaster or accident or under such circumstances that the order of deaths cannot be established by proof, then I direct that for purposes of this Will, my said Wife shall be presumed to have predeceased me. In the event that any other beneficiary of this Will and I or any other person upon whose death such beneficiary shall become entitled to receive either income or principal under this Will shall die in a common disaster or accident or under such circumstances that the order of deaths cannot be established by proof, then I direct that for purposes of this Will such beneficiary shall be deemed to have predeceased me or such other person as the case may be.

NINTH: If upon my death any part of my estate shall vest in absolute ownership in a minor, or if at the termination of any of the trusts created by this Will all or any part of any of the trusts created by this Will or if all or any part of the principal of any of the trust funds shall vest in absolute ownership in a minor, I authorize and empower my Trustees or Executors, as the case may be, to continue to hold said principal for the benefit of such minor during his or her legal minority or until the age of twenty-one (21) years, whichever shall be greater, to invest the same and keep the same invested and to collect the income thereof and in the sole and unreviewable discretion of the said Executors or Trustees, as the case may be, either to accumulate the income or pay over the net income arising therefrom to the minor to whom said principal shall belong or to his or her parent or legal guardian, or to the person with whom such minor resides, or to apply said income and such sum or sums out of principal, as in their sole and absolute discretion they deem necessary or advisable to said infant's care, education, maintenance, and support. The authority thus accorded to my Executors or Trustees, as the case may be, shall be construed as a power only and shall not operate to suspend the absolute ownership of such principal by such minor or to prevent the absolute vesting thereof in such minor. The rights, powers, privileges, and immunities granted in this my Last Will and Testament to my Executors and/or Trustees shall apply to the administration and investment of any funds held by my Executors or Trustees in accordance with this power, and they shall have the same rights to compensation for so acting as if any such trust had continued and said principal had not vested.

TENTH: I hereby nominate, constitute, and appoint my wife, , and my attorney, , as the Co-Executors of my Last Will and Testament and as the Co-Trustees of the Trusts herein established. Should predecease me, fail to qualify as such Co-Executor, and/or Co-Trustee or having qualified, shall for any reason fail to continue to act as such Co-Executor, and/or Co-Trustee then I hereby nominate, constitute, and appoint my attorney, , as Co-Executor and/or Co-Trustee in his place.

I direct that none of the persons named herein as Guardian, Executor and/or Trustee, original or successor, shall be required to give any bond or other undertaking for the faithful performance of their duties as Guardian, Executor, and/or Trustee, or as successor.

ELEVENTH: I confer upon my Executors and/or Trustees, original or successor, with respect to the management and administration of any property, real or personal, the following discretionary powers, without limitation by reason of specification, and in addition to the powers conferred upon them by statute or by general rules of law:

(1) I authorize and empower my Executors and/or Trustees to retain and continue any investments which I may own at the time of my death. In the making of new investments I direct that my Executors and/or Trustees shall not be restricted or limited to such legal investments as are provided for the investment of trust funds by any statutes now in force or which may hereafter be enacted, and I specifically authorize my Executors and/or Trustees to invest the assets of my estate and/or the corpus of any trust fund or any part hereof in a discretionary common trust fund, to purchase or acquire in exchange or otherwise real estate, mortgages, stocks, bonds, and securities other than those constituting legal investments for trust funds and to invest and keep invested therein any part of my estate or of the trusts herein created. My Executors and Trustees shall not be

held accountable or liable for any loss, depreciation, or damage sustained by reason of the retention, acquisition, or disposition of any investments pursuant to the provisions of this paragraph.

(2) I authorize and empower my Executors and/or Trustees in their discretion and without leave of Court to sell at public or private sale or to lease without public bidding and without restriction or limitation as the length of term (even though for a period longer than authorized by statute or longer than the duration of any trust herein created) or to mortgage or pledge any or all property coming into their hands, whether real or personal or mixed, at such times and upon such terms and conditions as in their judgment they may deem proper, and I authorize and empower them to sign, execute, acknowledge, and deliver any deeds, mortgages, conveyances, leases, and other papers that may be necessary in connection therewith.

(3) I authorize and empower my Executors and/or Trustees in their discretion to purchase property (a) on the foreclosure of any mortgage held by my estate, (b) on which my estate may own a mortgage or mortgages, (c) in which my estate shall have any interest, or any sale in partition, foreclosure, or otherwise or (d) which may be sold under any judgment in which my estate may have any interest, and I authorize and empower them to sign, execute, acknowledge, and deliver any deeds, mortgages, conveyances, leases, or other papers that may be necessary in connection therewith.

(4) I authorize and empower my Executors and/or Trustees to compromise, settle, or arbitrate any claim or demand in favor of or against my estate.

(5) I authorize and empower my Executors to join with my wife in executing and filing a joint Income Tax Return and agree with her as to the shares or proportions of the tax shown thereon which are to be paid respectively by my estate and by her. My Executors shall not be held accountable or liable for any error of judgment as to the filing of a separate or a joint return or as to the apportionment of the tax on a joint return.

(6) I authorize and empower my Executors and/or Trustees to vote in person or by proxy upon any and all stocks or other securities held by them; to exercise any rights to subscribe for or to convert into stocks or bonds or other securities of any corporation (whether a going concern or in liquidation or in reorganization or under any other circumstances or conditions whatsoever) for other real or personal property distributed by the same corporation or any other corporation which shall be formed as a reorganization of or in combination, merger or consolidation with the original corporation; to become a party to any plan of reorganization, merger, or consolidation or to become a depositor with and/or give power of attorney to any committee of bondholders or other security holders or creditors formed for the purpose of mutual protection in connection with any plan of corporate financing or reorganization or to represent or enforce the rights of security holders or creditors in connection with any defaults by the corporation or any reorganization or insolvency of the corporation; to accept any new or substituted security

of whatever nature in place of the defaulted or previosly held security; to make any payments necessary to obtain such new or substituted security, and generally to exercise in respect to any securitites held by them the unrestricted rights of a personal owner thereof, in accordance with their best judgment and discretion.

(7) I authorize and empower my Executors and/or Trustees to borrow money, from others or from themselves whether to pay taxes, make subsciptions, exercise options, pay assessments, or to accomplish any other purpose of any nature incidental to the administration of my estate or of any of the trusts herein created, and to mortgage or pledge as security therefor any securities or other property held by them.

(8) So far as I may be legally permitted to do so, I authorize and empower my Executors and/or Trustees to cause any stocks, bonds, or other securities at any time held by them to be in bearer form or to be registered in the name of a nominee or nominees.

(9) I authorize and empower my Executors and/or Trustees to hold and retain so long as to them may seem proper, as part of my estate and trust estate, any real, personal, or mixed property, or any interest therein, of which I may die seized or possessed, or to which I may be entitled at the time of my death, notwithstanding that the same may not be of the kind, character, legal, proper or permissable for the investment of funds or trust funds under the laws of the State of New York, or any other State and without regard to the proportion that any of said property may bear to the entire amount of my estate and trust estate, or of the trusts in which same are held.

(10) I authorize and empower my Executors and/or Trustees to form any corporation, partnership, general or limited, or association, and to sell, convey, exchange, contract, lease, assign, transfer and set over, or otherwise dispose of to said corporation, partnership, or association any or all of my estate, and to accept therefor property, real or personal, stocks, notes, bonds, debentures, mortgages, securities, or other evidences of indebtedness from said partnership, corporation, or association including the stock of any such corporation, common or preferred, in payment or part payment therefor, and to become directors and officers of any such corporation and with full power and authority on the part of any such corporation and my estate and trust estate to transact any business, including the making of any loans, with or without pledge, mortgage, or security between my estate and trust estate and said corporation, with full power and authority on the part of either the corporation or my estate and trust estate to become maker, endorser, guarantor, and surety for each other in respect to any matter whatsoever, and said corporation may be organized under the laws of any State selected by said Executors and/or Trustees with all the powers incident to corporations organized under the laws of such State.

(11) I authorize and empower my Executors and/or Trustees to continue any business of mine and the operation thereof and any interest that I may have either

individually or as a partner, stockholder in any business, firm, enterprise, association, partnership, whether general or limited, company, or corporation of whatsoever nature and wherever same may be situated, for so long a time and upon such terms and conditions and in such manner as my said Executors and/or Trustees may deem advisable and beneficial and for the best interest of my estate and trust estate, and for that purpose to retain and permit to be employed therein any capital or investment which shall at my death be employed therein, and generally to act in all matters relating to any such business or interest as herein mentioned as if they owned the same, or were beneficially interested in or entitled to the same.

(12) I authorize and empower my Executors and/or Trustees to carry out any contracts or agreements that I may have entered into with any person or persons, partnership, stockholders, or corporation in connection with any such business, interest, partnership, firm, association or corporation, or affecting or concerning any stock owned or held by me, and to extend and to continue the same or enter into any other agreement or arrangement that they may deem advisable and for the best interest of my estate and trust estate.

(13) I authorize and empower my Executors and/or Trustees to form any firm, partnership, association, company, or corporation with or concerning any business in which I may have any interest, as herein mentioned, and to participate in, consent to, or oppose any plan of liquidation, consolidation, reorganization, merger, or similar plan in connection with or concerning the said business or interest with any other business, firm, association, partnership, or corporation.

(14) I authorize and empower my Executors and/or Trustees to discontinue, liquidate, dissolve, and dispose of any business, firm, association, partnership, corporation, or any stockholdings or interest that I may have in the same.

(15) I authorize and empower my Executors and/or Trustees to apportion between principal and income all stock dividends and liquidating or extraordinary dividends or distributions. Without limiting the absolute discretion of my fiduciaries, I desire that all such dividends and distributions be allotted to principal except to the extent that my fiduciaries shall determine that they were declared or made in lieu of regular cash dividends or distributions.

(16) I authorize and empower my Executors and/or Trustees at any time and from time to time, to appoint for the time being an agent or attorney to make, execute, and deliver any transfer or other instructions, or to do any ministerial act necessary or proper to be done in the administration of my estate.

(17) I authorize and empower my Executors and/or Trustees to employ such attorneys, clerks, agents, accountants, and custodians, and to obtain such investment or other advice, in the transaction of the business of my estate and in the administration of any trust hereunder as my Executors or Trustees, as the case may be, may deem necessary or advisable, and to make such payments and disbursements therefor as they deem reasonable and proper.

(18) Except as otherwise expressly provided in this Will, I authorize and empower my Executors and/or Trustees to pay any pecuniary legacy hereunder, whether in trust or otherwise, and to make any distribution pursuant to this my Will, in whole or in part, in securities or other property owned by me at the time of my decease or thereafter acquired by my Executors or Trustees, subject to the applicable provisions of this Will, which shall fully govern with respect to the bequest therein provided for, and in making such payment or distribution in securities or other property, I direct that valuation placed thereon by my Executors or by my Trustees shall be binding and conclusive on all persons interested in my estate, subject only to the power of a court of competent jurisdiction to pass on such valuation.

(19) My Trustees may at any time and from time to time during the course of the administration of any trust created pursuant to this Will, render an account of their proceedings with respect to such trust to every person who is then of full age and sound mind and who is then currently entitled to be paid the net income of such trust or who then may be entitled in any future contingency to have paid over to him or to her all or any part of the principal of such trust and to every duly appointed guardian of the property of every such person who is not then of full age and who has such a guardian. If the persons to whom such an account is so rendered by my Trustees include both at least one person (or the guardian of one person) who may be entitled in any future contingency to have paid over to him or to her all or any part of the principal, the written approval of such account by all the persons to whom the account is so rendered (including any such guardians) shall be binding and conclusive upon all persons then having or thereafter acquiring or claiming any interest in the subject matter of such account and shall be a complete discharge to my Trustees with respect to all matters set forth in such account as fully and to the same extent as though such account had been judicially settled and allowed by a judgment or order or decree of a court of competent jurisdiction in an action or proceeding in which all persons so having, acquiring or claiming any interest in the subject matter of such account were duly made parties and were duly represented. The foregoing provisions of this paragraph shall not be deemed to limit the right of my Trustees to have any such account judicially settled despite such written approval.

TWELFTH: (A) I hereby direct that no disposition charge or encumbrances on any interest in my estate, or on any part thereof, by any beneficiary under the Will by way of anticipation shall be valid or in any way binding upon my Executors or Trustees, and no beneficiary shall have the right to assign, transfer, encumber, or otherwise dispose of such income or principal, or any part thereof until the same shall be paid to such beneficiary by my Executors or by my Trustees, and no income or principal or any part thereof shall be liable to any claim of any creditors of any such beneficiary.

(B) The right of any beneficiary to any payment of income or principal shall be in every case subject to any charges or deduction which my Executors or my

Trustees may make against the same under the authority granted to my Executors or to my Trustees by any law or by any provision of this Will.

THIRTEENTH: The powers and authority hereinbefore granted to my Executors and/or Trustees may be exercised without obligation to or authority from any court or judge, and, to the extent permitted by law, they shall not be liable or responsible for any loss which may be suffered except where the same is due to their dishonest or malicious acts.

FOURTEENTH: The words "child," "children," and "issue," wherever used in this Will, shall include not only the child, children, and issue of the person or persons designated, but also the legally adopted child or children of such person or persons.

IN WITNESS WHEREOF, I have hereunto set my hand and seal the day of , 19 .

____

The foregoing instrument consisting of ( ) pages, including this page, was on the day above signed, sealed, published, and declared by , the above-named Testator, as and for his Last Will and Testament, in the presence of us and each of us, who at his request, and in his presence and in the presence of each other, have hereunto subscribed our names as attesting witnesses, this day of , 19 .

____________________ residing at ____________________

____

____________________ residing at ____________________

____

____________________ residing at ____________________

____

SAMPLE POWER OF APPOINTMENT TRUST

(A) Should my wife, , survive me, then I give, devise, and bequeath the entire balance and residue of my Estate to my Trustees, hereinafter named, to hold IN TRUST NEVERTHELESS, to invest the same and to keep the same invested, to collect the income thereof and to pay over and distribute the net income arising therefrom to my wife, , during her lifetime. I expressly direct that all of the income from the corpus of this Trust shall be paid to my wife at least quarterly.

(B) I hereby authorize and empower my Trustees to pay out of the principal of the trust fund created under this Paragraph " " so much of the principal from time to time in whole or in part to my wife, , as they in their sole and unreviewable discretion may determine for the health, comfort, and welfare of my said wife or such sums may be applied for her proper support, maintenance, health, or comfort.

(C) I hereby authorize and empower my wife from time to time during her lifetime by appropriate instrument in writing to appoint all or part of the principal of this trust fund in such proportions and subject to such terms and conditions in trust or otherwise, in fee or less than in fee, as my wife alone and in her sole discretion may determine, and I direct my Trustees upon receipt of written notice of any such appointment to distribute the principal thus appointed in accordance with such notice.

(D) Upon the death of my wife, I direct that the principal of the trust fund or so much thereof as may be remaining in the hands of my Trustees as well as any income accrued but unpaid at the date of her death, shall be paid over to such person or persons (including her estate) in such proportions and in any manner in trust or otherwise, in fee or less than in fee, as she may in her Last Will and Testament appoint, specifically referring to this power.

(E) Upon the death of my wife, any of the principal and income remaining in this Trust which has not been validly and effectively appointed by her shall be distributed pursuant to Paragraph " " herein and shall follow the dispositions of Paragraph " " hereof in all respects as to income and principal.

Part 3

HANDLING CONCERNS DURING MARITAL DISHARMONY

CHAPTER 7

Safeguarding the Client's Interests

SITUATION

Herb and Ann Jones are 30 and 29 years old respectively. Herb works and earns $45,000, while Ann does not work. They have been married 10 years and have two children, ages 8 and 7. They jointly own bank accounts worth $200,000 and jointly own a house worth $150,000. In addition, Herb solely owns stocks worth $150,000. These stocks were bought with income earned by Herb after he married Ann. The first nine years of their marriage were harmonious. However, during the last year relations between them have become extremely strained. Herb began beating Ann several months ago and last month Ann discovered that Herb had a paramour.

DETERMINE WHAT CLIENT DESIRES

Ann comes to you, her attorney, to discuss the difficulties she has encountered with Herb. She informs you that at this juncture she believes that her marriage with Herb can be salvaged. She and Herb are discussing their marriage problems. Herb has agreed not to see his paramour, and he has accepted her suggestion to visit a marriage counselor on a regular basis. However, Ann is still concerned that her marriage with Herb will falter. She asks you for advice as to how she can protect herself in the event of a divorce.

PROTECTING CLIENT'S ASSETS

Ann must be warned that Herb has access to the bank accounts held in joint name and may decide to transfer the money held in these accounts to accounts held solely by him. Such an action by Herb is a distinct possibility considering the shakey status of their marriage. If Herb does invade the joint accounts, move out of the house, and refuse to provide financial assistance to Ann, she will find herself in an untenable position. Not only will she have difficulty procuring the finances necessary to maintain the household with her two children but she may not be able to procure the finances necessary to adequately fight Herb in a divorce action.

In view of the foregoing, Ann would be best advised to take half of the assets in the joint accounts and place them in an account held solely by her. Ann's removal of assets in the joint accounts will probably create more friction with Herb. However, Ann must be protected financially and the only means by which she can attain financial security is to remove some of the assets from the joint account.

CONSTRUCTING A RECONCILIATION AGREEMENT

Appropriateness of Agreement

If Ann and Herb's marriage was doomed to failure, it would make no sense to attempt to construct a reconciliation agreement. Ann, in this posture, would probably be best advised to consider negotiating a separation agreement with Herb with a view toward attaining a divorce. However, since the parties seem willing to give the marriage a chance despite the difficulties encountered, a reconciliation agreement is in order.

Drafting Agreement

In drafting a reconciliation agreement as Ann's attorney, you should address the same concerns that are addressed in drafting an antenuptial agreement. (See Chapter 3 for a detailed discussion of these considerations.) Also, you should address the custody, visitation, and support of the children issues in the event of a divorce, which considerations would not be addressed in the antenuptial agreement. (A detailed discussion of these considerations appears in Chapter 11.) Indeed, should Herb and Ann's marriage falter and they decide to divorce, the reconciliation agreement could at the very least serve as the basis for the separation agreement.

Dividing the assets. Through the reconciliation agreement, you might wish to attempt to provide Ann with an amount of assets equal to that possessed by Herb. In the instant case, since all the family assets are owned jointly except the $150,000 in stocks owned by Herb, you would attempt to have Herb transfer these stocks from his name into joint name. There would be no gift tax consequences from such a transfer. Also, the basis of the stock would remain the same—being transferred from Herb's sole ownership to their joint ownership—and then there would be no capital gain and resulting income tax consequences. The significance of such a transfer would depend on whether Herb and Ann reside in a community property, equitable distribution, or common law state. In a community property state, a divorce would lead to the same result as that bargained for in the reconciliation agreement, i.e. half the value of these stocks acquired after the marriage would be Herb's and half would be Ann's. On the other hand, in a common law state, Herb would retain all of the stocks upon divorce and Ann would get nothing. In an equitable distribution state, Herb might be entitled to 75% of the value of the stocks and Ann might receive 25%.

Specific bequest in will. Also, in the reconciliation agreement, you might wish to provide a clause which mandates that Herb make a certain specific bequest to Ann in his Will. Or, you might demand that at Herb's death a certain percentage of the assets passing through his Will flow to Ann. You should provide that the consideration for any transfers from Herb to Ann—whether pursuant to a Will or the reconciliation agreement—is the fact that Ann will consent to continuing to live with him as his wife.

A sample reconciliation agreement follows which will save you time and effort in drafting a reconciliation agreement for Ann.

SAMPLE RECONCILIATION AGREEMENT

AGREEMENT, dated this day of , 19 , by and between , residing at , County of and State of , hereinafter referred to as the "HUSBAND", and , residing at , County of and State of , hereinafter referred to as the "WIFE".

WITNESSETH:

WHEREAS, the HUSBAND and WIFE were married in County, State of , on 19 ; and

WHEREAS, there are no children of this marriage and none are expected; and

WHEREAS, the parties have experienced certain marital difficulties and problems; and

WHEREAS, the parties are desirous of reconciling these marital problems and resuming a normal marital relationship; and

WHEREAS, the parties are desirous of entering into a contractual relationship which will set forth certain present transactions as well as their future rights and obligations concerning property division and support in the event of a Divorce, Separation, or Annulment involving the HUSBAND and WIFE;

NOW, THEREFORE, in consideration of the sum of TEN ($10.00) DOLLARS and of the mutual promises and covenants hereinafter set forth, the parties agree to the following present transactions and terms as well as certain promises and terms in the event of a future Annulment, Separation, or Divorce as follows:

ARTICLE I

The parties agree that all debts presently existing which were incurred in the HUSBAND'S name alone or in the WIFE'S name alone, as well as all future debts which are incurred in the HUSBAND'S name alone or the WIFE'S name alone, shall remain as an individual debt of the party so incurring the debt and at no time hereafter will the other party have any responsibility to pay debts so incurred by the other, and the HUSBAND and WIFE shall hold each other harmless and indemnified in this connection.

ARTICLE II

In the event of a dissolution of the marriage at a future date, the parties have agreed on the following terms, which terms are to take effect immediately on the date a Summons for Divorce, Separation, or Annulment is served by one party on the other.

FIRST: At such time as either party serves the other with a Summons seeking dissolution of the marriage, he and she agree to waive, release, and relinquish any and all rights which he or she might otherwise have as a surviving spouse under the statutes and common law now or hereafter in effect in any jurisdiction in the property and estate of the other, including but not limited to a distributive share in the event of intestacy, the right of election to take against the Will, the right of election to take against testamentary substitutes, homestead rights, the right to act as Administrator or Executor or other fiduciary, curtesy, widower's allowances, equitable distribution, and community property. Both parties immediately upon service of a Summons for Divorce, Separation, or Annulment, waive, release, and relinquish any and all rights which he or she may have acquired by reason of their marriage to each other, in any property owned by him or her at any time, or by his or her estate upon his or her death, including but not limited to curtesy, homestead rights, equitable distribution, and community property.

SECOND: A. All outstanding bills, debts, and charges for necessaries incurred by the WIFE up to the date of the entry of a decree for Divorce, Separation, or Annulment, shall be the sole responsibility of the WIFE, and she will be liable to pay for same.

B. All outstanding bills, debts, and charges for necessaries incurred by the HUSBAND up to the date of the entry of a decree for Divorce, Separation, or Annulment, shall be the sole responsibility of the HUSBAND, and he will be liable to pay for same.

THIRD: All items of personalty, furniture, furnishings and the like that are situated at any marital residence at the time of the service of a summons seeking to dissolve the marriage shall be the subject of negotiations by the parties, but in the event they are unable to reach an accord on the division of such items of personalty, then the dispute shall be submitted to the American Arbitration Association in New York City for a determination.

FOURTH: In the event a child is born out of this marriage, then the question of who shall have custody of that child, and the visitation privileges of the non-custodial parent, and the question of who shall be responsible for the support of the child, shall be negotiated by the parties, but in the event they are unable to reach an accord on these issues, then such disputed issues shall be submitted to the American Arbitration Association in New York City for a determination.

FIFTH: A. The WIFE warrants and represents that her approximate income at the present time from all sources is $. In consideration of the terms and provisions contained in this agreement the WIFE agrees that she will not seek alimony, maintenance, or support for herself from the HUSBAND and she hereby waives her right to any past, present, or future alimony, maintenance, and support.

B. The HUSBAND warrants and represents that his income at the present time from all sources is $, and that in the future his income from employment could increase very substantially. In consideration of the terms and provisions contained in this agreement the HUSBAND agrees that he will not seek alimony, maintenance, or support for himself from the WIFE and he hereby waives his right to any past, present, or future alimony, maintenance, and support.

SIXTH: A. The parties warrant and represent that as of the date of the execution of this Agreement there are no assets "Separate Property" in the HUSBAND'S or WIFE'S name alone or in their joint name, which were obtained by him or her prior to their marriage or purchased with funds acquired prior to the marriage or through gifts or inheritances from a third party. "Separate Property" is defined in amended Section 236 of the New York Domestic Relations Law, which took effect July 19, 1980, also known as the Equitable Distribution Law.

B. The parties further agree that in the event either party acquires any "Separate Property" in the future, then at the time of the service of a summons for Divorce, Separation, or Annulment, which ever party had title to the asset at the time of the service of a summons shall retain sole ownership of that asset, including any appreciation in value and any interest or income earned thereon, and the non-titled spouse shall have no rights or claims against that asset.

SEVENTH: A. The parties warrant and represent that the following assets are the only substantial "Marital Property" owned by him or her or jointly owned as defined in amended Section 236 of the Domestic Relations Law, which took effect July 19, 1980, also known as the Equitable Distribution Law, and they have agreed that in consideration of the covenants and promises contained in this Agreement, this marital property is to be distributed as follows at such time either party serves a Summons for Divorce, Separation, or Annulment on the other party:

Asset	Today's approx. value	How presently held	Final disposition
Checking Account	$	HUSBAND	HUSBAND
Savings Account # ____________ , at ____________ Bank in	$	HUSBAND	HUSBAND
Checking account # ____________ , at	$	WIFE	WIFE

B. The parties agree that the above provided distribution of assets shall include any and all increases in the value of the designated asset, as well as to include any and all accumulated dividends and interest, through and including the date of the service of the Summons for Divorce, Separation, or Annulment.

C. The parties further agree that in the event of any sale, exchange, assignment, or transfer of the above designated assets, then any and all monies and assets received from such sale, exchange, assignment, or transfer, shall belong to that party who was to receive the original asset as provided for above.

D. The parties further agree that in the year either party acquires any "Marital Property" in the future, then at the time of the service of a Summons for Divorce, Separation, or Annulment, whichever party has title to the asset at the time of the service of such summons shall retain sole ownership of that asset, including any appreciation in value and any interest or income earned thereon, and the non-titled spouse shall have no rights or claims against that asset.

EIGHTH: The parties further agree that the rights to exclusive occupancy of any rented apartment at the time of the service of a Summons for Divorce, Separation, or Annulment shall be determined by terms of the outstanding lease or, in other words, if the lease is in the name of the HUSBAND alone, then he alone shall be entitled to sole and exclusive occupancy of the premises, or if the lease to said premises is in the WIFE'S name alone, then she shall be entitled to sole and exclusive occupancy of that apartment.

In the event at the time of the service of the summons the lease is in both names, then the parties shall endeavor to negotiate a settlement of who shall have the right to the lease and exclusive occupancy of such apartment, but in the event they are unable to reach an accord on this issue, then this dispute shall be submitted to the American Arbitration Association.

NINTH: The parties agree that as concerns all future acquired assets whether they are deemed "Marital Property" or "Separate Property", which are held in joint name of the parties at the time of the service of a Summons for Divorce, Separation, or Annulment, their jointly owned assets are to be divided equally between them.

TENTH: Concerning the distribution of assets provided for in Paragraphs Sixth, Seventh, Eighth, and Ninth of this Agreement, the parties acknowledge the fact that such distribution was arrived at on the basis that each party had been furnished with all information requested by the other and on the basis that each had the opportunity to make full and complete examination of the other's income, property, assets, and financial affairs.

ELEVENTH: The parties further agree that in the event an action is brought by either party for Divorce, Separation, or Annulment, each party will be respectively responsible to pay any and all legal fees for any and all representation in the matter which shall be inclusive of negotiations which might lead to a separation agreement and/or fees incurred in litigation.

ARTICLE III

FIRST: The parties acknowledge the fact that the HUSBAND has been represented and advised by independent counsel in the making of this agreement and that his attorneys were
, and
that the WIFE has been represented and advised by independent counsel in the making of this Agreement and her attorney was , with offices at , .

SECOND: Each party agrees that he and she shall be solely responsible to pay any and all counsel fees charged by his or her respective attorneys for negotiations leading up to the execution of this Agreement and for representation at the Closing of this Agreement.

ARTICLE IV

FIRST: Nothing contained in this Agreement shall be construed to prevent either party from instituting any suit, action, or other legal proceeding in this or any other jurisdiction for a Divorce, Separation, or Annulment against the other by reason of facts which heretofore occurred or which may hereafter occur. In the event that an action, suit for other legal proceeding for Divorce, Separation, or Annulment shall be instituted at any time by either party against the other, in the State of New York, or in any other jurisdiction, it is agreed that:

A. Neither of the parties shall cause or request that any provision be inserted in the final judgment or decree of the Court which shall be inconsistent with any of the provisions of this Agreement.

B. To the extent possible and appropriate, the terms and provisions of this Agreement shall be incorporated by reference into any final judgment or decree obtained in a Divorce or Separation action and shall survive such final judgment or decree.

C. This Agreement shall in no way and under no circumstances merge in any such judgment or decree of Divorce or Separation.

SECOND: Both the legal and practical effect of this Agreement in each and every respect and the financial standard of the parties has been fully explained to both parties by their own counsel, and they both acknowledge that it is a fair Agreement and is not the result of any duress or undue influence exercised by either party upon the other, or by any other person or persons upon either, and they further agree that this Agreement contains the entire understanding of the parties. There are no representations, promises, warranties, covenants, or undertakings other than those expressly set forth herein.

THIRD: Each of the parties hereto agrees further at any time and from time to time to make, execute and deliver all instruments necessary to effectuate the provisions of this Agreement.

FOURTH: For the purpose of this Agreement, all notices or other communications given or made hereunder shall, until written notice to the contrary, be mailed or given directly to the WIFE and directly to the HUSBAND at their respective aforementioned addresses, or at any other address which either party may subsequently designate in writing.

FIFTH: All matters affecting the interpretation of this Agreement and the right of the parties shall be governed by the laws of the State of New York. Each of the parties agree that the provisions of this Agreement may be enforced in jurisdictions other than New York where either party may reside in the future and that each party hereby agrees to submit himself or herself to said jurisdiction for that purpose.

SIXTH: All of the provisions of this Agreement shall be binding upon the respective heirs, next of kin, executors, administrators, and assigns of the parties hereto.

SEVENTH: This Agreement shall be executed in duplicate, each of which so executed shall be deemed an original and shall constitute one and the same Agreement.

EIGHTH: The failure of either party at any time or from time to time to exercise the rights herein reserved to either party shall not be deemed to constitute a relinquishment of his or her right to exercise the same in the future.

NINTH: There can and shall be no modification of this Agreement, no waiver of any provision thereof, right hereunder or condition therein, or release from any obligation imposed hereby, except by written instrument duly executed.

TENTH: If any provision of this Agreement is held to be invalid or unenforceable, all other provisions shall nevertheless continue in full force and effect.

ARTICLE V

The parties agree that this Agreement shall remain in full force and effect for five (5) years following the date of its execution by both parties, and thereafter, if an action for Divorce, Separation, or Annulment has not been instituted by either party within five (5) years from the date of the execution of this Agreement, this Agreement shall be null and void.

IN WITNESS WHEREOF, the said parties hereto have, after consultation with their own counsel relative to the matter herein set forth and agreed upon, having been advised fully and fairly as to all of the facts and circumstances herein set forth, have hereunto set their hands and seals this day of , 19 .

WITNESSETH:

______________________ ______________________

Witness for

______________________ ______________________

Witness for

STATE OF NEW YORK)
) ss.:
COUNTY OF NEW YORK)

On this day of , 19 , before me personally came , to me known and known to me to be the person described in and who executed the foregoing Agreement and acknowledged that he executed the same.

____
NOTARY PUBLIC

STATE OF NEW YORK)
) ss.:
COUNTY OF NEW YORK)

On this day of , 19 , before me personally came , to me known and known to me to be the person described in and who executed the foregoing Agreement and acknowledged that she executed the same.

____
NOTARY PUBLIC

Legal Validity of Agreement

Just as was true in preparing the antenuptial agreement, it must be assured that the reconciliation agreement is constructed pursuant to bargaining between yourself, the attorney for Ann, and an attorney representing Herb. Additionally, as was also true in the antenuptial situation, there must be no overreaching. Complete disclosure of assets and liabilities—both present and potential—by both parties is essential.

CHAPTER 8

How to Construct a Troubled Marriage Will

SITUATION

George and Renee Jones, ages 50 and 45 years respectively, have been married 27 years. They both work and have one son, age 21 years. Although married, George and Renee have been living apart for 7 years. George lives in New York, while Renee lives in California, and they have not spoken to each other for 2 years. Neither George nor Renee owns any real estate and each separately owns assets worth $400,000.

DETERMINE WHAT CLIENT DESIRES

For personal and religious reasons, neither George nor Renee wishes to divorce. Additionally, neither George nor Renee wishes to enter into a formal documented separation. They each earn sufficient salaries to meet their needs and need not address child support or custody considerations since their sole child has attained the age of majority.

George does understand that since he is married to Renee, she will probably be entitled to a portion of his estate when he dies. However, he wishes to write a Will which bequeaths as much as possible to his son. George comes to you, his attorney, for advice on how to accomplish these goals.

APPROPRIATENESS OF WILL

George is a perfect candidate for the troubled marriage Will. This type of Will is reserved for the client who is having extensive marital difficulties with his spouse, but does not desire or is not ready for a divorce. The Will is for that client who wishes to assure that upon his death, his spouse will receive the minimum amount of assets permissible under state law.

The client who opts for a troubled marriage Will must understand that by doing so, he or she is essentially forfeiting the estate tax advantages available through the marital deduction. The marital deduction permits an individual to bequeath an unlimited amount to his spouse without tax consequences. However, it is axiomatic that the estate tax advantages available through the federal unified gift and estate tax credit can still be utilized. Through the use of this credit, beginning in 1987, no federal tax would be paid on estates up to $600,000. Thus, you can advise George that if he dies tomorrow, he need not utilize the marital deduction to avoid the payment of federal estate tax on his $400,000 estate.

In the event George at some future date decides to divorce Renee, the need for a troubled marriage Will will disappear. Once they are no longer married, Renee can have no claim on George's estate at his death. This is, of course, provided that George does not, through any agreement, e.g., a separation agreement, give Renee any claims on his estate.

DRAFTING THE WILL

In drafting the troubled marriage Will for George, particular attention must be paid to what, if any, vested rights his spouse may have in his estate under state law. Generally, the spouse can either take what is bequeathed in the Will or can elect to take a certain statutorily-designated share of the estate (right of election). In some states, if the Will provides for the spouse to receive a certain minimum amount, the spouse may lose his or her right of election. In New York, for example, if the spouse receives a $10,000 bequest plus the income for life from a trust whose principal is an amount at least equal to the wife's elective share minus any assets bequeathed or otherwise flowing to her, the spouse cannot claim the right of election.

Once the spouse's elective share is determined or the amount and type of bequests necessary to deprive the spouse of his or her elective share is determined, you should construct a Will which provides for these minimum bequests. By proceeding in the foregoing manner, your client's

Will should go unchallenged. Either the spouse will not challenge the Will by taking his or her elective share, since the elective share will not result in any financial advantage, or the spouse will be prevented from challenging the Will by taking an elective share since he or she will have no right of election.

Selecting a Trustee or Executor

Another point that should be made on the drafting of the troubled marriage Will pertains to the selection of a trustee or executor. It is imperative that your client choose an executor and/or trustee whose loyalties are toward your client. In this regard, your client should definitely not choose anyone who is a relative or friend of the client's spouse. Certainly, your client should not choose the spouse. You, as George's attorney, might be a good choice. Also, your client should avoid the selection of individuals that have business dealings with the spouse and might possess divided loyalties due to the business relationship. For example, you should not choose your accountant for the position of executor or trustee if that accountant is also your spouse's accountant.

In the event George divorces Renee, he need not concern himself with providing any bequests to her. He can rewrite his Will, cut her out entirely, and bequeath his property to whomever he wishes.

In order to aid you in preparing a troubled marriage Will, the following sample Will is provided. The sample Will assumes that George resides in New York. It provides for a $10,000 outright bequest to Renee and the establishment of a trust with the trust income to flow to Renee for her life.

SAMPLE TROUBLED MARRIAGE WILL

I, , a resident of the County of and State of New York, being of sound and disposing mind, do hereby make, publish, and declare this to be my Last Will and Testament.

FIRST: I hereby revoke any and all Wills and Codicils heretofore made by me.

SECOND: I direct that all of my just debts, funeral and testamentary expenses be paid as soon as practicable after my decease from my residuary estate. I direct that all estate, inheritance, succession, and transfer taxes and duties, including not only those upon property hereby devised or bequeathed, but also those, if any, imposed or assessed with respect to the proceeds of life insurance, and those, if any, imposed or assessed at or upon or by reason of my death with respect to any other property which for the purpose of the taxes enumerated in this paragraph may be considered or treated as part of my gross estate, shall be a charge upon and payable out of my residuary estate.

THIRD: Should I be married to at the time of death, and should and I have not entered into a Separation Agreement or other Agreement whereby my said wife, , has waived her interest in my Estate and/or she has waived her right of election as against my Estate, and should said survive me, then under such circumstances only:

(A) I give, devise, and bequeath to my said wife, , the sum of TEN THOUSAND ($10,000.00) DOLLARS, absolutely and free of trust, and

(B) I further give, devise, and bequeath to my said wife, , that share of my estate to which she would be entitled by virtue of her right, pursuant to the laws of the State of New York, to elect to take against the provisions of my Will (without requiring her to assert such right of election) less the aggregate value of any other property passing to my wife that will be taken on account of such elective share, without regard to whether or not such property passes to my wife by my Will or otherwise, to my Trustees, hereinafter named to hold in Trust for the following uses and purposes:

(1) To hold, manage, invest, and reinvest the said property, collect and receive the income therefrom, and pay the net income to my wife, , during her lifetime.

(2) Upon the death of my said wife, my Trustees shall pay over and distribute the principal then remaining in the said Trust Fund and the undistributed income then remaining in the said Trust Fund to the Trustees as provided in Paragraph "FIFTH" of this my Last Will and Testament.

(C) It is my express and absolute direction and desire that should and I *not* be married at the time of my death, or should and I have entered into a Separation Agreement or other Agreement whereby she has waived his interest in my Estate and/or has waived her right of election as against my Estate, or should she have predeceased me then, under any of the aforesaid circumstances, this bequest to , shall lapse and shall be included in my residuary estate pursuant to Paragraph "FOURTH" herein.

FOURTH: All of the rest, remainder, and residue of my estate, real, personal and/or mixed, wherever situate and whensoever acquired (or my entire residuary estate should my wife, , not survive me or should we not be married at the time of my death, or upon her death pursuant to Paragraph "THIRD" herein), I give, devise, and bequeath to my Trustees, hereinafter named, IN TRUST NEVERTHELESS, and I direct my Trustees to hold the principal of the trust fund coming into their hands, for the benefit of my son, , should he be living at the date of my death, (or should my said son have predeceased me but leave issue him surviving, then such issue should take his or her parent's share in equal parts, per stirpes, and not per capita, to be held in trust all pursuant to the provisions herein) to dispose of in a single trust fund, if possible, for the benefit of each of my said son (or his issue) as follows:

(1) With respect to each part set apart for my son or his issue: I give, devise, and bequeath such part to my Trustees to invest the same and keep the same invested and to apply so much of the income arising therefrom and so much of the principal of the trust as in the sole and unreviewable discretion of my Trustees may be advisable for the education, health, maintenance, and support of my son and to accumulate the balance of said net income, if any, until said son shall have attained the age of twenty-one (21) years, at which time all accumulations of income from that portion of the trust for my said son shall be paid over and distributed to my said son.

(2) Thereupon I direct my Trustees to continue to invest and keep invested so much of the principal of said trust fund as may be remaining in their hands and to pay the net income arising therefrom quarterly to my said son until my said son shall have attained the age of twenty-six (26) years, at which time I direct that all undistributed income from that portion of the trust for said son together with one-third (1/3) of the principal then remaining in that portion held for said son shall be paid over to said son.

During this period, the Trustees may apply so much of the principal of the trust and the income arising therefrom as in the sole and unreviewable discretion of the Trustees may be advisable for the education, health, maintenance, and support of my said son.

(3) Thereupon I direct my Trustees to continue to invest and keep invested so much of the principal of said trust fund as may be remaining in their hands and to pay the net income arising therefrom quarterly to my said son until such son shall have attained the age of thirty-two (32) years, at which time I direct that all of the undistributed income from that portion of the trust for said son together

with all of the principal then remaining in that portion held for said son shall be paid over to said son.

During this period the Trustees may apply so much of the principal of the trust and the income arising therefrom as in the sole and unreviewable discretion of the Trustees may be advisable for the education, health, maintenance, and support of my said son.

(4) In the event that my said son should die before attaining the age of thirty-two (32) years, then upon the death of said son, the principal of said trust fund as may be remaining in the hands of my Trustees, together with accrued but unmatured income thereon and accumulations of income, if any, shall continue to be held in trust for the issue of said son surviving said son, per stripes, pursuant to the provisions of this Paragraph.

(5) Should my said son or his issue have attained the age of thirty-two (32) years at the time of my death then he or they shall receive his or their applicable aforesaid portion absolutely and free of trust.

(6) I direct my Trustees to pay out of the principal of this Trust for the benefit of my said son, , the sum of Twenty Thousand ($20,000.00) Dollars if, as, and when my said son attends college.

(7) Upon my son, or his issue, if applicable, attaining the age of thirty-two (32) years, the trust created pursuant to Paragraph "FOURTH" herein shall terminate and come to an end and all corpus and income then held shall be distributed, free of trust.

FIFTH: Upon the termination or change of beneficiary of any trust herein created through the decease, after my decease, of the person entitled to receive the income, there shall be no apportionment to the executor or administrator of such person of any accrued but unmatured income. Said accrued but unmatured income shall, upon the maturity and collection of the several respective items thereof, belong in its entirety to the person or persons entitled to receive the income of the particular trust fund, that is to say, to the remainderman or remaindermen in any case where the principal of the trust shall vest in fee, or to the next beneficiary in any case where the trust shall continue for the benefit of a successive or further beneficiary.

SIXTH: In the event that any beneficiary of this Will and I or any other person upon whose death such beneficiary shall become entitled to receive either income or principal under this Will shall die in a common disaster or accident or under such circumstances that the order of deaths cannot be established by proof, then I direct that for purposes of this Will such beneficiary shall be deemed to have predeceased me or such other person as the case may be.

SEVENTH: If upon my death any part of my estate shall vest in absolute ownership in a minor, or if at the termination of any of the trusts created by this Will all or any part of any of the trusts created by this Will or if all or any part of the principal of any of the trust funds shall vest in absolute ownership in a minor, I authorize and empower my Trustees or Executors, as the case may be, to continue to hold said principal for the benefit of such minor during his or her legal minority or until the age of twenty-one (21) years, whichever shall be greater, to invest the same and keep the same invested and to collect the income thereof and in the sole and unreviewable discretion of the said Executors or Trustees, as the case may be, either to accumulate the income or pay over the net income arising therefrom to the minor to whom said principal shall belong or to his or her parent or legal guardian, or to the person with whom such minor resides, or to apply said income and such sum or sums out of the principal, as in their sole and absolute discretion they deem necessary or advisable to said infant's care, education, maintenance, and support. The authority thus accorded to my Executors or Trustees, as the case may be, shall be construed as a power only and shall not operate to suspend the absolute ownership of such principal by such minor or to prevent the absolute vesting thereof in such minor. The rights, powers, privileges, and immunities granted in this My Last Will and Testament to my Executors and/or Trustees shall apply to the administration and investment of any funds held by my Executors or Trustees in accordance with this power and they shall have the same rights to compensation for so acting as if any such trust had continued and said principal had not vested.

EIGHTH: (A) I hereby nominate, constitute, and appoint my wife, ______, as the Guardian of the person and property of the infant children of our marriage. Should she either predecease me, fail to qualify, or having qualified, should for any reason fail to continue to act as such Guardian, then I appoint my sister-in-law, ______, as the Guardian in her place.

(B) I hereby nominate, constitute, and appoint my friend, ______, and my attorney, ______, as the Co-Executors of my Estate and as the Co-Trustees of the Trusts herein established. Should either predecease me, fail to qualify, or having qualified, fail to act or continue to act as Co-Executor and/or Co-Trustee, then I hereby nominate, constitute, and appoint my attorney as Co-Executor and/or Co-Trustee in his place.

(C) I direct that none of the persons named herein as Guardian, Executor and/or Trustee, original or successor, shall be required to give any bond or other undertaking for the faithful performance of their duties as Guardian, Executor, and/or Trustee, or as successor.

NINTH: I confer upon my Executors and/or Trustees, original or successor, with respect to the management and administration of any property, real or personal, the following discretionary powers, without limitation by reason of specification, and in addition to the powers conferred upon them by statute or by general rules of law.

(1) I authorize and empower my Executors and/or Trustees to have full discretion, upon my death, to continue, discontinue, sell, and/or otherwise deal in my business interests which I may own at the time of my death.

(2) I authorize and empower my Executors and/or Trustees to retain and continue any investments which I may own at the time of my death. In the making of new investments I direct that my Executors and/or Trustees shall not be restricted or limited to such legal investments as are provided for the investment of trust funds by any statutes now in force or which may hereafter be enacted, and I specifically authorize my Executors and/or Trustees to invest the assets of my estate and/or the corpus of any trust fund or any part hereof in a discretionary or common trust fund, to purchase or acquire in exchange or otherwise, real estate, mortgages, stocks, bonds, and securities other than those constituting legal investments for trust funds and to invest and keep invested therein any part of my estate or of the trusts herein created. My Executors and Trustees shall not be held accountable or liable for any loss, depreciation, or damage sustained by reason of the retention, acquisition, or disposition of any investments pursuant to the provisions of this paragraph.

(3) I authorize and empower my Executors and/or Trustees in their discretion and without leave of Court to sell at public or private sale or to lease without public bidding and without restriction or limitation as the length of term (even though for a period longer than authorized by statute or longer than the duration of any trust herein created) or to mortgage or pledge any or all property coming into their hands, whether real or personal or mixed, at such times and upon such terms and conditions as in their judgment they may deem proper, and I authorize and empower them to sign, execute, acknowledge, and deliver any deeds, mortgages, conveyances, leases, and other papers that may be necessary in connection therewith.

(4) I authorize and empower my Executors and/or Trustees in their discretion to purchase property (a) on the foreclosure of any mortgage held by my estate, (b) on which my estate may own a mortgage or mortgages, (c) in which my estate shall have any interest, or any sale in partition, foreclosure, or otherwise or (d) which may be sold under any judgment in which my estate may have any interest, and I authorize and empower them to sign, execute, acknowledge, and deliver any deeds, mortgages, conveyances, leases, or other papers that may be necessary in connection therewith.

(5) I authorize and empower my Executors and/or Trustees to compromise, settle, or arbitrate any claim or demand in favor of or against my estate.

(6) Should I be married at the time of my death, I authorize and empower my Executors to join with my wife in executing and filing a joint Income Tax Return and agree with her as to the shares or proportions of the tax shown thereon which are to be paid respectively by my estate and by her. My Executors shall

not be held accountable or liable for any error of judgment as to the filing of a separate or a joint return or as to the apportionment of the tax on a joint return.

(7) I authorize and empower my Executors and/or Trustees to vote in person or by proxy upon any and all stocks or other securities held by them; to exercise any rights to subscribe for or to convert into stocks or bonds or other securities of any corporation (whether a going concern or in liquidation or in reorganization or under any other circumstances or conditions whatsoever) for other real or personal property distributed by the same corporation or any other corporation which shall be formed as a reorganization of or in combination, merger, or consolidation with the original corporation; to become a party to any plan of reorganization, merger, or consolidation or to become a depositor with and/or give power of attorney to any committee of bondholders or other security holders or creditors formed for the purpose of mutual protection in connection with any plan of corporate financing or reorganization or to represent or enforce the rights of security holders or creditors in connection with any defaults by the corporation or any reorganization or insolvency of the corporation; to accept any new or substituted security of whatever nature in place of the defaulted or previously held security; to make any payments necessary to obtain such new or substituted security, and generally to exercise in respect to any securities held by them the unrestricted rights of a personal owner thereof, in accordance with their best judgment and discretion.

(8) I authorize and empower my Executors and/or Trustees to borrow money, from others or from themselves whether to pay taxes, make subscriptions, exercise options, pay assessments, or to accomplish any other purpose of any nature incidental to the administration of my estate or of any of the trusts herein created, and to mortgage or pledge as security therefor any securities or other property held by them.

(9) So far as I may be legally permitted to do so, I authorize and empower my Executors and/or Trustees to cause any stocks, bonds, or other securities at any time held by them to be in bearer form or to be registered in the name of a nominee or nominees.

(10) I authorize and empower my Executors and/or Trustees to hold and retain so long as to them may seem proper, as part of my estate and trust estate, any real, personal, or mixed property, or any interest therein, of which I may die seized or possessed, or to which I may be entitled at the time of my death, notwithstanding that the same may not be of the kind, character, legal, proper or permissible for the investment of funds or trust funds under the laws of the State of New York, or any other State and without regard to the proportion that any of said property may bear to the entire amount of my estate and trust estate, or of the trusts in which same are held.

(11) I authorize and empower my Executors and/or Trustees to form any corporation, partnership, general or limited, or association, and to sell, convey, ex-

change, contract, lease, assign, transfer, and set over, or otherwise dispose of to said corporation, partnership, or association any or all of my estate, and to accept therefor property, real or personal, stocks, notes, bonds, debentures, mortgages, securities, or other evidences of indebtedness from said partnership, corporation, or association including the stock of any such corporation, common or preferred, in payment or part payment therefor, and to become directors and officers of any such corporation and with full power and authority on the part of any such corporation and my estate and trust estate to transact any business, including the making of any loans, with or without pledge, mortgage, or security between my estate and trust estate and said corporation, with full power and authority on the part of either the corporation or my estate and trust estate to become maker, endorser, guarantor, and surety for each other in respect to any matter whatsoever, and said corporation may be organized under the laws of any State selected by said Executors and/or Trustees with all the powers incident to corporations organized under the laws of such State.

(12) I authorize and empower my Executors and/or Trustees to continue any business of mine and the operation thereof and any interest that I may have either individually or as a partner, stockholder in any business, firm, enterprise, association, partnership, whether general or limited, company, or corporation of whatsoever nature and wherever same may be situated, for so long a time and upon such terms and conditions and in such manner as my said Executors and/or Trustees may deem advisable and beneficial and for the best interest of my estate and trust estate, and for that purpose to retain and permit to be employed therein any capital or investment which shall at my death be employed therein, and generally to act in all matters relating to any such business or interest as herein mentioned as if they owned the same, or were beneficially interested in or entitled to the same.

(13) I authorize and empower my Executors and/or Trustees to carry out any contracts or agreements that I may have entered into with any person or persons, partnership, stockholders, or corporation in connection with any such business, interest, partnership, firm, association, or corporation, or affecting or concerning any stock owned or held by me, and to extend and to continue the same or enter into any other agreement or arrangement that they may deem advisable and for the best interest of my estate and trust estate.

(14) I authorize and empower my Executors and/or Trustees to form any firm, partnership, association, company, or corporation with or concerning any business in which I may have any interest, as herein mentioned, and to participate in, consent to, or oppose any plan of liquidation, consolidation, reorganization, merger, or similar plan in connection with or concerning the said business or interest with any other business, firm, association, partnership, or corporation.

(15) I authorize and empower my Executors and/or Trustees to discontinue, liquidate, dissolve, and dispose of any business, firm, association, partnership, corporation, or any stockholdings or interest that I may have in the same.

(16) I authorize and empower my Executors and/or Trustees to apportion between principal and income all stock dividends and liquidating or extraordinary dividends or distributions. Without limiting the absolute discretion of my fiduciaries, I desire that all such dividends and distributions be allotted to principal except to the extent that my fiduciaries shall determine that they were declared or made in lieu of regular cash dividends or distributions.

(17) I authorize and empower my Executors and/or Trustees at any time and from time to time, to appoint for the time being an agent or attorney to make, execute, and deliver any transfer or other instructions, or to do any ministerial act necessary or proper to be done in the administration of my estate.

(18) I authorize and empower my Executors and/or Trustees to employ such attorneys, clerks, agents accountants and custodians, and to obtain such investment or other advice, in the transaction of the business of my estate and in the administration of any trust hereunder as my Executors or Trustees, as the case may be, may deem necessary or advisable, and to make such payments and disbursements therefor as they deem reasonable and proper, it being my present wish and desire that   be the attorney for my Estate and for my Trusts, herein created.

(19) Except as otherwise expressly provided in this Will, I authorize and empower my Executors and/or Trustees to pay any pecuniary legacy hereunder, whether in trust or otherwise, and to make any distribution pursuant to this my Will, in whole or in part, in securities or other property owned by me at the time of my decease or thereafter acquired by my Executors or Trustees, subject to the applicable provisions of this Will, which shall fully govern with respect to the bequest therein provided for, and in making such payment or distribution in securities or other property, I direct that valuation placed thereon by my Executors or by my Trustees shall be binding and conclusive on all persons interested in my estate, subject only to the power of a court of competent jurisdiction to pass on such valuation.

(20) My Trustees may at any time and from time to time during the course of the administration of any trust created pursuant to this Will, render an account of their proceedings with respect to such trust to every person who is then of full age and sound mind and who is then currently entitled to be paid the net income of such trust or who then may be entitled in any future contingency to have paid over to him or to her all or any part of the principal of such trust and to every duly appointed guardian of the property of every such person who is not then of full age and who has such a guardian. If the persons to whom such an account is so rendered by my Trustees include both at least one person (or the guardian of one person) then currently entitled to be paid all or any part of such net income and at least one person (or the guardian of one person) who may be entitled in any future contingency to have paid over to him or to her all or any part of the principal, the written approval of such account by all the persons to whom the account is so rendered (including any such guardians) shall be binding and con-

clusive upon all persons then having or thereafter acquiring or claiming any interest in the subject matter of such account and shall be a complete discharge to my Trustees with respect to all matters set forth in such account as fully and to the same extent as though such account had been judicially settled and allowed by a judgment or order or decree of a court of competent jurisdiction in an action or proceeding in which all persons so having, acquiring, or claiming any interest in the subject matter of such account were duly made parties and were duly represented. The foregoing provisions of this paragraph shall not be deemed to limit the right of my Trustees to have any such account judicially settled despite such written approval.

(21) To the extent practicable, my Executors may exercise the election provided by Section 642(g) of the Internal Revenue Code of 1954 or its equivalent section, so that expense deductions as therein provided shall be deductions from the income of the estate for income tax purposes rather than from the gross estate for estate tax purposes.

TENTH: (A) I hereby direct that no disposition charge or encumbrances on any interest in my estate, or on any part thereof, by any beneficiary under this Will by way of anticipation shall be valid or in any way binding upon my Executors or Trustees, and no beneficiary shall have the right to assign, transfer, encumber, or otherwise dispose of such income or principal, or any part thereof until the same shall be paid to such beneficiary by my Executors or by my Trustees, and no income or principal or any part thereof shall be liable to any claim of any creditors of any such beneficiary.

(B) The right of any beneficiary to any payment of income or principal shall be in every case subject to any charges or deduction which my Executors or my Trustees may make against the same under the authority granted to my Executors or to my Trustees by any law or by any provision of this Will.

ELEVENTH: The powers and authority hereinbefore granted to my Executors and/or Trustees may be exercised without obligation to or authority from any court or judge, and, to the extent permitted by law, they shall not be liable or responsible for any loss which may be suffered except where the same is due to their dishonest or malicious acts.

TWELFTH: The words "child," "children," and "issue," wherever used in this Will, shall include not only the child, children, and issue of the person or persons designated, but also the legally adopted child or children of such person or persons.

THIRTEENTH: Wherever applicable the masculine and feminine genders, and the singular and plural, are used interchangeably in this my Last Will and Testament.

IN WITNESS WHEREOF, I have hereunto set my hand and seal the day of , 19 .

____

The foregoing instrument consisting of pages, including this page, was on the day above signed, sealed, published, and declared by , the above-named Testator, as and for his Last Will and Testament, in the presence of us and each of us, who at his request, and in his presence and in the presence of each other, have hereunto subscribed our names as attesting witnesses, this day of , 19 .

____________________ residing at ____________________

____

____________________ residing at ____________________

____

____________________ residing at ____________________

____

Part 4

CONCERNS DURING MARITAL BREAKDOWN

CHAPTER 9

How to Solve Immediate Problems

SITUATION

Peter and Virginia Jones' marital problems have escalated and have become irreconcilable. Peter and Virginia have decided to divorce. Peter has moved out of the house which he shares with Virginia, and their two children, ages 12 and 10. He now lives by himself in an apartment several miles away from the house. However, when he becomes drunk, he returns home and assaults Virginia. Further, Peter has vowed that Virginia will not obtain one cent of his money at divorce and that he will spend it all before the divorce can be finalized. And, although Virginia neither works nor has control over any assets—all of the family assets are in Peter's sole name—Peter has refused to provide for her or the children's financial support during the pending divorce. Finally, Peter has threatened to take them by force from Virginia and travel with them to parts unknown.

DETERMINE CLIENT'S NEEDS

Virginia is completely distraught. She needs and wants help to prevent Peter from dissipating his assets, beating her, and removing the children. She wants custody of the children and financial assistance for herself and the children while the divorce is pending. To prevent further confrontations with Peter—both verbal and physical—she desires exclusive occupancy of the house. She comes to you, her attorney, for advice and help to solve these immediate problems.

Checklist of Immediate Needs

In the event Virginia is too distraught to precisely verbalize her needs and desires, the following checklist will enable you to assure that all of her immediate needs are resolved.

1. Financial needs vs. financial assets and income.
   A. Income and assets available to client.
   B. Money required for divorce action, i.e., attorney and evaluation fees.
   C. Money required for children's support and support of wife during pendency of divorce.
2. Custody of children
   A. Who has custody (mother or father)?
   B. Is present custody arrangement satisfactory to both parties?
   C. If client has custody, has spouse threatened to forcibly obtain physical custody?
   D. Has client's spouse threatened to remove children from state?
3. Assets controlled by client's spouse
   A. What assets are controlled by spouse?
   B. Does client have claims to any of these assets at time of divorce?
   C. Has spouse been spending assets recklessly, attempting to hide or transfer assets, so as to deprive client of his/her share of them at divorce?
4. Occupancy of home
   A. Who presently occupies home (husband or wife, husband and wife)?
   B. Is present occupancy situation satisfactory?
   C. Is one spouse assaulting the other spouse, verbally or physically, so as to require separate living quarters?
   D. Does either spouse have alternate living quarters available?

HOW TO SECURE RESTRAINING ORDERS

Virginia is definitely in need of immediate judicial intervention to prevent Peter from dissipating his assets, absconding with the children, and assaulting her. (A sample motion which includes requests for this relief is annexed at the end of this chapter. The sample motion papers consist of an order to show cause, which can be your notice of motion to the other party, an affidavit, and an order.)

In almost every state jurisdiction, in the court having jurisdiction over domestic relations matters (e.g., the Supreme Court in New York), an immediate ex-parte (i.e., done for, in behalf of, or on the application of one party only), restraining order regarding the removal or dissipation of assets can be obtained if the moving party can show that his or her spouse is attempting to prevent the assets from being available for distribution at divorce. [In the ex-parte proceeding, your motion papers would consist of an affidavit and order, which order would be submitted to the court for its signature and approval. You would not need an order to show cause or other document giving your opponent advance notice of the relief you are seeking. If your state jurisdiction does not enable you as Virginia's attorney to utilize an ex-parte proceeding to obtain any of the relief discussed in this section, you can move to obtain the relief by ordinary motion where you would serve your motion papers (i.e., notice of motion document and affidavit) on Peter and thereby bring him into the proceeding.] This test would be met by proof that the spouse is removing the assets to unjustifiably spend or otherwise dissipate them, to secrete them, or transfer them to another state.

In Virginia's case, Peter's declaration that he intends spending all of the assets before divorce would probably enable her to meet the burden of proof. Virginia's sworn affidavit, submitted to the court with her motion papers (see sample motion at the end of the chapter) outlining Peter's declaration would be sufficient to meet her burden of proof. However, if Peter submits a sworn affidavit denying he made such a claim, the court might accept Peter's statement and deny Virginia's relief. Virginia would have a much greater chance of success if she were able to submit an affidavit by a disinterested party (e.g., someone who is a family friend with friendship ties to both her and Peter) who overheard Peter assert his declaration.

In most jurisdictions, a spouse can immediately obtain an ex-parte restraining order to prevent the removal of children if there is good reason to believe that the other spouse intends to abscond with them.

In Virginia's case, Peter's threat that he will forceably remove the children to parts unknown, should enable Virginia to obtain a temporary restraining order in this regard. Again, Virginia's sworn affidavit, submitted to the court with her motion papers (see sample motion at the end of the chapter) outlining Peter's declaration would be sufficient to meet her burden of proof. But, as discussed previously, Virginia's chance of success would be enhanced if she could submit an affidavit by a disinterested party who overheard Peter's declaration. In this case the court would not be in the position of choosing between Virginia's claim and Peter's possible denial of that claim.

The fact that Peter has been beating Virginia will enable her to obtain an ex-parte restraining order or order of protection to prevent assaults. Incorporated in this restraining order or order of protection might be a provision barring Peter from the house. This would be particularly appropriate in the instant case since Peter is no longer living in the house.

Once Virginia possesses this order of protection or restraining order, Peter would suffer grave consequences should he decide to continue his beatings. Not only might he be subject to sanctions (e.g., a contempt citation and possible confinement) by the court that issued the order, but he might very well subject himself to an arrest and prosecution for the assault.

Checklist for Procedures to Follow to Obtain Restraining Orders

The following checklist will aid you to quickly and effectively obtain restraining orders for Virginia.

1. Accumulate proof that Peter will dissipate his assets and will abscond with the children. Also accumulate proof that Peter has been beating and will continue to beat Virginia. In this vein, determine if Peter is still living with Virginia and whether he has alternate living quarters.
2. Determine if your state permits ex-parte proceedings for obtaining restraining orders.
3. If state permits ex-parte proceedings to procure restraining orders file affidavits in support of order and proposed order in court. (See sample motion papers at the end of the chapter. The order to show cause annexed at the end of the chapter to give notice to Peter of proceeding is not required in ex-parte proceeding.)
4. If state does not permit ex-parte proceeding to obtain restraining orders, file an order to show cause or notice of motion and affidavits in support of motion in court. Serve these documents either personally or by mail on Peter. (See sample motion papers and affidavit of service at the end of the chapter. These sample motion papers include an order to show cause which would require Peter to respond to motion more quickly than if a notice of motion had been filed. Some courts will permit notice to be served by a notice of motion while others will require that Virginia proceed by an order to show cause. If Virginia can proceed by a notice of motion, a notice of motion can be prepared for her by utilizing the sample notice of motion annexed in Chapter 13 in "Sample Motion for and Order of Garnishment.")
5. Obtain signed restraining order from the court and serve the order either personally or by mail on Peter. (Sample order and affidavit of service are attached at end of chapter.)

6. If Peter does not obey restraining order, go back to court and obtain an order of contempt from court. This order may contain financial penalties and/or confinement. (See the end of Chapter 13 for a sample motion for and order of contempt.)

HOW TO SECURE TEMPORARY ORDERS

Virginia would be well advised to obtain certain temporary orders. She should move in a state court which has jurisdiction over domestic relations matters for *pendente lite* (i.e., pending the suit, during litigation) relief to obtain temporary custody of the children, temporary child support, temporary visitation rights, temporary alimony, temporary exclusive possession of the house, interim legal fees, interim accountant's fees, and interim fees to enable Virginia to hire expert witnesses to evaluate the parties' real estate, pension plans, businesses, etc. (A sample motion which includes requests for this relief is annexed at the end of this chapter.)

In every jurisdiction where the children are residing with one spouse and are in need of financial assistance, the courts will award temporary custody of the children to that spouse. The courts will also extract support payments from the other spouse. Of course, the spouse with custody must prove to the court that he or she does not have sufficient financial resources to meet the financial needs of the children and that the other spouse has such resources.

If one spouse requests temporary alimony to live and financial assistance for fees relating to the divorce action, the other spouse will be required to provide temporary alimony and this financial assistance. Of course, this relief will only be provided if the moving party can establish that he or she does not have sufficient income and assets to commence the divorce action or live in a manner reasonably akin to what he or she had been accustomed, and the other spouse has sufficient income and assets to meet these needs.

Courts are generally reluctant to permit one spouse temporary exclusive posssession of the house. This occurs because courts strongly feel that no individual should be forced out of his or her home. However, if the moving party can establish that the other spouse no longer resides in the house or can establish that he or she is in actual physical danger by being in close proximity to the other spouse, courts will grant the moving party's application for temporary exclusive possession of the premises.

In Virginia's case, since Peter has essentially abandoned her and the children, only returns home to assault her, provides no financial assistance to Virginia and/or the children, and Virginia has no assets of her own, she should have little trouble obtaining all of the relief outlined above.

In the event Peter had succeeded in removing the children from Virginia's physical custody before she could obtain any judicial relief regarding legal custody, etc., and assuming for arguments sake that he brought the children to his apartment, where he precluded Virginia from seeing them, Virginia should seek a writ of habeas corpus. This writ can be obtained from the particular state court which has jurisdiction over domestic relations matters. For example in New York this writ can be obtained from the New York Supreme Court. (A sample petition for and order sustaining a writ of habeas corpus is included at the end of this chapter.) By the issuance of this writ, Peter would be forced to produce the children at court. When the children are produced, the court would contemperaneously hold a hearing to determine temporary custody, support, and visitation.

If Peter had taken the children to a location outside the state, Virginia could utilize the Uniform Child Custody Act to obtain relief, if the state to which Peter had removed the children were a signatory to this Act. That other state would compel Peter to return with the children to the original state of residence. Then, the local court in the state of original residence would make a determination as to temporary custody, support, and visitation.

If that other state is not a signatory to the Uniform Child Custody Act, Virginia must commence an action in that state where the children are located and that state would determine custody, child support, and visitation. Virginia would commence this action in the state court having jurisdiction over domestic relations matters. You, as Virginia's attorney can pursue this action by motion—where you can prepare this motion by using the portions of the sample motion annexed below pertaining to custody, child support, and visitation—or by petition for habeas corpus—where you can utilize the sample petition annexed below to prepare this petition.

In order to help you prepare for Virginia a motion and order regarding injunctive and other temporary relief, the following sample motion and order are provided. Also, a sample writ of habeas corpus is attached to enable you to address the child abduction situation.

SAMPLE MOTION AND ORDER FOR TEMPORARY CUSTODY, SUPPORT, ETC.

At a Special Term. of the State of New York, held in and for the County of ______ at the , New York, on the day of

PRESENT:

HON. ______________________
Justice.

---------------------------------------x

______________________ : Index No. ______

Plaintiff, : ORDER TO SHOW CAUSE

-against- :

______________________ :

Defendant. :

---------------------------------------x

Upon reading and filing the affidavit and the statement of net worth of ______ , both sworn to on ______ , and upon all papers and proceedings herein,

LET, ______ , the , show cause before at a Special Term of this Court, to be held at , County, , on the day of , at (time) , or as soon thereafter as counsel can be heard, why this Court should not issue an order which:

1. Prevents , or his agents, from in any way disposing or encumbering the following assets.
2. Restrains from beating, assaulting, or in any other way abusing .

3. Gives temporary legal custody of the children of the parties to , while this action is pending. should be awarded the following visitation rights:

   The above requests are made under N.Y. Domestic Relations Law, Section 240.

4. Requires that pay during the pendency of this action the sum of $ per week for her support and maintenance, and $ per week for the support and maintenance of the parties children. These requests are made under Domestic Relations Law, Sections 236 and 240.
5. Requires that pay for the medical and dental expenses of and the children. This request is made under Domestic Relations Law, Sections 236 and 240.
6. Requires that maintain life insurance (whose death benefits are not encumbered) for the benefit of , in the sum of $, disability insurance covering , and medical insurance through for the benefit of .
7. Provides with the exclusive possession of the marital residence, located at , (and everything contained in the residence), to include payment of mortgage payments, home insurance, utility bills, and water bills, and the automobile, to include furnishing any insurance required for the automobile. These requests are made under Domestic Relations Law Sections 234, 236, and 240.
8. Requires the payment of interim accountant's appraisers' and attorneys' fees with the proviso that leave be granted to apply for any further sums which may be needed.
9. Grants any additional relief that this Court may deem to be just and proper.

ORDERED, that pending the hearing of the instant motion, or his agents shall not in any way dispose of or encumber the following assets, shall not beat, assault, or in any way abuse , and shall not remove the children of the parties from their present living quarters.

SUFFICIENT reason appearing, let personal service of a copy of this order and the papers upon which it was granted, together with the summons and complaint, on or before the day of , be deemed sufficient.

ENTER:

____

AFFIDAVIT

COURT OF THE STATE OF
COUNTY OF

---x

, :

Petitioner, : Index No.

-against- : AFFIDAVIT

, Respondent. :

---x

STATE OF)
) ss.:
COUNTY OF)

, being duly sworn deposes and says:

1. I am the in the above entitled action and make this affidavit in support of my motion for .
2. An action for divorce was commenced by on , by the service of the attached summons and complaint.
3. My husband and I were married on . We have children, ages . Currently I reside in the marital residence at and my husband resides at .
4. My husband earns $ and has the following assets. My income and assets are as follows .
5. I require a restraining order preventing my husband from beating me because
6. My husband should be prevented from disposing or in any way encumbering the above listed assets because .
7. I should have custody of the children because
8. I and my children should receive $ for our support and maintenance because
9. My husband should be required to pay for interim accountants', appraisers', and attorneys' fees in the sum of $, because
10. My husband should pay for medical and dental expenses for myself and the children of our marriage because

11. My husband should provide insurance as follows: , because

12. I should be provided exclusive possession of the marital residence and automobile, and should acquire home and auto insurance required, and pay mortgage payments, utility bills, and water bills for the marital residence because

WHEREFORE, based on the foregoing I respectfully request that this Court issue an order which

____

Sworn to before me this
day of , 19 .

____

ORDER

PRESENT: HON. ________________________________
Court of the State of
, County of

---X

, : ORDER

Plaintiff, :

-against- :

, :

Defendant. :

---X

The plaintiff herein, , has duly moved this Court for an order requesting

NOW, on motion of , attorneys for , it is ORDERED, ADJUDGED, and DECREED that

ENTER:

____

SAMPLE HABEAS CORPUS PETITION, WRIT, AND JUDGMENT

Court, State of
County of

--x

In the Matter of the Application of

: Index #

Petitioner,

PETITION FOR A WRIT OF HABEAS CORPUS

For a Writ of Habeas Corpus to determine custody of ,
a child presently held by

Respondent. :

--x

TO:

The petition of alleges and establishes that:

1. Petitioner is the mother of , a child whose age is
2. Respondent, , is the father of said child
3. The said child has been living with petitioner at for months.

4. Respondent has been living at , for months.
5. On the day of , 19 , respondent improperly seized the said child and brought the child to .
6. The said child desires to live with petitioner.
7. Petitioner and said child have requested that respondent return the child to petitioner's abode.
8. Respondent has refused to do so and is forcibly and wrongfully detaining said child.
9. No court or judge of the U.S. has exclusive jurisdiction to order the release of said child.
10. Respondent has no right to retain custody of said child and his detention of said child is illegal.
11. No previous application has been made for this writ in this or any other court.

WHEREFORE, your petitioner requests that a writ of habeas corpus issue, which directs the respondent to produce the said child before this Court and that said child be ordered delivered to petitioner at on , and any other relief which the Court feels is just and proper.

Dated: , 19 .

____

VERIFICATION

STATE OF)
) ss.:
COUNTY OF)

, being duly sworn, deposes and says:

That she is the person who signed the foregoing petition; that the same is true as to her own knowledge except as to matters therein stated to be alleged on information and belief; that as to those matters she believes them to be true.

____

Sworn to before me this
day of , 19 .

____

WRIT OF HABEOUS CORPUS

Court of the State of
, County of

______________________________________x

In the Matter of the Application of

, : Index #

Petitioner, : WRIT OF HABEAS CORPUS

For a Writ of Habeas Corpus to
Determine Custody of ,
child presently held
by ,
Respondent. :
______________________________________x

GREETING:

WE command you, that you produce the body of , a child who is claimed to be held and detained by you, together with the time and cause of such detention, before , a Judge of this Court, at , on , to do and receive what shall at this time and place be considered as to said child, and you should at this time and place have this writ.

WITNESS, HON. , Judge of this Court, this day of , 19 .

By the Court,

____
Clerk

JUDGMENT

PRESENT: HON.

Court of the State of
, County of

---x

In the Matter of the Application of | Index No.

Petitioner, | JUDGMENT

For a Writ of Habeas Corpus to
determine custody of , a child
presently held by ,

Respondent.

---x

A writ of habeas corpus having previously been issued on the petition of , commanding to produce the body of , together with the time and cause of the detention of , and having been brought before this Court on , and an examination into the reasons and basis of such detention by having been had, and it appearing that respondent has no lawful cause for the detention of said child and that petitioner rather than respondent should have custody of said child, because

NOW, after hearing , Esq., attorney for petitioner, and , Esq., attorney for respondent, and reading and filing the writ, with proof of service, the verified petition of , and the sworn return of , it is:

ORDERED, ADJUDGED, AND DECREED that the said writ of habeas corpus be sustained and that respondent release from his custody, and that custody be vested in petitioner.

E N T E R :

____

SAMPLE AFFIDAVIT OF SERVICE

STATE OF)
) ss.:
COUNTY OF)

, being duly sworn, deposes and says:

That I am not a party to the instant action and am over the age of 18 years.

That on , I served a true copy of the within , upon at , by (personally delivering the copy to at) (mailing the copy in a sealed envelope in a post office box regularly maintained by the United States Government at , addressed to at .)

Sworn to before me this
day of 19 .

____

CHAPTER 10

Helping Clients with Legal Alternatives

SITUATION

Cathy Jones has been married for 30 days to Ken Jones. Before they were married, Ken assured Cathy that he wished to have children. However, once married, Ken told Cathy that he did not want and would not have children. And, he has refused to have sexual relations with her to assure that she does not become pregnant. Cathy now knows that Ken's pre-marriage declarations regarding children were only made because he knew that Cathy would not marry him if she knew his true desires.

DETERMINE WHAT CLIENT DESIRES

Cathy wants to end her relationship with Ken. This is so not only because of his lack of desire to have children and sexual relations, but she has discovered that Ken has a mistress. However, Cathy is in a quandary as to how she should end it. Because of religious and personal convictions, she would rather not live under the stigma of being a divorced woman. Also, she would rather not have to air her reasons for terminating her relationship with Ken. Indeed, although she might consider divorce despite its stigma, she would not consider this option if she was not only burdened by its stigma, but was required to air her reasons for terminating her relationship with Ken. Not only would the airing of this "dirty laundry" be extremely difficult for her to handle, it would also devastate her family.

Cathy has heard that she might be able to obtain a legal separation from Ken or obtain separate maintenance without going through the trials and tribulations of a divorce proceeding. However, she is not clear as to exactly what her status will be after she has pursued relief through these means, or whether she will be in a better financial position by pursuing a legal separation or separate maintenance as opposed to a divorce. Finally, Cathy wonders whether she can and should pursue an annulment and what will be the advantages and disadvantages of pursuing this avenue.

DIVORCE, ANNULMENT, LEGAL SEPARATION, SEPARATE MAINTENANCE

Cathy contacts you, her attorney, for advice as to what is needed to accomplish each of these legal alternatives i.e.: *divorce, annulment, legal separation,* or *separate maintenance.* She queries you as to what remedy would best serve her needs—both emotional and financial.

Divorce

No-fault divorce. The general rule today is that a divorce will be granted without the establishment of a fault ground and the airing of "dirty laundry." Most states, although requiring the establishment of one of several divorce grounds, include incompatibility or the irretrievable breakdown of the marriage as one of these grounds. In some states, after the party seeking the divorce meets certain residency requirements and establishes that he or she has not lived together with his or her spouse for a certain period of time, he or she is entitled to a divorce under the incompatibility ground. In other states, the incompatibility ground is established by showing that the parties involved in the divorce proceeding have not shared the same bed for a certain period of time. In short, under the incompatibility ground, a divorce can be obtained without the need for delving into potentially highly embarrassing material. And, the bitterness engendered by the previously perceived need to throw accusations back and forth, will very likely be avoided. The states with incompatibility or like grounds are Alabama, Alaska, Arizona, California, Colorado, Connecticut, Delaware, District of Columbia, Florida, Georgia, Hawaii, Idaho, Indiana, Iowa, Kansas, Kentucky, Louisiana, Maine, Maryland,

Massachusetts, Michigan, Minnesota, Mississippi, Missouri, Montana, Nebraska, Nevada, New Hampshire, New Jersey, New Mexico, North Dakota, Ohio, Oklahoma, Oregon, Pennsylvania, South Carolina, South Dakota, Tennessee, Texas, Vermont, Washington, Wisconsin, and Wyoming.

Grounds for a fault divorce. Today, only a few states do not have an incompatibility or like divorce ground. That is, only a few states might require as a condition to the granting of a divorce that one of the marriage partners was responsible for some egregious conduct. Generally, these fault grounds include adultery, cruel and inhuman treatment, desertion, or confinement. Confinement may constitute either jail or placement in a psychiatric institution. The states that do not have an incompatibility or like divorce ground are Arkansas, Illinois, New York, North Carolina, Rhode Island, Utah, Virginia, and West Virginia.

Choosing divorce. In light of the above, Cathy should seriously consider divorcing Ken. She should be able to avoid the need to establish a fault ground for divorce since most states have no-fault grounds. Even if she presently resides in a state which only has fault grounds, she should be able to bring an action for divorce in a state that has no-fault grounds by either becoming a permanent or temporary resident of that state. It must be pointed out that the other state may only have jurisdiction to grant the divorce and may have no jurisdiction to distribute the marital property, determine child support and alimony, and award child custody. (See Chapter 12 for detailed discussion re jurisdiction.) However, Cathy is not concerned with child custody and support since there are no children involved. Further, she probably would not be entitled to a large alimony award or distribution of marital property since she has been married to Ken for such a short period of time. And, she could always return to her home state to petition for any alimony or marital property distribution to which she might be entitled. Thus, considering the above, the only detriment Cathy might suffer by being divorced would be the social stigma of that divorce.

On the other hand, Cathy obviously wants a marriage relationship and children. She cannot attain these ends unless she is not married to Ken. She may not be able to break the marriage bond between herself and Ken unless she divorces him.

Cathy might be left with balancing between the stigma of a divorce and having children in another happy marriage. If this becomes her choice—particularly considering that she does not appear to be overly concerned with the stigma of a divorce—she should be advised to initiate a divorce proceeding.

Annulment

An annulment totally vitiates the marriage. That is, after an annulment is granted, the law does not recognize that the marriage ever existed.

Grounds for annulment. The grounds for an annulment are fraud or duress. To establish duress, it must be proved that the party raising this ground was forced against his or her will to enter into the marriage. Fraud can be established by proving that the other spouse made material misrepresentations concerning age, religion, financial status, or desire to have children. The most prevalent fraud claim involves the one spouse's pre-marriage declaration that he or she wishes to have children, followed by his or her post-marriage refusal to carry out this promise.

In order to obtain an annulment of the marriage, it is imperative that annulment proceedings be commenced within a reasonable time period after the ground justifying an annulment has been discovered. In seeking an annulment, the moving party does not forfeit the rights to which he or she would be entitled if he or she had attempted to terminate the marriage relationship by a divorce proceeding. In other words, in an annulment proceeding, the distribution of any marital property, alimony, child support, and custody will be addressed.

Choosing annulment. From the foregoing, it is apparent that an annulment is a viable alternative for Cathy. Ken's refusal to have children after promising such, provides Cathy with a ground for the annulment of the marriage. By obtaining an annulment, Cathy will obtain the same financial advantages regarding alimony and distribution of marital property as exist in a divorce proceeding. She will not, however, have the stigma that a divorce entails but will legally return to the status that she enjoyed before her marriage to Ken. However, it must be pointed out that she may have to disclose all her reasons for terminating her relationship with Ken in seeking the annulment of the marriage. If such disclosure bears too heavily upon herself and her family, annulment may not be a viable alternative.

Legal Separation

Legal separation, unlike divorce or annulment, does not change the marital status. Thus, by legal separation, there is no freedom to remarry. Moreover, since the marital status is not changed, the couple can still file joint tax returns if they so desire, take advantage of the gift tax exemption for gifts to spouses, and take advantage of other tax benefits available to married couples.

Grounds for legal separation. A legal separation can either be achieved by contract or court order. If the legal separation is obtained pursuant to a court order, the grounds for obtaining the separation are generally the same as those available regarding obtaining a divorce. If one resides in a no-fault state, the separation can be accomplished by establishing incompatibility. If one resides in a fault state, the separation can only be obtained by establishing one of the fault grounds.

Rights and responsibilities. The remedies that are sought in the legal separation proceeding are the same as those sought in the divorce or annulment proceeding. That is, whether the parties are seeking a legal separation, divorce, or annulment, they are seeking child custody and support, division of assets, etc. Moreover, whether one is attempting to obtain a permanent legal separation, divorce, or annulment, an attempt should be made to enter into a separation agreement which defines the rights and responsibilities of the parties. Indeed, the legal separation agreement that might be consummated pursuant to a permanent legal separation could be exactly the same separation agreement that should be consummated in contemplation of a divorce or annulment. Of course, some of the concerns that exist when drafting the permanent legal separation agreement might be different from those that exist when drafting an agreement in the divorce or annulment context. For example, when drafting the permanent legal separation agreement it is imperative that estate rights be fully addressed. If one spouse does not contract away in the separation agreement the other spouse's inheritance rights, that other spouse will retain them. However, this is not as crucial a concern when drafting the separation agreement in contemplation of a divorce or annulment. Even if you do not address inheritance rights in the separation agreement in contemplation of divorce or annulment, these rights will end since after the divorce or annulment neither spouse will possess, by law, any inheritance rights regarding the estate of the other.

Divorce after a legal separation. Assuming that after a legal separation is obtained one of the spouses wishes a divorce, it might be extremely easy to obtain a divorce. In some states, the legal separation status can—practically speaking—be almost immediately converted to the divorce status within a prescribed period of time. In New York, for example, the separation agreement or judgment of separation can be converted by either party into a divorce judgment provided that both parties lived separate and apart for one year and have substantially complied with all the terms of the separation agreement or separation decree.

Choosing legal separation. In Cathy's case, if she does not want to divorce because of the stigma involved in that proceeding and does not want an annulment because she may have to divulge the intimate reasons for seeking the annulment, she may wish to consider the legal separation route. Cathy should be able to obtain a legal separation without any embarrassment. She will certainly avoid any possibility of embarrassment if she can convince Ken to enter into a separation agreement. If she cannot convince Ken to enter into such an agreement, she would avoid embarrassment if she lived in a no-fault jurisdiction. Even if she did not, she should be able to obtain at some point in the future a separation decree in a state that possesses no-fault grounds. If after Cathy obtains her separation agreement or decree she decides she wants to marry someone else, she can always decide to change her status from that of legal separation to divorce. She probably would not be able to obtain an annulment at that point since an annulment proceeding must be commenced within a reasonable time after the ground justifying the annulment has been discovered.

Separate Maintenance or Support

In some states (e.g., N.Y., N.J., New Hampshire, Florida, Connecticut, California, Ohio, Texas, Maine, Utah), even though there are no active proceedings for divorce, annulment, or separation, one of the spouses can bring a separate action for alimony/maintenance and/or child custody and support. Moreover, such can be done on either a temporary or a permanent basis. The spouse may wish to pursue this option if he or she is in need of financial assistance but does not want to jeopardize his or her inheritance rights by pursuing a divorce, annulment, or legal separation or cannot establish any of the grounds necessary for a divorce, annulment, or legal separation.

Choosing separate maintenance. In Cathy's case, she might find that the embarrassment of a divorce or annulment outweighs its viability. Also, she might find that she can only avoid embarrassment via a legal separation by moving—at least temporarily—to another state. If she does not wish to change her residence, she might decide that a legal separation is not for her. Assuming *arguendo* that she is in need of financial assistance, separate maintenance and support might be the answer for her. As is also true in the case of the permanent legal separation, she can always decide at a later date to seek a divorce.

CHAPTER 11

How to Negotiate the Terms of Separation

SITUATION

Bruce and Maryvonne Jones, ages 35 and 30 respectively, have determined that their marriage is in a state of chaos. They are not certain as to whether they wish to divorce. However, they are certain that at the present time they no longer desire to live together. They have decided to enter into a separation agreement at this point and plan to review their situation in approximately one year to determine whether they will or will not divorce.

Bruce approaches you, his attorney, and requests that you negotiate with Maryvonne's attorney to create a separation agreement. Bruce tells you that Maryvonne can have custody of their 10 year old child and that he will make child support payments. He also tells you that Maryvonne can have use of their home for herself and the child and that he will move into one of several apartments that he owns. Further, he tells you that Maryvonne can have a fair share of the assets that were acquired by him and her since they were married 15 years ago. Finally, he tells you that considering he earns $100,000 a year, while Maryvonne earns $15,000 a year, he expects to make support payments to Maryvonne.

Bruce queries you as to what analysis, calculations, and findings are necessary before a separation agreement can be finalized. In other words, he wants you to explain to him in detail the mechanics that are involved in drafting a separation agreement for himself and Maryvonne. He is not interested in what course of action he must take if he does not enter into a separation agreement with Maryvonne. In other words, he is not interested in how you, as his attorney, would handle a contested permanent separation, annulment, or divorce. (See Chapter 12 for discussion re contested permanent separations, annulments, and divorces.)

Checklist of Separation Agreement Considerations

Initially, you should inform Bruce that negotiations re the separation agreement involve detailed consideration of the following items.

1. Maintenance and/or alimony.
2. Child support.
3. Pre-separation standard of living of wife and children.
4. Needs of wife and children based on pre-separation standard of living.
5. Present and projected income of husband and wife.
6. Fringe benefits for children.
7. Property evaluation, valuation, and distribution.
8. Use of home.
9. Custody and visitation.
10. Outstanding bills.
11. Medical coverage and life insurance.
12. Estate consequences.
13. Tax returns, taxes, tax exemption, and tax audits.
14. Legal fees.
15. Misc. contract provisions.

A detailed perusal of the foregoing items encompasses the remainder of the chapter.

HOW TO DETERMINE MAINTENANCE AND/OR ALIMONY AND CHILD SUPPORT

Key to Support Determination

You should inform Bruce that the key to a determination of the support obligations depends on three factors. They are:

1. The pre-separation standard of living of Maryvonne and the child,

2. The needs of Maryvonne and the child based on the pre-separation standard of living, and
3. The present and projected income of Bruce and Maryvonne.

Calculations

In calculating the actual support to which Maryvonne and the child are entitled, you must first consider the cost of the following to them:

CHECKLIST OF NEEDS

1. Food, clothing, and mortgage (i.e., principal, interest, taxes) or rent.
2. Home expenses to include but not be limited to household furnishings (repair and replacement cost), garage, home owners' insurance, exterminator, utilities, swimming pool, T.V.—cable, sprinkler system, repairs, water, painting, (amortize this expense) gardener, maid, snow removal, and telephone.
3. Medical doctors, dentist, optometrist, psychiatrist, psychologist, and drugs not covered by insurance.
4. Cleaners, laundry, and tailor.
5. Automobile, i.e., loan payments, repairs, maintenance, gasoline, and insurance.
6. Beauty parlor and/or barber shop.
7. Pet, i.e., veterinarian, food, and grooming.
8. Newspapers and magazines.
9. Private lessons (e.g., piano, dance) tutors, lunch money, camp, private school, gifts to children, and birthday parties.
10. Medical and life insurance premiums.
11. Contributions to charities and holiday gifts.
12. Entertainment, vacations, clubs, summer or vacation home, boat maintenance, and airplane maintenance.
13. Transportation, e.g., taxis, buses, subway, and commuting.

After you have calculated the above, you will have arrived at a figure which depicts the gross needs of Maryvonne and the child based on their standard of living. Assume for arguments sake that in Maryvonne's case the figure is $2,500.00. From this figure e.g., $2,500.00, you must deduct any amounts included in Maryvonne's gross needs which are not expenses that she will incur. For example: (a) if the existing house is sold and they move to a new location where they incur less expenses, the difference in house expenses should be deducted; (b) if Maryvonne does not drive, any car expense should be deducted; or (c) if Bruce pays directly for the child's camp, tutoring, etc., these expenses should be deducted. Assume for argument's sake that Maryvonne's deductible amount will be $500 per week. The figure calculated after these deductions will depict Maryvonne's net needs; e.g., $2,500.00 minus $500 or $2,000.

From Maryvonne's net needs (e.g., $2,000) you must deduct her after-tax income. Additionally, if she receives a distribution of property as a result of the separation agreement, you must take a deduction which takes into account the income potential of the property.

For example, if Maryvonne receives a $100,000 piece of property you could estimate the income Maryvonne would receive if she had $100,000 in the bank. If the then prevailing interest rate was 8% you could assume that the $100,000 amount has an income value of $8,000 per year. If Maryvonne would pay $2,000 in taxes on this $8,000 in income, you could assume that her net income from this amount was $6,000 a year and you would take a deduction in this amount. This final figure arrived at after the above deductions depict Maryvonne's net net needs. Assume that in Maryvonne's case her deduction for after-tax income and distribution of property is $1,000, and her net net needs are thus, $1,000.

Maryvonne will not necessarily obtain from Bruce her net needs. You must factor into this figure Bruce's after tax income. For example, if Bruce's after tax income is $1,500 a week and Maryvonne's net net needs are $1,000 a week, Maryvonne would never obtain her full net net needs. If a court were deciding support payments to Maryvonne in this situation, it might give Maryvonne 50% of Bruce's $1,500 weekly salary if she had two children, 35–40% if she had one child and 25% if she had no children.

Termination of Child Support

Generally, child support ends when the child reaches the age of majority. At common law that age was 21. Today, most states by statute have reduced the age of majority to 18 or 19. For example, the age of majority is 18 in New York, Arizona, California, Connecticut, Delaware, Georgia, Hawaii, Idaho, Illinois, Kansas, Kentucky, Louisiana, Maine, Michigan, New Jersey, New Mexico, North Carolina, North Dakota, Oklahoma, Pennsylvania, Rhode Island, South Dakota, Tennessee, Vermont, Virginia, West Virginia, and Wisconsin. It is 19 in Iowa, Montana, and Nebraska. However, the termination of child support date can be the subject of negotiation. The separation agreement can provide that child support ends when the child finishes college, marries, is fully employed, joins the army, etc.

If child support is provided for several children and support ceases for one child, the decrease in the total child support is not necessarily a figure which is calculated by determining what percentage that particular child is of all of the children. For example, if there are two children receiving child support, support is not necessarily cut in half when support obligations re one child terminates. You may want to negotiate for a sum in excess of 1/2 to provide greater flexibility in the case of the younger child.

Termination of Alimony

There is no set formula for the termination of alimony payments. You may want to negotiate to end alimony when Bruce dies, when Maryvonne remarries, or when Maryvonne resides with an unrelated male. In some states, one or more of these factors may be required to be a termination date for alimony. Considering that Maryvonne is fairly young and working, you may want to negotiate for the termination of alimony on a certain date. If Maryvonne was older e.g., 60-65, and not working, she probably should receive alimony for the remainder of her life, unless, of course, she remarries.

Cost of Living Adjustment

Many separation agreements contain a clause which provides an adjustment for alimony or child support for any increase or decrease in the cost of living. If Maryvonne's attorney insists on such a clause, you, as Bruce's attorney, should limit an increase to the actual augmentation in Bruce's salary for that particular year. For example, if the cost of living has increased by 10%, but Bruce's income has only increased by 5%, the alimony and/or child support payments should only increase by 5%.

Escalation or De-escalation Clause

Another typical clause in the separation agreement pertains to increases or decreases in one spouse's income which are not related to the cost of living. You may wish to place a clause in the separation agreement which calls for a particular increase in Bruce's support payments, for a particular increase in his income, and a corresponding decrease in his support obligations, if Maryvonne's income goes up by that particular amount or Bruce's income decreases by that particular amount.

For example, if Bruce's income—after taking into account increases for the cost of living—increases by x dollars, perhaps Maryvonne's support payment should increase by 25% of x dollars. On the other hand, if Maryvonne's income increases by x dollars or Bruce's income decreases by x dollars, Maryvonne's support payments shall decrease by 25% of x dollars.

Tax Consequences

You should make Bruce aware that any child support payments he makes will never be tax deductible to him and will never be taxable to Maryvonne. On the other hand, alimony payments will be tax deductible to Bruce and taxable to Maryvonne if they are less than $15,000 per year. For any amount in excess of $15,000, it will be tax deductible to Bruce and taxable to Maryvonne only if the alimony is to be paid for more than 3 calendar years. Otherwise, this excess will not be taxable to Maryvonne and will not be tax deductible to Bruce.

Note. It should be noted that the $15,000 and 3 year numbers detailed above were instituted in the 1986 Tax Reform Act. Prior to this Act the respective numbers were $10,000 and 6 calendar years.

It should also be noted that as of the 1986 Tax Reform Act, Bruce would not be able to deduct any permanent alimony payments if these payments are made while Bruce is living under the same roof as Maryvonne. However, the living under the same roof rule does not apply if the payments in question are temporary alimony payments pending a divorce, annulment, or permanent separation.

HOW TO NEGOTIATE FRINGE BENEFITS FOR CHILDREN

There exist certain expenses for the child that Maryvonne may want Bruce to pay directly, or Bruce may want to pay directly, rather than have these expenses covered by the child support payment. These expenses might include the cost of nurseries, camp, private lessons, private school, and college.

As to camp and private schools, it may be appropriate for each parent to pay one-half (1/2) of the expenses. Also, a maximum amount for these expenses should be designated. Further, Bruce may wish to possess the right to select the camp or school. As to private lessons, perhaps Bruce should pay the entire amount. Bruce should arrange for a maximum limit for these expenses and may wish to demand that his consent be obtained before this expense is incurred.

College expenses should include tuition, books, room and board, registration and lab fees, spending money, and travel expenses from the college to the custodial parents residence approximately four times each year. A maximum amount for college should be designated. The maximum amount might be the expenses charged by a particular State university at the time the child enters college. Bruce may also wish to negotiate that he will only be responsible for one-half (1/2) of the college expenses, and that he will have the right to select the school that the child attends.

The fringe benefit expenses should be dependant on Bruce's financial ability to pay them. The separation agreement should stipulate who will resolve any dispute as to Bruce's financial ability to pay. Perhaps such a dispute should be resolved by an arbitrator. Perhaps it should be resolved by the courts.

HOW TO DETERMINE DISTRIBUTION OF PROPERTY

Procedure for Determining Right to a Distribution

As discussed in Chapter 3, spousal rights to a distribution upon the breakup of a marriage depend on whether the state having jurisdiction over the distribution is a common law, community property, or equitable distribution state. (See Chapter 3 for list detailing which states are common law, community property, or equitable distribution states.)

In the common law state, all assets in Bruce's name would be his, all assets in Maryvonne's name would be hers and all assets in joint name would be shared 50–50. In the community property and equitable distribution states, the distribution would depend on what is deemed to be marital property.

The general rule is that marital property constitutes all property acquired after the marriage except gifts and inheritances. Of course, as discussed in Chapter 3, there are certain exemptions to the general rule. For example, a certain percentage of post-marriage gifts or inheritance may be classified as marital property. Also, significant appreciation in the value of certain pre-marriage property may be classified as marital property.

In community property states each spouse will be entitled to a 50% share of the marital property. In the truly equitable distribution state each spouse starts with 0% of the marital property, and certain factors determine what total % of the marital property each spouse will receive. For example, after an analysis of certain factors, a court might determine that one spouse is entitled to 75% of the marital property while the other is entitled to 25%.

These factors may include the age of the parties, the income of the parties, the quantity of separate property each spouse possesses, the present and future ability of each spouse to earn income, the health of the parties, the length of the marriage, the standard of living of the parties, the nature of the assets, the tax consequences of any transfer, the contribution of each spouse to the marriage and particular assets, what income a particular spouse would have earned if not married, the housing needs of the spouse taking custody of the children, any wasteful distribution of assets by one spouse to avoid an equitable distribution, and which party is more at fault in regard to the demise of the marriage.

Note. It should be noted that some of the states that have embraced the equitable distribution concept, have not embraced it in its entirety. Instead of commencing with a notion that each spouse starts with 0% of the marital property before an analysis of the factors, some states commence with a notion that each spouse is entitled to a 50% distribution of the marital property. Indeed, unless an analysis of the factors indicates a strong need for other than a 50–50 split, the marital property will be divided equally.

How to Evaluate and Valuate Assets

There is no need to undergo an extensive evaluation and valuation of assets in a common law state since title to property determines post-separation ownership. However, even in a common law state there may be a need for some evaluation and valuation.

For example, Bruce and Maryvonne may jointly own a stamp collection, set of china, or real estate that can not be divided. There will be a need to place a value on these assets so that a distribution can be made, they can be divided to arrive at a 50–50 split. Or, one spouse may keep possession of a certain asset or assets and compensate the other spouse with cash so as to arrive at a 50–50 split.

The real need for a valuation and evaluation of assets occurs in community property and equitable distribution jurisdictions. Before it can be determined to what each spouse is entitled, it must be determined what assets are marital assets and what value they have. Only after a dollar value is placed on the total accumulation of marital property can a dollar value be given for the prospective share of each spouse.

Note. In arriving at the total value to be placed on the marital property, it might be appropriate to consider liabilities in addition to assets.

Some states feel that it is appropriate to consider liabilities in the evaluation while others do not.

Checklist of Possible Marital Items

The type of items that might be considered in arriving at a figure for marital property are as follows:

1. Hobbies, e.g., stamp, coin, train, etc.
2. Automobile, boat.
3. Real estate.
4. Clothing and furs.
5. Outstanding liens.
6. Artworks, antiques, and jewelry.
7. Household furnishings to include furniture, china, etc.
8. Stocks and bonds.
9. Mortgages owned.
10. Security deposit on apartment.
11. Savings, checking and money market accounts, and certificates of deposit.
12. IRA accounts, pension plans, profit sharing plans, and life insurance cash surrender value.
13. Tax shelters.
14. Potential value of apartment that may become co-op.
15. Professional degrees (only some states, e.g., New York, place a value on professional degrees).
16. Value of business or appreciation in value of business.

In determining the value of many of the items listed above, professional help will be needed. For example, an actuary will probably be required to determine the value of certain pension plans. Also, an expert will be required to determine the cash surrender value of life insurance policies or the value of real estate. Certainly, an expert will be required to determine the value of any business, or the appreciation in the value of any business, that is deemed to be marital property. In formulating a separation agreement, it is common practice for both sides to agree on the selection of a particular expert for the valuation of a particular asset. A sample letter, which will help you confirm the use of a particular expert for the valuation of certain of Bruce's and Maryvonne's marital property, follows.

SAMPLE LETTER FOR CONFIRMATION OF PARTICULAR EXPERT

This letter will serve to confirm the following arrangement which was agreed upon by the parties concerning our getting joint evaluations of assets:

1. We will jointly request that gives us the evaluations.
2. We will request that evaluate the following:
   A. Evaluation of partnership interest in his law firm.
   B. Evaluation of partnership interest in the building owned by the partnership.
   C. Evaluation of private practice which includes executor and trustee commissions, as well as legal fees on certain estates which he handles privately with the firm's consent.
   D. Evaluation of capital account at the firm.
   E. Evaluation of savings, tax shelters, and securities.
   F. An evaluation of Keogh Plan.
   G. Evaluation of surrender value of life insurance owned by
   H. Evaluation of pension plan interest.
3. is to be fully responsible to pay for all services rendered in this connection.
4. It is agreed that neither nor are to be bound by any conclusions, figures or facts contained in the evaluations.
5. It is further agreed that under no circumstances, should this case not be settled, will these evaluations be introduced into evidence or submitted to any Judge, whether he be a trial Judge or a Judge discussing settlement, and it is agreed that neither side will use or anyone in his office as an expert witness at a trial of this case.
6. The deadline for these evaluations is to be . Please have and yourself sign two copies of this letter and then return them to me as quickly as possible so that I can get to sign a copy of this letter, sending one fully executed copy back to your office. Thereafter, both you and I are to contact and ask him to go ahead and make these evaluations.

Yours very truly,

After the gross value of the marital assets is determined, certain adjustments must be made. For example, as to any real estate considered, it might be necessary to deduct any capital gains taxes and brokerage commissions that would have to be paid if the real estate were converted into a cash asset. Also, the amount of any capital gains tax that would have to be paid on the appreciation in the value of the stocks, should be deducted. Additionally, the income that would have to be paid on pension plan assets should be deducted. Once these deductions are made, you will have a figure which represents the net value of the marital assets. From this net asset value, you can determine the dollar amount to which each spouse is entitled.

How To Determine Who Gets What Assets

Your duties re the distribution of property does not end with the determination of each spouse's prospective share. You must then negotiate with Maryvonne's attorney to determine which spouse will obtain or retain title and/or possession to what particular asset.

Distribution of personal property. As to personal effects, [e.g., furniture, towels, linens, silverware, etc.] the separation agreement should contain a provision which provides in detail who will keep what items. Also, it should be determined when the personal effects will be moved and who will bear the expense of moving them.

Retained right in pension plan. Bruce may desire to give Maryvonne a certain percentage of his pension to satisfy a portion of her prospective share. An actuary should be used to determine the present value of a certain percentage of Bruce's pension. The present value amount would then be deducted from Maryvonne's prospective share.

If Maryvonne is not to be included as a beneficiary of Bruce's pension until he retires, certain steps have to be followed to insure that she is not deprived of her pension rights. First, the separation agreement must (a) identify Maryvonne as an alternate payer of the pension and detail her full name and address, (b) set forth Maryvonne's interest in Bruce's pension plan, e.g., 5%–10%, and (c) set forth the details of the payout to Maryvonne. Second, a court order must exist which contains a Qualified Domestic Relations Order, i.e., an order which contains the information detailed in A–C above.

If Bruce and Maryvonne eventually obtain a divorce, the divorce judgment or decree would be the court order that would contain the Qualified Domestic Relations Order. If Bruce and Maryvonne remain separated under this separation agreement and take no judicial action as to their matrimonial situation, Maryvonne should, with notice to Bruce, move for a Qualified Domestic Relations Order in her state court which has jurisdiction over matrimonial actions. For example, in New York, the Supreme Court would be such a court. The sample motions included in Chapters 9 and 14 will enable Maryvonne's attorney to prepare the motion and order required to provide Maryvonne relief in this regard.

Distribution of solely held real property. As to titled property that is solely held, the general rule is that the title holder will retain legal title to that asset and will have physical possession of it after separation. There is one major exception to this rule. Where the asset is the family home and there are children, courts generally will hold that the custodial parent—although not the titled owner—should be permitted physical possession of the home until the youngest child reaches the age of majority, or the custodial parent remarries. This occurs because courts are reluctant to move the children out of the house. However, where the home is the only marital asset, some courts will force a sale of the house and distribute the proceeds of the sale. This occurs because these courts are reluctant to deprive the noncustodial parent of his or her marital share until the children attain majority.

In view of the foregoing, you may wish to entertain serious negotiations with Maryvonne's attorney as to the occupancy of the house. In this vein, you should determine not only who should have physical occupancy of the house and for how long, but you should determine who will be responsible for any mortgage payments, maintenance expenses, and taxes.

Note. Likewise, if the marital residence were an apartment, you should ascertain who would receive the security deposit, and who would pay the rent. And, in the event the apartment building becomes a co-op or a condominium, it should be made clear who would have the right to purchase it.

Distribution of jointly held real property. If the house is jointly owned where Bruce and Maryvonne are to share in the proceeds of its sale, and Maryvonne—being the custodial parent—is to retain physical possession of the house for a period of time, provision must be made in the separation agreement for the subsequent sale. First, a firm deadline for the sale must be incorporated in the agreement. Next, it must be understood that no encumbrance will be placed on the residence. What you don't want is a situation where Maryvonne will use the property as collateral for a loan which will result in a lien being placed on it and will affect the ability to sell it. Further, you may wish to provide that Bruce will receive a certain sum from the sale and Maryvonne will receive the remainder of the sales price. Or, you may wish to provide that each will receive a certain percentage of the sales price and that the home will not be sold for less than certain specified amount. If the sale is to occur at a point far in the future, it may be better to establish that a particular real estate broker will establish a certain fair market price below which the house can not be sold.

Tax Note. It should be noted that under the 1986 Tax Reform Act, once a couple is divorced, the house owned by the couple must be sold within 18 months after the divorce for the party residing in the house at divorce to be able to roll over to his or her new primary residence any capital gain earned on the marital residence. For example, assume Bruce and Maryvonne contributed $50,000 each five years ago for the purchase of their home, and that the house was sold for $200,000. Further assume that one week after the sale Bruce purchases a new house for $300,000. Bruce would have realized a $50,000 capital gain, i.e. an increase from $50,000 to $100,000 for his share of the house. If the house was sold within 18 months of the divorce, Bruce could reduce his basis in his new primary residence by the amount of his capital gain and avoid the payment of a capital gains tax. (The above assumes, of course, that the new residence bought by Bruce costs at least $200,000.) However, if the old residence was sold more than 18 months after the divorce, Bruce would have to pay taxes on his $50,000 capital gain even though he had bought a new primary residence.

In light of the above tax consequences, Bruce may not want to have Maryvonne reside in the house an extended period of time after the divorce. He might want to insist that the home be sold within 18 months of divorce. Of course, if Bruce and Maryvonne only remain separated and do not obtain a divorce, this tax consequence of the 1986 Tax Reform Act would not affect Bruce.

Final Asset Distribution Negotiation

After a credit is given for the assets given to or retained by Bruce, and those given to or retained by Maryvonne, it must be determined what is still owed to Bruce or Maryvonne. If, for example, a large amount of assets, are still due to Maryvonne, you may want to negotiate with Maryvonne's attorney for the transfer into her name of some of Bruce's assets. Or, you may wish to have Bruce give Maryvonne a cash award—which is called a distributive award—to make up the difference. Such an award is commonly ordered by the state courts that determine the distribution of property in matrimonial actions. For example, in New York, this court could be the New York Supreme Court. This award has been determined to be tax free and should not be classified as alimony. This has been held to be true even in circumstances where a court might permit payment of the award over a period of years because the party ordered to make the payment has no liquid assets.

PROCEDURES FOR DETERMINING CUSTODY AND VISITATION

Although Bruce has decided that Maryvonne can have custody of their child, you should inform him that if he desires custody and such is in the child's best interest, he will obtain custody. Courts—keeping in mind of course who is the most fit parent—attempt to ascertain what is in the child's best interests in awarding custody.

Even though Bruce may not desire to seek sole custody of their child, he may wish to consider joint custody. Under a joint custody arrangement, each parent would have custody of the child for a particular length of time.

For example, one parent may have custody of the child for one week and then the other parent will have custody for a week. The key to a joint custody arrangement is that the parents live in close proximity to each other and that relations between them are cordial. Bruce should be aware that in some states there exists a presumption of joint custody. Thus, in these states, if Bruce desires joint custody of the child, he should be able to achieve this end without much fanfare.

Joint Responsibility

You should advise Bruce that despite his desire not to seek joint custody he may very well desire joint responsibility re decisions pertaining to the child's education, health, religion, social life, etc. Through this arrangement the child resides with one parent for most of the year. However, all important decisions re the child are jointly made.

Visitation Rights

In regard to visitation of the child once Maryvonne has custody, a typical arrangement that Bruce can expect to obtain is as follows. Bruce would visit with the child one week day evening every week as long as the visitation does not interfere with the child's education. In addition, he would have visitation with the child every other weekend from Friday to Sunday. Also, the child would be with him every other school holiday, alternate winter and spring school vacation periods and from 2 to 4 weeks during the summer. It may also be appropriate to provide that the child be with Bruce every other religious holiday.

If relations between Bruce and Maryvonne were strained, it would be best to provide for all visitation at a location away from Maryvonne's home. Also, under this situation, it might be best to provide that some of the visitation be telephone conversations.

In reviewing whether overnight visitation is appropriate, the age of the child is crucial. If the child is an infant and Bruce does not feel he can properly care for the child during an overnight stay, perhaps overnight visitation should not begin until the child is 2, 3, or 5 years old.

In negotiating custody and visitation, provision should be made for what will happen if the custodial parent moves a great distance. Perhaps custody should be given to the other parent. Perhaps the visitation rights of the noncustodial parent should be extended to encompass longer blocks of time. Further, it might be appropriate to hold the custodial parent responsible for any transportation expenses which relate to transporting the child to the noncustodial parent's residence. An exception to the above might exist if the custodial parent moves in order to remarry or due to health reasons.

OTHER CHILD RELATED CONCERNS

Some final notes should be made as to child related concerns. A clause should be placed in the separation agreement that the child's name will not be changed. Additionally, each parent should agree that he or she will not deprive the other of access to the child and will not injure the child's opinion as to the other. Further, if one parent has knowledge that the child is ill, the other should be informed. Also, each parent should be kept informed by the other as to the whereabouts of the child. Moreover, each parent must be entitled to full information regarding the child from any school or physician.

Any arrangement re custody and visitation incorporated in the separation agreement need not be a final one. You may want to insert a proviso into the arrangement that after a certain period of time custody and/or visitation will be renegotiated.

RESPONSIBILITY FOR OUTSTANDING BILLS

Any outstanding loans and bills that were incurred during the marriage should be addressed in the separation agreement. As to debts for luxuries, the spouse that incurred the bill should be responsible for paying it. Since Bruce earns a far greater income than Maryvonne, he should be responsible for most, if not all of the debts incurred for necessaries. This should be true even if Maryvonne was personally responsible for the debt relating to necessaries.

RIGHT TO MEDICAL COVERAGE

Bruce is responsible for providing medical coverage [e.g., Blue Cross, Blue Shield, Major Medical] for Maryvonne after the separation agreement is consummated. However, it is important to note that this obligation ends if and when they divorce. As to medical coverage for their child, this coverage should last until the child is 19 years old. If the child enters college, the coverage should last until the child finishes college, with a maximum age limit of 22.

In regard to any medical bills incurred in excess of that covered by medical insurance, Bruce should be permanently responsible for this expense. It may be appropriate to incorporate a deductible into any proviso relating to these medical expenses. For example, perhaps Maryvonne should be responsible for the first $100 of excess expenses incurred by her and the first $100 of excess incurred by the child. Also, Bruce may want to include a maximum limit on his responsibility and he may want the right to select the doctor who will provide the medical care. Bruce should consider excluding from this coverage the cost of psychiatrists and cosmetic surgery. Bruce may not want to include the cost of orthodontists and other dental care for Maryvonne and/or the child.

LIFE INSURANCE ENTITLEMENTS

There is no legal requirement that Bruce provide life insurance for Maryvonne or the child. However, Maryvonne may attempt to negotiate for life insurance to cover her alimony payments and any distributive award to which she might be entitled. For example, if Maryvonne is to receive alimony for five years, she may want term life insurance with a decreasing term. As Bruce makes alimony payments, the amount of the life insurance will decrease. As to the child, Maryvonne may desire life insurance to cover any payments (e.g., support and college), Bruce will make. The life insurance might continue until the child is emancipated or finishes college.

A typical clause contained in the separation agreement which pertains to life insurance policies would require that Bruce provide proof that the policy is in existence upon demand for such proof by Maryvonne. Also, Maryvonne may justifiably demand that if Bruce does not keep the policy in force and he dies, his estate will be responsible for the benefit that would have been provided by the policy.

ESTATE PROVISIONS

Bruce may want to modify his Will to bequeath a certain amount of his estate upon his death to his child. He may desire to negotiate with Maryvonne for the insertion of a similar bequest provision in her Will. Maryvonne may attempt to negotiate with Bruce for the insertion in his Will of a provision which bequeaths a certain amount to her. However, Bruce should be aware that in making such a request, Maryvonne does not stand on firm ground. It is rare for a wife to ever be granted such a request.

DETERMINING WHO IS RESPONSIBLE FOR INCOME AND CAPITAL GAINS TAXES, TAX EXEMPTIONS, AND TAX AUDITS

The responsibility for income and capital gains taxes, tax exemptions, and tax audits is strictly a matter for negotiations. If Bruce wishes to be concerned only with taxes on his income and assets, he should negotiate for the filing of separate returns. If he files a joint return with Maryvonne—which can be done until the date of divorce—he must negotiate with her as to responsibility for the payment of taxes, right to refunds, and liability for deficiencies that are determined after a tax audit.

If separate returns are to be filed, it must be understood that neither spouse has an absolute right to claim the child as an exemption on the tax return.

Any rights one spouse may have can be contracted away to the other. Generally, the spouse that is responsible for the bulk of the expenses relating to the support of the child, should be entitled to claim the child as an exemption on his or her tax return.

A sample letter which will help you confirm any arrangements negotiated between Bruce and Maryvonne re tax returns and related problems follows.

SAMPLE LETTER FOR CONFIRMATION OF STATUS RE TAX RIGHTS AND LIABILITIES

Dear

As I advised you in our telephone conversation of , we feel that it would be in the best interests of Mr. and Mrs. to sign and file joint tax returns for the tax year .

If Mrs. agrees to our suggestion, then we are agreeable to the following conditions, which are standard in this type of an arrangement.

1. Mr. will be personally responsible to pay any and all taxes due on the tax returns, which might include any penalties and interest.

2. In the event there is any refund on the tax returns, both parties agree that they are to be divided between them on an equal basis.

3. Mr. will make the arrangements for the preparation of the tax returns, and in the event there are any accounting fees, he will be personally responsible to pay same.

4. The Husband and Wife acknowledge the fact that by signing and filing these tax returns neither concedes in any respect the truth, completeness or accuracy of any of the statements made by the other on said returns, including, without limiting the foregoing, the income reported or any of the deductions or other data.

5. Despite such signing and the filing of such joint return both parties are to be completely free in all respects to introduce evidence concerning the assets, income, expenses, and deductions of the other, in connection with any pending or future action or preceding between them, or otherwise.

6. No claim is to be made by the Husband and Wife that on the basis of said joint return the Wife or Husband is in any way estopped from presenting to the Court such evidence as he or she may desire concerning the assets, income, expenses, and deductions of the other for said year or for any other year.

7. After these tax returns are filed, in the event there shall be any additional tax assessment, penalties, interest, or additional balance of any kind whatsoever required, then the Husband shall be solely responsible to pay same unless such additional assessment arose from Mrs. failure to declare income or the taking of improper expenses by her, and then under those circumstances she shall be responsible to pay the assessment, penalty, and interest resulting therefrom.

8. There shall be sent to you, as attorneys for the Wife, a copy of any communications, notices, or reports received by the Husband with respect to said returns.

9. Simultaneously with the execution and delivery of said joint income tax returns, the responsible party shall make payments of any amounts due and owing the appropriate taxing authorities thereunder.

10. No modification or waiver of the terms and conditions and of this Letter of Agreement is to be valid unless in writing signed by the Wife and the Husband.

If the foregoing correctly sets forth the agreement concerning this joint income tax return and the terms and conditions pursuant to which said returns are to be executed and filed, will you please sign on the counterpart of this letter, and this letter, when executed by both parties and their counsel, will be and constitute an agreement.

Very truly yours,

______________________________ Esqs.

Attorneys for Husband

The foregoing is hereby agreed to in all respects:

____

Attorney for Wife

____

Husband

____

Wife

LEGAL FEES

There is no set formula for the determination as to what, if any, legal fees Bruce will pay in regard to the separation agreement. You and Maryvonne's attorneys should enter into serious negotiations to resolve this issue.

MISCELLANEOUS PROVISIONS

There exist numerous important miscellaneous clauses that Bruce may wish to incorporate into the separation agreement. First, Bruce may want a diminutive clause. Under the clause, if Bruce suffers a severe change in financial status, he will have the right to petition the court or an arbitrator to reduce his support payment.

Next, Bruce may want to insert a provision into the separation agreement which mandates that it merge into any subsequent divorce decree. Under such a clause, Bruce will be better able to subsequently effectuate a judicial reduction of any alimony payments if his income goes down. Of course, Maryvonne would be better able to effectuate a judicial increase of alimony payments if her income is reduced or Bruce's is increased. (See Chapter 14, "Judicial Modification of Support Obligations" for more detailed discussion.)

Another clause which might be appropriate would provide open access to each party's books and records. Further, a statement should be included which specifies that if one party reneges as to any provisions in the contract and the other party is forced to commence a lawsuit, the guilty party will be responsible for all legal fees.

The separation agreement should also include a statement that both parties are represented by counsel, know what they are signing, and are satisfied with the agreement. The manner by which communication between the parties will be made should be specified. Further, the contract should note that any changes in the contract must be in writing, that there will be three original copies—one for the court, one for the wife, one for the husband—and that the contract will be binding on heirs, estate administrators, etc. A provision should also be added stating that the failure of a party to exercise his or her rights at a particular time does not constitute a waiver of these rights in the future. Additionally, it should be stated that if any of the contract provisions are held to be invalid, all other provisions will remain in full force and effect. Finally, the state where laws will govern the contract should be stated.

In order to ease your task of constructing a separation agreement for Bruce, a sample separation agreement has been attached herein.

SAMPLE SEPARATION AGREEMENT

AGREEMENT made this day of , 19 , between , presently residing at , , State of New York, hereinafter sometimes referred to as the "WIFE", and , presently residing at , County of New York, City and State of New York, hereinafter sometimes referred to as the "HUSBAND".

W I T N E S S E T H

WHEREAS, the parties are HUSBAND and WIFE and were married in the County of , State of New York, on ; and

WHEREAS, there are three (3) CHILDREN of the marriage, unemancipated and presently under the age of twenty-one (21), namely, , born , 19 , age , , born , age , and , born , age , hereinafter sometimes referred to as the "CHILDREN"; and

WHEREAS, the parties are experiencing disputes and irreconcilable differences; and

WHEREAS, the parties desire to confirm and make arrangements in connection with the settlement of all questions relating to their property rights and other rights and obligations growing out of the marriage relation;

NOW, THEREFORE, in consideration of the promises and of the mutual covenants and undertakings herein set forth, the parties covenant and agree as follows:

FIRST: The HUSBAND and WIFE shall live free from interference, authority, or control, direct or indirect, by the other. Each may reside at such place as he or she may select. Each may for his or her separate benefit, engage in any employment, business, or profession he or she may choose.

SECOND: The parties shall not harass or interfere with each other, by any means whatsoever.

THIRD: The HUSBAND and WIFE covenant and represent that neither he nor she has heretofore incurred or contracted, nor will he or she at any time in the future incur or contract, any debt, charge, or liability whatsoever, including bills for necessities, for which the other party, their legal representatives, or their property or estate are now or may become liable. The WIFE and HUSBAND further covenant at all times to keep the other party and their estate free, harmless, and indemnified of and from any and all debts, charges, and liabilities heretofore and hereafter contracted by him or her.

FOURTH: Subject to the provisions of this Agreement, each party has remised, released and forever discharged, and by those presents does, for himself or herself and his or her heirs, legal representatives, executors, administrators, and assigns, remise, release and forever discharge the other of and from all causes of action, claims, rights, or demands he or she heretofore ever had or now has against the other, including all causes of action, claims and rights which might exist or might have existed, except any or all cause or causes of action for divorce.

FIFTH: Subject to the provisions of this Agreement, each of the parties may in any way dispose of his or her property of whatsoever nature, real or personal, and each of the parties hereto, for himself or herself and for his or her heirs, legal representatives, executors, administrators, and assigns, hereby waive any right of election which he or she may have or hereafter acquire regarding the estate of the other or to take against any Last Will and Testament of the other, whether heretofore or hereafter executed, as provided by Section 5–1–1 of the New York Estates, Powers and Trusts Law, or as may now or hereafter be provided for in any law of the State of New York or any other state or territory of the United States or any foreign country, and renounces and releases all interest, right of claim, or right of dower and curtesy, or otherwise, that he or she now has or might otherwise have against the other on the property of whatsoever nature, real or personal, of the other under or by virtue of the laws of any state or country, and each will, at the request of the other or his or her legal representatives, executors, administrators, and assigns, execute, acknowledge, and deliver any and all deeds, releases, or any other instruments necessary to bar, release, or extinguish such interest, rights, and claims, or which may be needful for the proper carrying into effect of any of the provisions of this Agreement. Each of the parties renounces and relinquishes any and all claims and rights that he or she may have or hereafter acquire to act as executor or administrator of the other party's estate.

SIXTH: The parties have divided up all personal effects, furnishings, and household goods previously situated at the former marital residence at ______, ______ New York, to their mutual satisfaction.

Henceforth, each of the parties shall own, have, and enjoy, independently of any claim or right of the other party, all items of personal property of every kind, nature, and description and wheresoever situate, which are now owned or held by them or which may hereafter belong or come to the HUSBAND or the WIFE, with the full power to the HUSBAND or the WIFE to dispose of same as fully and effectually in all respects for all purposes as if he or she were unmarried.

SEVENTH: The parties have carefully weighed the question of the custody of the CHILDREN. In doing so, they have been guided solely by considerations touching upon the CHILDREN'S health, welfare, and well-being. They are convinced that the following disposition will be in the CHILDREN'S best interests:

A. The WIFE shall have sole custody of the CHILDREN.

B. The HUSBAND shall have the following visitation with each CHILD, until each CHILD attains such CHILD'S sixth birthday:
   (i) Every Wednesday evening from 6 P.M. until 9 P.M.
   (ii) Every Sunday from 10 A.M. until 9 P.M.

C. The HUSBAND shall have the following visitation with each CHILD, after each CHILD attains his or her sixth birthday:
   (i) Every Wednesday evening from 6 P.M. until 9 P.M.
   (ii) Three Sundays per month from 10 A.M. until 9 P.M.
   (iii) One weekend each month from Friday at 6 P.M. until Sunday at 9 P.M., provided the HUSBAND notifies the WIFE by no later than the 5th of each month as to whether he intends to exercise this visitation privilege and if so which weekend he intends to visit with the CHILD or CHILDREN.
   (iv) Alternate Christmas and Easter school vacation periods each year. The HUSBAND shall give the WIFE three (3) months notice if he does not intend to exercise this visitation privilege.
   (v) Two consecutive weeks each summer provided the HUSBAND gives the WIFE three (3) months notice as to which two weeks he wishes to exercise this visitation right.

D. The HUSBAND shall take the CHILDREN with him away from the WIFE'S residence during the above visitation periods, and at all times he shall keep the WIFE fully informed as to the state of health, welfare, and whereabouts of the CHILDREN during all of the visitation periods heretofore provided.

E. The HUSBAND agrees that the above provided visitation rights shall not be construed as a waiver of the absolute right of the WIFE to complete custody of the CHILDREN. Failure of the HUSBAND to take the CHILDREN on any given visitation period shall not affect his future visitation rights.

F. The parties shall consult with each other with respect to all matters affecting the welfare of the CHILDREN, whose well-being, education, and development shall at all times be the paramount consideration of the HUSBAND and WIFE.

G. The parties shall exert every reasonable effort to maintain free access and unhampered contact between each CHILD and each of the parties and to foster a feeling of affection between each CHILD and the other party. Neither party shall do anything which may estrange the CHILDREN from the other party or injure the opinion of the CHILDREN as to their mother or father, or which may hamper the free and natural development of each CHILD'S love and respect for the other party.

H. The WIFE and HUSBAND shall promptly inform each other with respect to any illness or accident of any CHILD and in the event that any such illness or accident causes a CHILD to be confined to bed or home (whether of the HUSBAND or WIFE) for more than forty-eight (48) hours, such other parent shall be entitled to visit the CHILD at reasonable times and for reasonable periods at such place of confinement.

I. Each party shall, at the time of the execution of this Agreement, give his and her address and residence telephone number to the other and shall cause prompt notice to be given to the other, in writing, of further changes of addresses and telephone numbers until the last of the children is emancipated as set forth in Paragraph Ninth.

J. Each party shall be entitled to complete and full information from any pediatrician, general physician, dentist, consultants, or specialists attending a CHILD for any reason whatsoever, and to have copies of any reports rendered by them or any of them sent to either and/or both parents.

K. Each party shall be entitled to complete and full information from any teacher or school giving instruction to the CHILDREN to which the CHILD/CHILDREN may attend, and to have copies of any reports rendered by them, or any of them, sent to either and/or both parents.

L. Each party shall have the right to communicate with the CHILDREN by telephone, or otherwise, and to receive telephone calls or other communications from the CHILDREN during reasonable hours so long as said communications do not interfere with said CHILDREN'S mealtimes, rest periods, or school work.

M. The parties may agree to further visitation privileges for the HUSBAND from time to time, but it shall be subject to both parties' consent.

EIGHTH: The HUSBAND shall pay the WIFE for her support, maintenance, and alimony:

A. The sum of   and 00/100 ($ .00) DOLLARS each week commencing on the first Friday following the execution by both parties of this Agreement.

B. The HUSBAND'S obligation under this Paragraph shall be reduced by one-third (1/3) as each CHILD becomes emancipated as defined in Paragraph Ninth of this Agreement.

C. The WIFE's remarriage shall not terminate the HUSBAND'S responsibility to pay maintenance or alimony to the WIFE.

D. The HUSBAND'S obligation under this Paragraph "EIGHTH" shall terminate upon the death of the WIFE, the death of the HUSBAND, or at such time as the last CHILD is emancipated, whichever event shall sooner occur, except for any arrearages.

NINTH: The HUSBAND shall pay the WIFE for the support and maintenance of each CHILD:

A. The sum of and 00/100 ($) DOLLARS per CHILD per week, the first weekly payment to be made to the WIFE on the first Friday following the execution by both parties of this Agreement.

B. The HUSBAND agrees to increase his payments for child support as follows:

The HUSBAND shall pay, commencing one year from the date of this Agreement, for five years, in addition to the DOLLARS per CHILD per week, an amount equal to the percentage difference of the Cost of Living increase, as computed from July 1st, to June 30th, for each of the five years. Such Cost of Living increase shall be predicated upon the U.S. Department of Labor Cost of Living Index for the New York metropolitan area. The HUSBAND'S responsibility for this Cost of Living increase shall never exceed an increase of 9% per annum, and whatever aggregate amount the HUSBAND must pay the WIFE during the last year of the cost of living increase shall continue until each CHILD is emancipated.

For example: HUSBAND pays $ per CHILD per week through , 19 . If the Cost of Living increases by 5% between 19 and June, 19 , the per CHILD per week becomes $ per CHILD per week from , 19 through 19 .

If the Cost of Living increases by 10% between , 19 and , 19 , the per CHILD per week can only be increased by 9% and becomes $ per CHILD per week from , 19 through , 19 .

If the Cost of Living increases by 8% between , 19 and , 19 , the per CHILD per week becomes per CHILD per week from , 19 through , .

Each subsequent year shall be calculated similarly with the amount payable for the year , 19 to , 19 to continue until each child is emancipated.

C. The HUSBAND further agrees that whenever his gross income, gross income as defined later in this Paragraph, exceeds the sum of $ per year, then commencing with that year, but not before , 19 , he shall increase whatever he is then paying as child support by twenty (20%) percent and from that date on his liability to pay child support shall be fixed at that increased sum.

D. The term "gross income" as herein used shall mean and include any and all income of the HUSBAND before taxes (excluding inheritances and capital gains). If the HUSBAND is not employed on a salary basis, but is in his own business or is employed as a "commission salesman," the term "gross income" as herein used shall also include his share of the gross earnings of the business or gross commissions before taxes, less proper deductions of the business or of a commission salesman for expenses, business losses and bad debts as may be recognized under the Federal Income Tax Law then in effect as allowable for deductions.

E. Within ninety (90) days after the close of each calendar year commencing with , and until such time as the HUSBAND'S gross income exceeds $ per year, the HUSBAND shall render to the WIFE, upon her request, a sworn detailed statement, in writing, setting forth his gross income for the previous calendar year and the sources from which derived. If the HUSBAND'S gross income is more than $ for the year, then the HUSBAND shall set forth a computation of the sum of money the WIFE shall be entitled to by reason of such gross income.

F. The WIFE shall have the right, commencing with , if she so elects, through an accountant or an attorney employed by her to check the HUSBAND'S annual statement against his records. The HUSBAND shall fully and promptly cooperate in permitting such check to be made, and he shall make available all pertinent books, records, and information, including his Federal and State Income Tax Returns. It is understood that the foregoing shall not be construed to permit the WIFE to examine the records of the HUSBAND'S employer, provided, however, that she shall have the right to request the HUSBAND'S employer to supply pertinent financial information, if the financial information required by this Paragraph is not furnished by the HUSBAND or if the HUSBAND fails to furnish the statement required by Paragraph NINTH "F".

G. Emancipation for the purpose of this Agreement shall be defined as follows:

   (i) CHILD attains the age of twenty-one (21), or if then attending college, until the age of twenty-two (22); or

   (ii) Marries; or

   (iii) Enters the armed services or Peace Corps; or

   (iv) Resides permanently away from the WIFE'S residence and during those periods when the CHILD so resides away; or

   (v) Becomes self-supporting; or

   (vi) Dies; whichever event shall sooner occur.

H. Payments for the support of each CHILD shall terminate on the WIFE'S or HUSBAND'S death or when the CHILD becomes emancipated as previously defined.

I. The parties acknowledge that pursuant to their oral agreement, the HUSBAND has been paying to the WIFE, during the period of their separation and at least as of , , all of the payments set forth in paragraphs Eighth and Ninth hereof to wit: and 00/100 ($) DOLLARS support and maintenance and and 00/100 ($) DOLLARS per week as support for each CHILD.

TENTH: A. The parties have filed joint tax returns for the tax year 19 and each party shall be solely responsible for his or her respective taxes due and owing for the tax year 19 . In the event of any refund on these 19 returns, the parties shall share such refund in equal shares.

B. In the event of any audits of previously filed joint returns, each party shall be responsible for and will pay all deficiencies, penalties, and interest charges attributable to his or her failure to declare income or for the taking of improper deductions and each holds the other harmless and indemnified in this connection.

C. The HUSBAND and WIFE agree that the HUSBAND shall have the right to declare the CHILDREN, and , as his exemptions under the applicable income tax laws, and the WIFE shall have the right to declare the CHILD, , as her exemption.

ELEVENTH: The WIFE will carry the CHILDREN until each CHILD attains the age of nineteen (19), but if at college, until the age of twenty-three (23), under the terms of her present or comparable medical and major medical insurance, provided such coverage is available to the WIFE through her employer at no cost to her. At any time that the WIFE must contribute to the cost of such medical insurance on behalf of the CHILDREN she shall immediately notify the HUSBAND in writing and from that time on the HUSBAND shall either carry the CHILDREN under Blue Cross/Blue Shield and Major Medical Insurance available to him, or provided the WIFE can obtain such coverage, shall reimburse the WIFE for the cost of the coverage for the CHILDREN as the HUSBAND elects. If the HUSBAND elects to reimburse the WIFE, then he shall do so within thirty (30) days of presentation of a written bill.

TWELFTH: The parties shall equally share the cost of necessary and reasonable uninsured medical, dental, orthodontic, prescription drugs, nurses, and psychotherapeutic expenses of the CHILDREN provided that the HUSBAND'S liability for such expense shall be conditioned upon the WIFE giving the HUSBAND reasonable prior notice of the condition for which treatment is sought, the professionals and facilities to be used, the treatment to be rendered, and the costs involved. The HUSBAND'S consent shall first be obtained in writing, except in cases of emergency when the giving of such notice or obtaining written consent is impossible or impractical, and such consent shall not be unreasonably withheld.

THIRTEENTH: In addition to the aforementioned, the parties agree to be responsible for and pay, pro-rated on their financial ability at the time, all expenses related to each CHILD'S attendance at college-level institutions, including room, board, books, tuition, and round trip travel between each CHILD'S residence and school four (4) times per year, only if such CHILD is a matriculating student at such institution and only until such time as such CHILD attains his or her twenty-third (23) birthday. The parties' responsibility under this Paragraph shall be further conditioned upon each consenting to the selection of College and the course of study, but such consent shall not be unreasonably withheld.

In the event of any dispute, claim, or problem arising under the terms of this Paragraph, or dispute as to what the parties pro-rata share should be for payment of the CHILDREN'S college expenses, then same shall be submitted to arbitration for a determination as provided for in Paragraph "FOURTEENTH" of this Agreement.

FOURTEENTH: In the event of any dispute or controversy between the parties concerning Paragraph Thirteenth of this Agreement, the parties shall seek amicably to settle and adjust such dispute or controversy and if they are not able to do so, such dispute or controversy shall be determined by arbitration before a board of three arbitrators, each party choosing one arbitrator and the two so chosen arbitrators selecting a third. The decision of the majority of the arbitrators shall be binding and shall be rendered in such form that a judgment may be entered thereon in the highest court of the forum having jurisdiction.

FIFTEENTH: A. The HUSBAND agrees to be responsible for and pay all premiums, dues, and assessments which may become due and payable on a certain life insurance policy on the HUSBAND'S life, described in detail below:

Policy no.	Company	Type	Face amount	Beneficiary
			\$ Per CHILD	WIFE as Trustee for each CHILD, until death.
			\$	WIFE until death

(i) The HUSBAND represents to the WIFE that the aforesaid policies are free, clear, and unencumbered; that all premiums due thereon have been paid; that they are now in full force and effect; that he has made the designation of beneficiaries as hereinabove provided.

(ii) The HUSBAND agrees that he shall not borrow against, pledge, or otherwise encumber these policies, he shall pay any and all dues, premiums, and assessments thereon; and he shall upon the request of the WIFE or her attorney exhibit receipts for same.

(iii) In the event upon the HUSBAND'S death, the beneficiaries do not receive the benefits provided for above, then the HUSBAND'S estate shall be liable for payment of these benefits.

B. The WIFE agrees to be responsible for and continue the existing, or comparable policies, on her life, described in detail below:

Policy no.	Company	Type	Face amount	Beneficiary
		Term	$,000.00	HUSBAND
		Term	$,000.00	until youngest CHILD is emancipated.

(i) The WIFE represents that the aforesaid policies are free, clear, and unencumbered; that all premiums due thereon have been and will be paid, that they are now in full force and effect; that she has made the designation of beneficiaries as hereinabove provided.

(ii) The WIFE agrees that she shall not borrow against, pledge, or otherwise encumber these policies; she shall pay any and all dues, premiums, and assessments thereon; and she shall upon the request of the HUSBAND, or his attorney, exhibit receipts for same.

(iii) In the event that upon the WIFE'S death, the HUSBAND does not receive the benefits provided for above, then the estate of the WIFE shall be liable for payment of these benefits.

(iv) The WIFE'S obligation to maintain the above life insurance policies as set forth in this paragraph Fifteenth "B" shall cease and this obligation shall be null and void upon the emancipation, as defined in paragraph Ninth hereof, of their youngest CHILD,

SIXTEENTH: A. The HUSBAND and WIFE warrant and represent that the following assets are the only substantial marital assets as of this date, owned by the parties either individually or jointly, other than those disposed of in this Agreement and they herewith agree to divide these assets by disposing of same as follows under the provisions of Section 236 of the Domestic Relations Law, as amended, which took effect on July 19, 1980, which act is referred to as the Equitable Distribution Statute of the State of New York.

Description of asset	Approximate value		How presently held	Agreed final disposition
	$		HUSBAND	HUSBAND
	$		HUSBAND and WIFE	WIFE
Auto	$	value loan		
	$	Equity	WIFE	WIFE
	-0-		WIFE	WIFE

B. The HUSBAND and WIFE have agreed to sell the premises at , , New York, which they own as tenants by the entirety, and enter into a contract for sale of the premises with a purchaser, at such time as the WIFE vacates the premises, marries, dies, when the youngest CHIID becomes emancipated, or at the WIFE'S sole discretion, whichever event sooner occurs.

It is further agreed that until such time as the sale of the premises is consummated and title passes to the purchaser, the WIFE will be permitted to occupy said premises.

Until such time as the HUSBAND and WIFE convey title to a purchaser the WIFE agrees to be solely responsible for and to pay all monthly installments of the mortgage principle and interest and taxes plus all operating expenses related to the house, including, but not limited to, heating, fuel, gardening, utilities, insurance, water, electric, maintenance, and all repairs. Should any of the aforementioned items of expense related to the said premises be unpaid when title to the house is conveyed, then that portion of the proceeds from the sale of the house that the WIFE or HUSBAND would be entitled to under the provisions of this paragraph shall be charged and made to pay for such unpaid items which he or she was obligated to pay or shall be paid over to the other if he or she had paid same.

The WIFE shall be responsible for maintaining the house in good order and condition.

In the event a contract for sale of this house is entered into by the parties before , and the house is sold to a third party purchaser, then the HUSBAND shall receive from such sale the sum of $ as payment in full for his assigning his interest in these premises to the third party purchaser, and the WIFE shall retain as her own the balance received.

In the event a contract for sale of these premises is not entered into before , then at such time as the house is sold the HUSBAND shall be entitled to receive 12% of the gross sales price, gross meaning the actual sales price before mortgage, taxes, brokerage fees, filing fees, and all other expenses related to the sale, and the WIFE shall receive the balance.

On any sale of these premises after , , in the event either party is unwilling to agree to a sales price acceptable to the other, then the premises shall be appraised by an appraiser acceptable to both parties or in the event of their inability to agree on an appraiser, then by an appraiser appointed by the then president of the local Realty Board. Provided that the appraised value of the property is less than or equal to the proposed sales price, the property shall be sold at the proposed sales price or for no less than such appraised price, and the parties hereto agree to execute all documents, including a deed to the premises, which may be necessary and proper to effectuate such sale.

In the event of a sale of the premises in accordance with the provisions of this Agreement, then the parties shall join in executing a contract of sale and in executing a conveyance in pursuance of said contract.

The provisions of this and the preceding paragraphs shall survive the death of the HUSBAND and WIFE, or either of them, that is to say that notwithstanding the death of the WIFE, the provisions hereof with respect to the sale of the property and the distribution and disposition of the proceeds thereof shall survive the WIFE'S death, and the portion of the sale price payable to the WIFE shall then be payable to the estate of the WIFE. In the event that the HUSBAND predeceases the WIFE, his estate shall similarly be entitled to receive the portion of the proceeds of the sale, if any, as if he were alive. The death of either of the parties shall not serve to make the survivor the sole owner of the property.

The HUSBAND and WIFE agree that the WIFE shall have first option to purchase the HUSBAND'S one-half (1/2) interest in the aforesaid premises. In the event the WIFE shall exercise this option before , then the WIFE shall pay the HUSBAND the sum of $, for the HUSBAND'S interest in the house. In the event the WIFE elects to exercise this option after , then the WIFE shall pay the HUSBAND a sum of money equal to 12% of the then Fair Market Value on these premises, but in the event they cannot agree upon a Fair Market Value, then the premises shall be appraised by an appraiser acceptable to both parties, or in the event of their inability to agree on an appraiser, then by an appraiser appointed by the then president of the local Realty Board, and whatever Fair Market Value price the appraiser establishes, the WIFE shall pay the HUSBAND the sum of money equal to 12% of such Fair Market Value.

In the event the WIFE at any time desires to exercise this option to buy the HUSBAND'S undivided one-half (1/2) interest, then she shall give written notice to him of such intent and the parties shall execute a written contract of sale within 60 days after delivery of such notice of intent. The contract of sale by the HUSBAND and WIFE shall provide for a title Closing within 30 days of the contract signing.

Should the WIFE exercise this option to buy the HUSBAND'S undivided one-half (1/2) interest then she alone will be responsible to pay off the existing mortgages on the premises, which mortgages have been incurred by the HUSBAND

and the WIFE, and she further agrees to hold the HUSBAND harmless and indemnified in this connection.

Any contract for the sale of these premises shall be drawn by the WIFE'S attorneys, but shall be approved by the HUSBAND'S attorneys. Any and all legal fees due on this real estate transaction shall be paid by the HUSBAND and WIFE individually and shall not be a charge against the proceeds of the sale.

The terms of this Agreement as relates to the sale of the said house shall make all prior agreements and contracts entered into by the HUSBAND and WIFE relating to the division and distribution of the proceeds of the sale of this real property null, void and of no effect.

The HUSBAND and WIFE agree that in the event they sell the premises to a third party purchaser each will be responsible to pay any capital gains tax assessed against his or her share of the net proceeds received. In the event the WIFE exercises her option to purchase the HUSBAND'S interest in these premises then the HUSBAND and WIFE agree that the HUSBAND will be responsible for and will pay any capital gains taxes due any taxing authorities with respect to his transfer of his one-half (1/2) interest in this real estate to the WIFE and any further capital gains taxes due any taxing authorities in the event of the future sale of this property by the WIFE will be the sole responsibility of the WIFE.

As the WIFE alone made all mortgage and tax payments on this residence in the year 19 , the parties agree that she alone will be entitled to take all tax benefits accruing from these payments on her Income Tax Returns for the tax year 19 , and so long as she continues to make these payments in the future all tax benefits accruing from such payments shall continue to be taken by the WIFE on all future tax returns.

C. The HUSBAND and WIFE warrant and represent that there are no assets which he or she owns and which would be construed as "SEPARATE PROPERTY" in accordance with the provisions of the amended Section 236 of the Domestic Relations Law, except for an engagement ring owned by the WIFE worth $ which she shall retain as her own.

D. The parties agree that they will either simultaneously with the execution of this Agreement or at a future date, execute whatever documents are necessary to effectuate the disposition of assets as provided for in this Paragraph SIXTEENTH.

E. The parties acknowledge that their respective attorneys have fully explained and discussed with them the content and meaning of the provisions of Domestic Relations Law Section 236 and that each fully understands the nature and extent of the claims he or she can make against the other and of the claims the other may make against him or her. The parties intend this Agreement to constitute an agreement pursuant to Domestic Relations Law Section 236. They intend this Agreement and its provisions to be in lieu of each of their respective rights, pursuant to all aspects of Domestic Relations Law Section 236.

SEVENTEENTH: The parties acknowledge the fact that each has the following debts incurred in his or her name solely and they have agreed that in consideration of the covenants and promises contained in this Agreement each will be responsible for and will pay the debt incurred in his or her own name respectively.

Date of debt	Creditor	Balance owing	Original debt	Description of debt	Date incurred by and to be paid by

The parties further agree to hold the other harmless and indemnified against any and all claims which might accrue against him or her as a result of the debt specified as being incurred by and to be paid by the other.

EIGHTEENTH: The parties acknowledge that each has been furnished with all information requested by the other, and that each has had the opportunity to make a full and complete examination of the other's income, property, assets, and financial affairs.

NINETEENTH: The HUSBAND and WIFE have agreed that each shall be responsible for and shall pay their own legal fees in full, due and owing their respective attorneys, for the preparation and execution of this Agreement and all negotiations prior thereto, as well as for any services rendered the HUSBAND or WIFE in any pending or future action for divorce or separation instituted by either party in any jurisdiction and each party herewith agrees to hold the other harmless from and indemnified against any and all claims and suits for such legal services rendered the other by any and all attorneys in this connection.

TWENTIETH: Nothing contained in this Agreement shall be construed to prevent either party from instituting any suit, action, or other legal proceeding in this or any other jurisdiction for a divorce or separation against the other by reason of facts which heretofore occurred or which may hereafter occur. In the event that an action, suit, or other legal proceeding for divorce or separation shall be instituted at any time by either party against the other, in the State of New York, or in any other jurisdiction, it is agreed that:

A. Neither of the parties shall cause or request that any provision be inserted in the final judgment or decree of the Court which shall be inconsistent with any of the provisions of this Agreement.

B. To the extent possible and appropriate, the terms and provisions of this Agreement shall be incorporated by reference into any final judgment or decree obtained in a divorce or separation action and shall survive such final judgment or decree.

C. This Agreement shall in no way and under no circumstances merge in any such judgment or decree of divorce or separation.

TWENTY-FIRST: Both the legal and practical effect of this Agreement in each and every respect and the financial standard of the parties has been fully explained to both parties by their own counsel, and they both acknowledge that it is a fair Agreement and is not the result of any duress or undue influence exercised by either party upon the other, or by any other person or persons upon either, and they further agree that this Agreement contains the entire understanding of the parties. There are no representations, promises, warranties, covenants, or undertakings other than those expressly set forth herein.

TWENTY-SECOND: Each of the parties hereto agrees further at any time and from time to time to make, execute, and deliver all instruments necessary to effectuate the provisions of this Agreement.

TWENTY-THIRD: For the purpose of this Agreement, all notices or other communication given or made hereunder shall, until written notice to the contrary, be mailed or given directly to the WIFE and directly to the HUSBAND at their respective aforementioned addresses.

TWENTY-FOURTH: The WIFE recognizes and acknowledges that the foregoing provisions are satisfactory and that they are reasonable and adequate and that they will assist her in providing for her own and the CHILDREN'S support. The WIFE accordingly hereby releases and discharges the HUSBAND absolutely and forever, for the rest of her life, from all claims and demands for any past maintenance and support for herself and the CHILDREN.

TWENTY-FIFTH: All matters affecting the interpretation of this Agreement and the right of the parties shall be governed by the laws of the State of New York.

TWENTY-SIXTH: All the provisions of this Agreement shall be binding upon the respective heirs, next of kin, executors, administrators, and assigns of the parties hereto.

TWENTY-SEVENTH: This Agreement shall be executed in triplicate, each of which so executed shall be deemed an original and shall constitute one and the same Agreement.

TWENTY-EIGHTH: The failure of either party at any time or from time to time to exercise the rights herein reserved to either party shall not be deemed to constitute a relinquishment of his or her right to exercise the same in the future.

TWENTY-NINTH: There can and shall be no modification of this Agreement, no waiver of any provision hereof, right hereunder or condition herein, or release from any obligation imposed hereby, except by written instrument duly executed.

THIRTIETH: If any provision of this Agreement is held to be invalid or unenforceable, all other provisions shall nevertheless continue in full force and effect.

THIRTY-FIRST: The parties agree that this Agreement shall be filed with the County Clerk, County of   or   , State of New York.

IN WITNESS WHEREOF, the said parties hereto have, after consultation with counsel relative to the matters herein set forth and agreed upon, having been advised fully and fairly as to all of the facts and circumstances herein set forth, have hereunto set their hands and seals the day and year first above written.

WITNESSES:

____________________ ____________________

____________________ ____________________

STATE OF NEW YORK)
) ss.:
COUNTY OF NEW YORK)

On this day of , 19 , before me personally came , to me known and known to me to be the person described in and who executed the foregoing Agreement and acknowledged that he executed the same.

____

NOTARY PUBLIC

STATE OF NEW YORK)
) ss.:
COUNTY OF NEW YORK)

On this day of , 19 , before me personally came , to me known and known to me to be the person described in and who executed the foregoing Agreement and acknowledged that she executed the same.

____

NOTARY PUBLIC

CHAPTER 12

How to Handle Litigation

SITUATION

Tony and Janet Jones have decided to divorce. They both live in New York and have lived there for the past ten years. However they have lived in separate residences for the past two years. Additionally their children, ages 15 and 10, have resided with Janet. No formal agreements have been entered into re division of property, alimony, child custody and support, etc.

Janet comes to you, her attorney, and informs you that Tony will not fight the divorce. Also, Tony has told her that she can have custody of the children, that he will not contest a reasonable evaluation re the distribution of property, and that he wants to provide reasonable alimony and child support. Janet has considered obtaining an out of state divorce and Tony has declared that he would consent to *in personam* jurisdiction (i.e., jurisdiction over the person) over him for the purpose of this action. (See discussion in following section "How To Establish Jurisdiction for Initiating Suit" for relief that can be obtained by *in personam* jurisdiction.) Tony is also amenable to having the divorce granted in New York.

In light of Tony's feelings re the divorce proceedings, Janet anticipates that it will be a smoothly conducted uncontested divorce. However, she is not certain that Tony will continue his benevolent attitude. She wishes to be prepared for what might be in store for her if the divorce proceedings turn into a hotly contested battle. Thus, she seeks advice from you, not only re the procedures involved in consummating an uncontested divorce—both foreign and domestic—but re the procedures involved in consummating a contested divorce.

HOW TO ESTABLISH JURISDICTION FOR INITIATING SUIT

The first query that you must address pertains to jurisdiction in the divorce action. If the court has *in personam* jurisdiction over the parties, it can grant the divorce, determine property rights, award alimony and child support, and decide custody and visitation issues. *In personam* jurisdiction over a party can be obtained if that party resides in the State or has sufficient contacts with the state, and is personally served. Further, even if the above requirements are not met, *in personam* jurisdiction can be obtained if the party consents to such jurisdiction. Each state has its own requirements as to how *in personam* jurisdiction can be obtained and your local state statute should be consulted to determine if you, as Janet's attorney, can obtain *in personam* jurisdiction over Tony.

If *in personam* jurisdiction can not be obtained in a particular state, you may not be able to settle matters involving property distribution, alimony and child support in that state. Again, you must look to your local state statute to determine under what circumstances property distribution, alimony, and child support can be obtained.

However, even if you cannot obtain *in personam* jurisdiction in a particular state, you can still obtain a divorce in that state if you can obtain *in rem* jurisdiction (i.e., jurisdiction over the thing which in the case of a divorce action is the divorce) in that state. Certain minimum requirements must be met before *in rem* jurisdiction can be obtained, which requirements would be substantially less than those required to obtain *in personam* jurisdiction. For example, in New York, *in rem* jurisdiction sufficient for granting the divorce can be obtained if the plaintiff in the divorce action has been a New York domiciliary for a year or two. Your particular state statute must be examined to determine what requirements must be met before you are entitled to obtain *in rem* jurisdiction.

Once you meet the requirements necessary for obtaining *in rem* jurisdiction, you can acquire such jurisdiction by publishing notice of the divorce action in a local newspaper and sending notice of the divorce action to your adversary's last known address by certified mail with return receipt requested.

As to child custody, the fact that you can only obtain *in rem* jurisdiction does not necessarily bar a finding on this issue. If the child resides in the state that is granting the divorce, the Court will most likely possess the power to resolve the custody issue. For example, such is true in New York.

In Tony and Janet's case, the fact that Tony resides in N.Y. would enable the court to exercise *in personam* jurisdiction over him.

UNCONTESTED DIVORCE

How to Accomplish a Domestic Divorce

If Tony and Janet wish to pursue a domestic divorce, i.e., a divorce in the state where they reside, there are certain basic procedures that they should follow no matter what state is the domicile.

First, they should enter into a separation agreement outlining the rights and obligations of the parties after divorce as to child custody, support, and visitation, alimony, property distribution, etc. (See Chapter 11 for sample separation agreement.) Then, after the separation agreement has ripened pursuant to the particular state statutory scheme, (in New York, for example, one must wait one year after the separation agreement is signed by the parties before the uncontested divorce action can be commenced), one of the parties should initiate an action by serving a summons and complaint for divorce on the other party. The other party should prepare a stipulation which acknowledges service of these documents, waives the right and time to answer the complaint, acknowledges the existence and proper execution for the separation agreement, acknowledges that the complaining party has substantially complied with the terms of the separation agreement, and consents to the entry of a divorce decree. The plaintiff should then prepare an affirmation of affidavit of regularity which notes the defendant's stipulation that the summons was served, and that the divorce will be uncontested. All documents should thereafter be filed by the plaintiff in a state court having jurisdiction over divorce actions e.g. the Supreme Court in New York. The court will ultimately issue a judgment of divorce which recognizes the rights and obligations contained in the separation agreement. (Samples of the above documents are annexed at the end of this sub-section "How to Accomplish a Domestic Divorce.")

Checklist for Consummating Uncontested Divorce

In order to help you quickly determine how to consummate an uncontested divorce, the following list is provided.

1. Enter into separation agreement.
2. After separation agreement ripens (e.g., 1 year in N.Y.) serve summons and complaint on other party.
3. Have other party prepare stipulation.
4. Prepare affidavit of regularity.
5. File all above documents in court having jurisdiction over divorce actions, e.g., the Supreme Court in N.Y.
6. Obtain judgment of divorce from court.

Each state will have procedures which supplement these basic procedures. For example, in New York the plaintiff would submit with the complaint an affidavit of fact which sets forth the facts of the case. Also, in New York, depending on where you reside in the state, the court may issue one document entitled "Decision" and another document entitled "Judgment." Or, the court may combine these two documents into one.

SAMPLE PLEADINGS APPLICABLE FOR DIVORCE ACTION

Sample pleadings applicable to New York to help prepare for an uncontested divorce follows. This includes a sample summons, complaint, plaintiff's statement of fact, affirmation of regularity, stipulation, notice of appearance, (notice would be by defendant and may not be necessary in uncontested proceedings), decision, and judgment.

SUMMONS

SUPREME COURT OF THE STATE OF
NEW YORK: COUNTY OF

____________________________________x

______________, :

Plaintiff, : *Summons*

-against- :

______________, :

Defendant. :

____________________________________x

To the above named defendant:

You are given notice that a civil action for divorce has been initiated against you, and you are summoned to serve upon plaintiff's attorneys, within twenty (20) days after the personal service of the summons and attached verified complaint, a notice of appearance. In the event you fail to enter an appearance in this case, a default judgment will be taken against you for the relief demanded in the verified complaint.

Dated:

____
Plaintiff's Attorney

VERIFIED COMPLAINT

SUPREME COURT OF THE STATE OF
NEW YORK: COUNTY OF

,	:	Index No.
Plaintiff,	:	*VERIFIED COMPLAINT*
-against-	:	
,	:	
Defendant.	:	

Plaintiff, by her attorneys, , complaining of defendant, alleges:

FIRST: At all times hereinafter mentioned and for more than two years prior to the commencement of this action, the plaintiff has been and still is a resident of the State of New York.

SECOND: At the time of the commencement of this action each of the parties is over the age of eighteen (18) years.

THIRD: The parties were married to each other, on ; in the County of , State of , by a .

FOURTH: There are no children in this marriage, and none are expected.

FIFTH: During recent years of the marriage, defendant has shown less and less affection toward plaintiff, and various arguments ensued.

SIXTH: The parties have not cohabited with each other as husband and wife for a period commencing on or about .

SEVENTH: During said period of time, defendant has not cohabited with plaintiff as husband and wife, despite plaintiff's willingness to do so.

EIGHTH: Defendant's refusal to engage in marital relations with plaintiff, as aforesaid, was not caused or provoked by any conduct on the part of plaintiff, and was without plaintiff's consent.

NINTH: Upon information and belief, defendant has not suffered from any disability which would prevent defendant from cohabiting with plaintiff.

TENTH: The conduct of defendant, as aforesaid, constitutes an abandonment of plaintiff by defendant.

ELEVENTH: Plaintiff has taken all steps solely within plaintiff's power to remove any barrier to defendant's remarriage.

TWELFTH: There is no judgment or decree against plaintiff in favor of defendant for a divorce, and no other action is pending between the parties in any Court of competent jurisdiction.

WHEREFORE, plaintiff demands judgment against defendant as follows:

a) of absolute divorce, dissolving forever the bonds of matrimony between plaintiff and defendant;

b) awarding plaintiff such other and further relief as to this Court seems just and proper.

Attorneys for Plaintiff

TO: ATTORNEY FOR DEFENDANT

INDIVIDUAL VERIFICATION

STATE OF NEW YORK)
) ss.:
COUNTY OF NEW YORK)

, being duly sworn, deposes and says: I am the plaintiff in the within action, have read the foregoing Verified Complaint, and know the contents thereof; that the same are true to deponent's own knowledge, except to the matters therein stated to be alleged on information and belief, and that as to those matters deponent believes them to be true.

____

Sworn to before me this
day of , 19 .

PLAINTIFF'S AFFIDAVIT

SUPREME COURT OF THE STATE OF
NEW YORK: COUNTY OF

____________________________________x

,	:	Index No.
Plaintiff,	:	*PLAINTIFF'S AFFIDAVIT*
-against-	:	
,	:	
Defendant.	:	

____________________________________x

STATE OF NEW YORK)
) ss.:
COUNTY OF NEW YORK)

, being duly sworn, deposes and says:

1. I am the plaintiff in this action and make this affidavit in support of my request for a judgment of divorce against defendant.

2. Both defendant and I are over the age of eighteen (18) years, and have resided in this state for a continuous period of more than one year immediately preceding the commencement of this action.

3. Defendant and I were married on ; in , by a .

4. There are no children and none are expected.

5. Since , defendant and I have not cohabited as man and wife despite my willingness to do so. Defendant's refusal to engage in marital relations with me was not caused or provoked by any conduct on my part, and was without my consent. Upon information and belief, defendant has not suffered any disability which would prevent defendant from cohabiting with me. Defendant's conduct continues to date and constitutes an abandonment of me.

6. On , defendant and I entered into a written Separation Agreement, which resolved all issues concerning property division, maintenance, and all other issues which existed between us at that time. The said Separation Agreement was duly executed by defendant and myself on

7. I have compared the signature on the copy of the Separation Agreement, dated attached to the Findings, and know them to be the signatures of the defendant and of myself.

8. I request that the Separation Agreement, dated , , attached to the Findings, be incorporated by reference in the judgment of divorce, and shall survive it, but shall not merge in it.

9. I have never brought any other action for divorce or annulment of this marriage, and on information and belief, defendant has never brought such action in any Court of competent jurisdiction against me. There is no other action now pending between the parties.

10. Defendant, our respective attorneys, and I, entered into a written Stipulation in which defendant appeared by his attorney, , and agreed to waive his rights and time to answer my complaint and stipulated to place this matter on the uncontested matrimonial calendar, immediately. This Stipulation containing the waiver, is to merge into the judgment and not to survive it.

11. I have taken all steps solely within my power to remove any barriers to defendant's remarriage.

WHEREFORE, I ask that this Court award me judgment against defendant, dissolving the bonds of matrimony between us and incorporating the terms and conditions of the parties' Separation Agreement, dated , 19 , but not merging that Separation Agreement into the judgment, and that I have such other and further relief as to this Court may seem just and proper.

____

Sworn to before me this
day of , 19 .

____

AFFIRMATION OF REGULARITY BY ATTORNEY

SUPREME COURT OF THE STATE OF
NEW YORK: COUNTY OF

, Plaintiff,	:	*AFFIRMATION OF REGULARITY BY ATTORNEY*
-against-	:	Index No.
, Defendant.	:	

I, the undersigned attorney at law, duly admitted to practice law in the State of New York, respectfully show:

I am associated with , attorneys for the plaintiff herein.

This is a matrimonial action.

The Summons with Notice was personally served upon the defendant herein within the State of New York, as appears by the Stipulation submitted herewith.

Defendant has appeared by .

Defendant has agreed, by the annexed Stipulation dated 19 , to waive his rights and time to answer plaintiff's Verified Complaint and to place this matter on the uncontested matrimonial calendar immediately.

WHEREFORE, I respectfully request that this action be placed on the undefended matrimonial calendar for trial.

I state, under the penalties of perjury, that the statements herein made are true, except as to such statements as are based on information and belief, which statements I believe to be true.

Dated: New York, New York
, 19

____

STIPULATION

SUPREME COURT OF THE STATE OF
NEW YORK: COUNTY OF

_______________________________________x

,	:	Index No.
Plaintiff,	:	*STIPULATION*
-against-	:	
,	:	
Defendant.	:	

_______________________________________x

IT IS HEREBY STIPULATED AND AGREED by and between the parties and their respective attorneys, as follows:

1. Defendant acknowledges that he was personally served with a Summons for Divorce in the above captioned matter in the State of New York, and hereby appears by his attorney, .

2. Defendant waives his rights and time to answer plaintiff's complaint and stipulates to place this matter on the uncontested matrimonial calendar, immediately.

3. The parties acknowledge that they have entered into a written Separation Agreement, dated , 19 which resolves all questions of maintenance, equitable distribution of the marital assets, counsel fees, and all other issues previously existing between them, with regard to this action.

4. The parties agree that the Separation Agreement, dated , 19 , shall be incorporated, by reference, in the judgment of divorce, and shall not merge in it but shall survive it.

5. The parties acknowledge that neither is in the military service of the United States or of the State of New York.

6. The parties agree that venue may properly be laid in the Supreme Court of the State of New York, County of New York.

Dated: New York, New York
, 19

PLAINTIFF

DEFENDANT

ATTORNEYS FOR PLAINTIFF

ATTORNEYS FOR DEFENDANT

STATE OF NEW YORK)
) ss.:
COUNTY OF NEW YORK)

On the day of , 19 , before me personally came , to me known and known to me to be the individual described in and who executed the foregoing Stipulation and duly acknowledged to me that he executed the same.

NOTARY PUBLIC

STATE OF NEW YORK)
) ss.:
COUNTY OF NEW YORK)

On the day of , 19 , before me personally came , to me known and known to me to be the individual described in and who executed the foregoing Stipulation and duly acknowledged to me that she executed the same.

NOTARY PUBLIC

NOTICE OF APPEARANCE

SUPREME COURT OF THE STATE OF
NEW YORK: COUNTY OF

,	:	
Plaintiff,	:	*Notice of Appearance*
-against-	:	Index #
,	:	
Defendant.	:	

NOTICE is hereby given that defendant , enters his [her] appearance in the above captioned case and that defendant has retained the undersigned as his attorney, and demands that a copy of the Complaint, and all the papers in this action, be served on defendant's attorney at the address listed below.

Dated:

Defendant's Attorney
(Attorney's address)

DECISION

At a Special Term of the New York State Supreme Court, at the County Court House, County, on , 19 .

PRESENT:

HON. ______________________________
Special Referee

______________________________x

, : Index No.

Plaintiff, : *DECISION*

-against- :

, :

Defendant. :

______________________________x

FINDINGS OF FACT

Upon reading and considering the papers submitted on 19 , I find that:

1. Residence is established, as required by Domestic Relations Law, Section 230;

2. The parties were married on , in New York City, , by a , and the marriage has not been terminated previously;

3. Process has been served to give personal jurisdiction of the defendant, and the defendant has appeared but, by Stipulation dated

19 , waived his rights and time to answer plaintiff's Complaint;

4. There are no children of this marriage;

5. The defendant's ability to pay and the needs of the plaintiff have been fully resolved by the Separation Agreement, dated , which was duly executed and acknowledged by the parties; and appropriate provisions for equitable distribution of marital property and maintenance have been made therein;

6. The parties entered into a Separation Agreement, dated , which was duly executed and acknowledged by the parties, and which is annexed. The Separation Agreement shall be incorporated, by reference, in the Judgment, and shall survive it, and shall not merge in it;

7. The grounds for divorce, which are alleged in the Verified Complaint, in accordance with Domestic Relations Law, Section 170, Subdivision 2, were proved as follows: During recent years of the marriage, defendant has shown less and less affection towards plaintiff, and various arguments ensued. The parties have not cohabited with each other as husband and wife for a period commencing on or about December of 1984. During said period of time, defendant has not cohabited with plaintiff as husband and wife, despite plaintiff's willingness to do so. Defendant's refusal to engage in marital relations with plaintiff, as aforesaid, was not caused or provoked by any conduct on the part of the plaintiff and was without plaintiff's consent. Upon information and belief, defendant has not suffered any disability which would prevent defendant from cohabiting with plaintiff. The conduct of defendant, as aforesaid, constitutes an abandonment of plaintiff by defendant.

CONCLUSIONS OF LAW

Plaintiff is entitled to a judgment dissolving the marriage, on the grounds set forth in Domestic Relations Law, Section 170, Subdivision 2.

These Findings of Fact and Conclusions of Law constitute my decision, as required by CPLR 4213 (b).

Dated: New York, New York
, 19 .

____
Special Referee

DIVORCE JUDGMENT

At a Special Term, Part 5A, of the New York State Supreme Court, at the County Courthouse, County, on , 19 .

PRESENT:

HON. ______________________
Special Referee

______________________x

, : Index No.

Plaintiff, : *DIVORCE JUDGMENT*

-against- :

, :

Defendant. :

______________________x

This action was submitted to me for consideration on , 19 .

The defendant was served within this state, personally, on , 19 .

Plaintiff presented a verified complaint.

Defendant appeared by his attorneys, , and by Stiuplation, dated 19 , waived his rights and time to answer the complaint.

The Court accepted written proof of nonmilitary service.

NOW, on motion of , Esqs., attorneys for plaintiff, it is:

ORDERED AND ADJUDGED that:

1. Plaintiff shall have judgment that the marriage of the parties is dissolved on the evidence found in the Findings of Fact and Conclusions of Law, in accordance with the Domestic Relations Law, Section 170, Subdivision 2:

2. The Separation Agreement, dated 19 , and duly executed and acknowledged by the parties, which is annexed to the Findings of Fact, shall be incorporated, by reference, in the Judgment, and shall survive.

3. Pursuant to the Separation Agreement, both parties waive all rights to support or maintenance from the other party.

4. That the Agreement entered into between the parties on , a copy of which is on file with the Court, shall be incorporated in this Judgment and shall survive and shall not be merged in this Judgment.

5. Each party may resume the use of his or her premarriage surname or any other former surname, to wit: .

ENTER:

____

Special Referee

____

Clerk

How To Accomplish a Foreign Divorce

Certain jurisdictions such as Nevada, the Dominican Republic, and Haiti have become popular places for consummating uncontested divorces. This is so due to the quickness and ease with which a divorce can be obtained there.

In order to accomplish the divorce in one of these foreign—out of state or out of country—jurisdictions, a separation agreement should first be entered into by the parties. Then, one of the parties will have to travel to the foreign jurisdiction to establish residence. Generally, the residence requirement encompasses a very short amount of time. The other party should sign an affidavit which authorizes the first party to appear on his or her behalf as his or her attorney in fact. Thereafter, the first party would file all documents necessary for the granting of a divorce in that foreign jurisdiction and would offer the separation agreement to the foreign court for findings as to the rights and liabilities of the parties re child custody, visitation and support, alimony, property division, etc. By proceeding in this manner, the divorce and divorce related determinations (i.e., custody, support, etc.) should be valid in the home state.

CONTESTED SEPARATION, ANNULMENT, AND DIVORCE ACTIONS

Preparation for Trial

Pre-trial disclosure. Just as in any action, the first task that you should undertake is the disclosure of information re the action which is held by your adversary.

Net Worth Statement. In this regard in the divorce action, you should initially obtain the other party's net worth statement and review his or her assets and liabilities. A sample demand for net worth statement follows.

SAMPLE DEMAND FOR NET WORTH STATEMENT

Court of
State of
________________________________x

,	:	*Demand For Net Worth Statement*
Plaintiff,	:	
		Index No.
-against-	:	
,	:	
Defendant.	:	

________________________________x

SIRS:

PLEASE TAKE NOTICE that plaintiff demands that within twenty (20) days the defendant serve on , attorney for plaintiff, a sworn statement of his (her) net worth. This statement will detail all of defendant's income and assets and will list all assets transferred during the last three years. This request is made pursuant to Domestic Relations Section 236. The defendant shall use the form outlined in NYCRR Section 202.16. Failure to comply with DRL Section 236 is punishable by the penalties listed in Civil Practice Law and Rules Section 3126.

Dated:

Yours, etc.
Attorneys for Plaintiff

To: Attorneys For Defendant.

Interrogatories. Then, you should serve a set of written interrogatories on your adversary. These written interrogatories will simply be questions pertaining to employment history, current employment, assets, liabilities, ownership of personal and real property, business interests, pension plans, etc. A sample set of interrogatories follows.

SAMPLE INTERROGATORIES

SUPREME COURT OF THE STATE OF
NEW YORK: COUNTY OF
______________________________________x

,	:	Index No.
Plaintiff,	:	*INTERROGATORIES*
-against-	:	
,	:	
Defendant.	:	

______________________________________x

S I R S :

The plaintiff/defendant requests that the plaintiff/defendant answer under oath, in accordance with Article 31 of the CPLR and DRL Section 236(B)4, the following interrogatories:

NOTE. Questions concerning marriage and children are with relation to the other party to this suit, unless otherwise indicated. When a question or part of a question is inapplicable, indicate same.

1. State your full name, age, residence and post office address, home telephone number, social security number, business address, and business telephone number.
2. State:
   Whether any dependent child is in need of unusual or extraordinary medical or mental care or has special financial needs, giving a detailed description of the condition which requires such care and the treatment required, to the best of your knowledge, including, but not limited to:
   - (i) Nature of treatment;
   - (ii) Name of treating doctor(s) and/or other professionals;
   - (iii) Cost of care; and
   - (iv) Estimated length of treatment.
3. As to yourself, state:
   (a) Your present health;
   (b) Whether you have any need of unusual or extraordinary medical care or special financial needs;

(c) Educational background, giving all schools attended and years of attendance, any degrees conferred, as well as any special training courses and employment skills;
(d) If you were married at the time you attended school or any special training course, indicate whether your spouse contributed to the cost of your education and/or support and living expenses and the amount thereof, and, if your spouse did not contribute to these, who paid for your education and/or support and living expenses;
(e) If you own or have been granted a license to practice any profession in this or any other state, indicate the nature of such license(s) and the approximate monetary value of such license.

4. If you have any disability(ies) which at any time renders or rendered you unable to perform work or limits or limited your ability to perform work, either now, in the past, or in the future, state:
(a) The nature of the disability(ies)
(b) The name and address of each treating physician for the past ten years for said disability(ies);
(c) The frequency of said treatment;
(d) The cost of said treatment;
(e) The nature of said treatment;
(f) The method of payment for said treatment, including the name of the payor.
Attach any medical reports concerning this disability(ies)

5. If you are not currently residing with your spouse, state the names, ages, and relationship to you of those persons with whom you reside at the above address, either on a permanent or periodic basis.

6. If your present primary residence is owned by you, state:
(a) the date the residence was acquired;
(b) from whom it was purchased;
(c) the purchase price;
(d) the downpayment;
(e) The source of the downpayment, showing contribution by both spouses, as well as any other persons;
(f) the amount of the original mortgage(s);
(g) the amount of the mortgage(s) as of the date of the service of the summons in this action;
(h) the amount of the mortgage(s) at the present time if different from (g) above;
(i) the name and address of the mortgagee(s) and the mortgage number(s), if any;
(j) the market value of the property at the time of the service of the summons in this action;
(k) the present market value of the property, if different from (j) above;

(l) the tax basis on the house when acquired;
(m) the adjusted tax basis on the house at the time of the service of the summons in this action;
(n) the current adjusted tax basis, if different from your answer to (m) above;
(o) the nature and dollar amount of any liens and/or encumbrances on the property not indicated in a previous answer(s);
(p) the current assessed valuation assigned the property for real property taxation purposes.
Attach copies of closing statement of purchase, deeds, and a copy of any appraisals obtained, as well as the most recent bill or bills for real estate taxes.

REAL ESTATE

7. If you have any interests in any real property other than indicated in the previous section for each such piece of real property, state:
(a) Street, address, County, and State where the property is located;
(b) Type of property, deed references, and your interest in the property (full or partial; type of tenancy; restraints on alienation);
(c) Zoning of the property;
(d) Date same was acquired;
(e) From whom it was purchased;
(f) The downpayment;
(g) The source of the downpayment, showing the contribution by both spouses and others;
(h) The amount of the original mortgage(s);
(i) The purchase price;
(j) The amount of the mortgage(s) as of the date of the service of the summons in this action;
(k) The amount of the present mortgage(s);
(l) The name and address of the mortgage(s) and the mortgage number(s), if any;
(m) The present market value of the property;
(n) The nature and dollar amount of any liens and/or encumbrances on the property which are not listed in a previous answer;
(o) The names and addresses of all co-owners and their interest in the property;
(p) Itemize all operation expenses, including but not limited to taxes, mortgage payments, insurance, fuel oil, gas, electric, water, and maintenance;
(q) The present assessed valuation assigned the property for real property taxation purposes;
(r) The exact nature and extent of your interest, if not listed in question 11(b);
(s) The tax basis on the property when acquired;

(t) The adjusted tax basis at the time of the service of the summons in this action;
(u) The names and mailing addresses of all tenants and occupants and the annual and/or monthly rental paid by each, and their relationship to you, if any.
(v) The source and amount of any income produced by the property, if not previously indicated.
Attach copies of the closing statement of purchase, deeds, and a copy of any appraisals obtained.

8. If you have sold or otherwise disposed of any real property in which you have had an interest within the last ten (10) years, state for each property, in detail, the same information as asked in interrogatory 11 above.
Attach copies of each closing statement of purchase and deed.
9. If you have executed any contracts to buy or sell real property within the last ten (10) years, indicate the location of the property, terms of the sale, and whether you were the purchaser or seller, and the name of the other party or parties.
Attach a copy of each such contract.
10. If you are the holder of any real property not disclosed in a previous interrogatory, state for each:
(a) The type of such property (whether real or personal);
(b) The location of such property;
(c) The date acquired;
(d) The net monthly rental to you from each piece of property;
(e) The gross monthly rental to you from each piece of property;
(f) The present value of such property.
11. As to your present employment, state:
(a) Name and address of your employer;
(b) Type of work performed, position held, and nature of work or business in which your employer is engaged;
(c) Amount of time you have been employed in your present job;
(d) Hours of employment;
(e) Rate of pay or earnings, setting forth, specifically, your gross and net average weekly salary, wages, commissions, overtime pay, bonuses, and gratuities.
Attach copies of all evidence of above payments, including pay stubs, W-2 forms, etc., for the past year.
12. State what benefits your employer provides for you and/or your family, inclusive, but not limited to, all of the following. Include a brief description of the benefit and whether your family is a beneficiary of the particular benefit.
(a) Health insurance plan;
(b) Life insurance coverage;
(c) Pension, profit sharing, or retirement income program;
(d) Expense and/or drawing accounts;

(e) Credit cards (include reimbursement for business expenses placed on your personal credit cards);
(f) Disability insurance coverage;
(g) Stock purchase options;
(h) Indicate whether you are required to pay for all or any part of the benefits listed in this interrogatory and the amount of those payments and/or contributions.

13. Describe any other property or other benefit furnished to you as a result of your present employment.
14. State and itemize all deductions taken from your gross weekly earnings or other emoluments, including but not limited to taxes, insurance, savings, loans, pensions, profit sharing, dues, and stock options.
15. State if you have an employment contract with any company, corporation, partnership, and/or individual at the present time or at any time during the last three (3) years. If there is or was such a contract of employment, state the terms thereof, or if written, attach a copy hereto.
16. As a result of your employment at any time during the marriage, are you entitled to receive any monies from any deferred compensation agreement? If so, for each agreement state:
(a) the date such agreement was made, or if in writing, executed. If written, attach a copy.
(b) the parties making or executing such agreement.
(c) the amount you are to receive under such deferred compensation agreement and when you are to receive same. Attach copies of evidence of such payment.
17. State whether you have filed Federal, State and/or Local income tax returns during the last five (5) years. If so, indicate the years during which the same was filed and whether Federal, State, or Local.
Attach copies of all such returns filed during the past five (5) years, if available.
18. State in which bank, savings account, or checking account your salary or other compensation is deposited, giving the name of the bank, branch, and account number. If said salary, bonus or other compensation checks are cashed or negotiated rather than deposited, indicate the name and branch of the bank(s) where said checks are regularly cashed or negotiated.
19. State whether you have received or are receiving any form of compensation, monetary or otherwise, from any work and/or services performed for other individuals, companies, corporations and/or partnerships outside the business in which you are regularly engaged. If so, state:
(a) the name and address of the individual, company, corporation and/or partnership from whom you are receiving or have received such compensation during the last five (5) years;
(b) the amount of the compensation received;

(c) the nature of the services rendered by you for said compensation. Attach copies of all 1099 forms, "miscellaneous income" received as a result of such work and/or services during the last five (5) years.

20. State whether your salary or other compensation will increase during the next year and/or contract period as a result of any union contract and/or employment contract or as the result of any regular incremental increase, or as a result of a promotion which you have received which is not yet effective.
21. Itemize all income benefits and other emoluments not already included in your answers to any preceding interrogatories, including but not limited to any other sources of income such as pensions, annuities, inheritances, retirement plans, social security benefits, military and/or veterans' benefits, lottery prizes, bank interest, dividends, showing the source, amount, and frequency of payment of each. Indicate whether each income benefit and/or emolument is taxable or nontaxable.

SELF-EMPLOYMENT

22. If you are self-employed or conduct a business or profession as a sole proprietor, partner or corporation, state the type of entity it is. (For purposes of this question, a corporation includes any corporation in which your interest exceeds twenty percent (20%) of the outstanding stock.)
23. If a partnership, list the names and addresses of all partners, their relationship to you, and the extent of their interest and yours in said partnership. Attach copies of any partnership agreements in effect at any time during the last five (5) years and all partnership tax returns filed during this period.
24. If a corporation, list the names and addresses of all directors, officers, and shareholders and the percentage of outstanding shares held by each. If any of the foregoing people are related to you, indicate the relationship. Attach copies of all corporate tax returns filed by the corporation during the past five (5) years.
25. State whether you have had an ownership interest(s) in any other corporation, partnership, proprietorship, or limited venture during the course of the marriage. If so, state:
    (a) the nature of such interest(s);
    (b) the market value of such interest(s);
    (c) the position held by you with respect to such interest(s), including whether you were an officer, director, partner, etc.;
    (d) the date of acquisition of your interest(s) and the market value of said interest(s) when acquired;
    (e) the value of said interest(s) on the date of your marriage if such interest(s) was acquired before your marriage;

(f) the date of termination of your ownership interest, if terminated;
(g) the total sales price of the business enterprise, if terminated;
(h) the amount of the compensation received by you and the form of the compensation if other than cash or negotiable instrument as a result of the sale and/or transfer;
(i) the terms of each agreement of sale;
(j) the income received by you from the business during the last year prior to the sale and/or transfer.

26. State for each business, partnership, corporation, and/or other enterprise in which you have an interest, the following:
(a) The amount of your contribution to the original capitalization;
(b) The amount of your contribution for any additional capitalization or loans to the business entity;
(c) The source from which monies were taken for capitalization and/or loans;
(d) Market value of the business entity at the time of the service of the summons in this action;
(e) The present market value of the business if different from (d) above;
(f) The market value of your share of the business entity at the time the summons was served in this action if different from (d) above;
(g) The present market value of your share of the business entity if different from (f) above;
(h) The market value of your share of and the total value of the business entity at the time of your marriage;
(i) Amount of loans and/or reimbursement of capitalization paid you by the business entity, at any time during the past five (5) years, stating the amount received, the date received, and the disposition of the proceeds;
(j) The present amount maintained in the capital account;
(k) The name and address of all banks in which the business has or has had, during the past five (5) years, checking and/or savings accounts, the account numbers of each account, the amount presently contained in each, the amount contained in each at the time of the service of the summons and the amount contained in each six months prior to the commencement of the action. If an account was closed prior to the time periods mentioned in this question, that is, prior to six months before the action was commenced, indicate the amounts in each such account for a three-year period prior to the closing account. State the destination of the amount that was in the account when closed;
(l) The total value of your capital account;
(m) Total value of all accounts receivable;
(n) The dollar value of all work in progress;
(o) The appreciation in the true worth of all tangible personal assets over and above book value;
(p) The total dollar amount of accounts payable;
(q) Set forth a list of all liabilities.

27. State the name and address of the following:
    (a) All personal and business accountants during the last five (5) years;
    (b) All personal and business or corporate attorneys consulted during the past five (5) years (except those attorneys representing you in this action);
    (c) Your stockbroker(s)
    (d) Your investment advisor(s).

PERSONAL ASSETS

28. Itemize all bank and savings and loan association accounts, time deposits, certificates of deposit, savings clubs, Christmas clubs, and checking accounts in your name or in which you have an interest presently or had had an interest during the past five (5) years, stating for each:
    (a) The name and address of each depository;
    (b) The balance in those accounts as of the date of the service of the summons in this action;
    (c) The present balance;
    (d) The balance four (4) months prior to the service of the summons in this action;
    (e) If there is any difference between your answers to (b), (c) and (d) above, specify when the withdrawals were made, who received the benefit of the withdrawals, who made the withdrawal and where the proceeds of the withdrawals went;
    (f) The name and address in which each account is registered, account numbers, and the present location and custodian of the deposit books, check registers, and/or certificates.
    Attach copies of the monthly statements of such accounts for the past five (5) years and copies of savings account books or savings books and check registers.
29. State whether you have a safe deposit box either in your name individually, or in the name of a partnership or corporation, and to which you have access, stating the following:
    (a) The location of the box and box number;
    (b) The name in which it is registered and who, in addition to yourself, has access to the box;
    (c) List the contents of said box in which you or your spouse claim an interest.
30. If you have any cash in your possession or under your control in excess of One Hundred Dollars ($100), specify:
    (a) The amount of the cash;
    (b) Where it is located;
    (c) The source of said cash.

31. For each vehicle of any nature in which you have any interest, including, but not limited to, automobiles, trucks, campers, mobile homes, motorcycles, snowmobiles, boats, and/or airplanes, state:
    (a) The nature of each vehicle;
    (b) Your interest therein;
    (c) The name in which the vehicle is registered;
    (d) The make, model, and year of each;
    (e) The price paid and the date acquired;
    (f) The principal operator of the vehicle since its purchase, if any;
    (g) The present location of the vehicle;
    (h) The name and address of any co-owners;
    (i) The present value of said asset.
32. State whether you own any horses or other animals with a value in excess of Two Hundred Fifty Dollars ($250). If so, state:
    (a) The date of purchase and purchase price of same;
    (b) The type of animals;
    (c) The market value at the time of the service of the summons in this action;
    (d) The present market value if different from (c);
    (e) The names and addresses of any co-owners and the percentage of their interest in same.
33. List all household goods, furniture, jewelry, and furs with a value in excess of Two Hundred Fifty Dollars ($250), in which you have an interest, stating for each:
    (a) The nature of each;
    (b) Your interest therein;
    (c) The price paid and the date acquired;
    (d) The present value of the asset;
    (e) Whether the asset is "marital property" or "separate property." If you claim the asset is separate property, state your reasons therefor.
34. State whether you own or have an interest in any collections or hobbies, including but not limited to art, stamps, coins, precious metals, antiques, books, and/or collectibles with an aggregate value in excess of Two Hundred Fifty Dollars ($250). If so, state:
    (a) The nature of each;
    (b) Your interest therein and the interest of any co-owners. Also state the names and addresses of all co-owners;
    (c) A complete itemization of each such collection, showing the price paid and the date acquired of each such collection. An "element" means a unit which is capable of being sold by itself;
    (d) The present value of each element of the asset;
    (e) The value of each such element, if owned prior to the marriage, at the time of the marriage;
35. State whether you are receiving or entitled to receive any royalty income. If so, state:

(a) The basis for such income, including the nature of any composition, copyright, work, or patent from which such income arose;
(b) The amount of such income yearly during the past five (5) years;
(c) The terms of any agreement in relation to such composition, work, patent, etc.
Attach copies of any royalty statement or other invoice, verifying such income.

36. State whether you have any legal actions pending for money damages, or whether you are entitled to receive any legal settlements or insurance recoveries. If so, state:
(a) The amount of money which you are demanding in your pleadings, or to which you are entitled as an insurance recovery or legal settlement;
(b) The court in which the action is or was pending, the caption of the case, and the index or docket number;
(c) Whether any other person has an interest in the insurance recovery, legal settlement, or pending action and, if so, the nature of their interest, name, and address;
(d) The circumstances resulting in your becoming entitled to the insurance recovery or legal settlement, or commencing the legal action.

37. State whether you have any HR10 or IRA arrangements. If so, state:
(a) The date of the creation of each such plan;
(b) The amounts contributed by you or on your behalf to each such plan;
(c) The current value of your account under each such plan.

38. State whether you are entitled to receive, or have received during the past five (5) years, any gambling awards or prizes, indicating the nature thereof, amount, when you are to receive same, and the date you became entitled to the award or prize.

39. State the names and addresses of all persons who owe you money not indicated in previous interrogatories. Also state as to each:
(a) The amount thereof;
(b) When said sum is due;
(c) The nature of the transaction that entitled you to receive the money and when the transaction took place.

STOCK ASSETS

40. Itemize all shares of stock, securities, bonds, mortgages and other investments, other than real estate not revealed in previous interrogatories, stating for each:
(a) Identity of each item as to type and amount of shares;
(b) Whose name they are registered in and the names of any co-owners and their interest therein;
(c) The source of the monies from which you purchased the item;

(d) The original price of each item;
(e) The market value at the time of the service of the summons in this action;
(f) The present market value of each item if different from (e) above;
(g) The amount of any dividends and/or other distribution received on a yearly basis;
(h) The present location and custodian of all certificates or evidences of such investments.
Attach hereto monthly statements of these securities for the past five (5) years.

41. State whether any of the shares of stock owned by you and listed in any of your previous answers to interrogatories is subject to any cross purchase or redemption agreement. If so, state:
(a) The date of such agreement;
(b) The parties to such agreement;
(c) State the event that will bring about the sale or transfer under the agreement;
(d) The sales price under such agreement.

42. Itemize all shares of stock, securities, bonds, mortgages, and other investments, other than real estate and business entities previously listed in your name or in which you have an interest, which you have sold in the last five (5) years, stating for each:
(a) The identity of each item as to type and amount of shares;
(b) Whose name they were registered in and the names of any co-workers and their interest therein;
(c) The source of the monies from which you purchased each item;
(d) The original price of each item and date of purchase;
(e) The market value at the time of the service of the summons in this action;
(f) Amount of dividends or other distribution received on a yearly basis;
(g) The date each was sold or transferred;
(h) To whom each was sold or transferred;
(i) The amount received for each such sale or transfer;
(j) The disposition and destination of the proceeds of said sale;
(k) If applicable, the value of each such item at the time of your marriage.

43. Itemize all shares of stock, securities, bonds, mortgages, and other investments which you have purchased but which is held nominally by third persons, stating for each:
(a) The manner in which the person is holding said investment;
(b) Identity of each item as to type and amount of shares;
(c) Whose name they are registered in and the names of any co-owners and their interest therein;
(d) The source of the monies from which you purchased each item;
(e) The original price of each item;
(f) The market value at the time of filing of the services of the summons;

(g) The present market value of each item;
(h) The value, if applicable, at the time of your marriage;
(i) The present location and custodian of all certificates or evidence of such investments;
(j) The amount of dividends or other distribution received on yearly basis. Attach hereto monthly statements of these securities for the past three (3) years.

44. Are you the holder of any mortgages, accounts receivable, notes, or other evidence of indebtedness not indicated in your answer to previous interrogatories? If so, for each such instrument, state:
(a) The type of instrument;
(b) The date of maturity of such instrument;
(c) The amount of interest payable to you yearly under such instrument;
(d) The nature of the sale or transaction (including the type of merchandise sold) from which the said instrument arose;
(e) The date the instrument was acquired by you.

45. State whether you have any money invested in any business ventures not answered in previous interrogatories, and for each such investment state:
(a) The nature of such investment;
(b) Your share of the interest therein;
(c) The original cost of such investment and the source of monies used for said investment;
(d) Amount of income yielded from the said investment;
(e) The present value of said investment.

46. If, during the course of your marriage, you have received any inheritances, state:
(a) From whom you inherited;
(b) The nature and amount of the inheritance;
(c) The disposition of any of the assets of the inheritance, tracing them, if possible, to the time of the service of the summons in this action;
(d) The value of the inheritance at the time of the service of the summons in this action;
(e) The present value of the inheritance.

47. State whether you expect to receive any inheritance. If so, state:
(a) From whom you expect to inherit;
(b) The nature and amount of inheritance.

48. State whether you have, during the last five (5) years, sold or transferred any interest in personal property valued in excess of Two Hundred Fifty Dollars ($250) and for each such sale or transfer state:
(a) Description of the property;
(b) The date of the sale or transfer;
(c) The method of transfer;
(d) The name and address of each purchaser or person receiving title;

(e) The amount received for said transfer or sale;
(f) The disposition or proceeds of said sale or transfer.

49. State whether you have made any gift of any money and/or personal property to friends, relatives, or anyone else during the past five (5) years of a value in excess of Two Hundred Fifty Dollars ($250). If so, state:
(a) The name and address of said person and the relationship of that person to you;
(b) The nature and value of the gift or the amount of money given;
(c) The date each gift was given;
(d) The reason for such gift.

TRUSTS

50. State whether you are the grantor, beneficiary, or holder of a power of appointment for any trust created by you, the members of your family, or any other persons or corporations. If so, state:
(a) The date of the trust instrument;
(b) The name of the settlor of each trust;
(c) The name of the beneficiary(ies) of each trust;
(d) The present amount of each trust corpus;
(e) The amount of the trust corpus at the time of the service of the summons in this action;
(f) The amount of the trust corpus at the time of your marriage, if applicable;
(g) Any restrictions on alienation to which such corpus is subject;
(h) The terms of each trust instrument;
(i) The income earned by the trust during the past five (5) years.
If there is a trust instrument, attach a copy hereto. If the trustee has rendered an accounting during the past five (5) years, attach a copy hereto.

51. List any and all property, assets, or things of a value in excess of Two Hundred Fifty Dollars ($250) which you hold in trust for anyone, stating for each:
(a) A description of the property, its location, and the name and address of the person for whom you hold same;
(b) The conditions or terms of the trust, including whether or not you are paid any commissions or other compensation for holding such property;
(c) How such property was acquired by you and whether you paid any part of the consideration therefor.

52. List any and all property or things of value of every nature or kind with a value in excess of Two Hundred Fifty Dollars ($250) which is held in trust for you or which is in the care and/or custody of another person, corporation, or entity for you, stating for each:
(a) The description of the property, its location, and custodian;
(b) The name and address of the trustee, if different from above;

(c) The conditions or terms of the trust;
(d) How such property was acquired and who paid the consideration therefor;
(e) The original cost;
(f) The value at the time if different from (f) above.
(g) The present value if different from (f) above.
Attach copies of any trust instruments or writings evidencing the above.

INSURANCE

53. List each life insurance policy, annuity policy, disability policy, or other forms of insurance not disclosed in a previous interrogatory, stating for each:
(a) The name and address of the insurance company;
(b) The policy number;
(c) Type of policy;
(d) The name and address of the owner of the policy;
(e) The name and address of the present beneficiary of the policy;
(f) If there has been a change of beneficiary in the last five (5) years, give the date of each change and the name and address of the former beneficiary;
(g) The date the policy was issued;
(h) The face amount of the policy;
(i) The annual premium and the name and address of the person paying the premium currently and for the past five (5) years;
(j) The cash surrender value of said policy;
(k) If any loans have been taken out against the policy, the date of each such loan, the person making such loan, the amount of the loan, and the purpose for which the proceeds were utilized;
(l) If said policy has been assigned, the date of the assignment, the name and address of each assignee;
(m) The present custodian of the policy;
(n) If any policy is supplied by an employer, whether it is a condition of employment and under what conditions it terminates.

54. State whether you have surrendered, transferred, or in any way terminated any form of insurance policy for the last five (5) years. If so, state:
(a) The name and address of the insurance company;
(b) The number of the policy;
(c) The type of policy;
(d) The name and address of the last and/or current owner of the policy;
(e) The name and address of the last and/or present beneficiary of the policy;
(f) The face amount of the policy;

(g) The cash surrender value of the policy at present or just prior to its being surrendered, transferred, or terminated;
(h) The person transferring, surrendering, or terminating said policy;
(i) If any cash was realized from the said transfer, termination, or surrender, the amount realized and for what purposes were the proceeds used.

PENSION AND DISABILITY

55. State whether you are entitled to any pension, profit sharing, and/or retirement plan. If so, state:
(a) The nature of the plan;
(b) The name and address of the entity or person providing the plan;
(c) Whether your interest in the plan is vested and, if not, the date and conditions under which the plan will vest;
(d) Whether the plan is contributory or noncontributory and, if contributory, the amount you contributed during the marriage;
(e) The amount you earned in the plan during the marriage;
(f) If you have the right to withdraw any monies from the plan, how much money you may withdraw and when;
(g) If you have withdrawn and/or borrowed any monies from the plan, indicate when and how much was borrowed and whether the money must be returned or repaid;
(h) If there are any survivor benefits, and give a brief description thereof.
Attach copies of all writings concerning the plan(s) in your possession or which are readily available from your employer or pension payor.
56. If you are entitled to any disability benefits, state:
(a) The nature of the disability;
(b) The dollar amount of the award;
(c) The date of payment of the award;
(d) Whether there are any survivor benefits, giving a brief description thereof;
(e) Whether any benefits or awards are presently being claimed by you, litigated, or are being reviewed, indicating the amount thereof if not included above.

EXPENSES

57. Itemize your average monthly expenses in detail. If any of the expenses include support of any other person outside your immediate family, set forth the name and address of such person, and the portion of each expense attributable to each such person supported. (*NOTE:* All weekly expenses must be multiplied by 4.333 to obtain the monthly expense.) If certain expenses are paid by your employer, spouse, or another party, so indicate by footnoting.

BUDGET EXPENSE

FOOD ________
CLOTHING ________
MORTGAGE(S) ________
PROPERTY TAXES ________
RENT ________
UTILITIES ________
FUEL OIL ________
TELEPHONE ________
GARBAGE COLLECTION ________
WATER ________
PLUMBING ________
ELECTRICIAN ________
DOCTORS ________
DENTISTS ________
ORTHODONTISTS ________
PSYCHIATRISTS ________
ATTORNEYS' FEES ________
DRUGS ________
HAIR CARE ________
DRY CLEANERS ________
LAUNDRY ________
VETERINARIAN ________
NEWSPAPERS ________
MAGAZINES ________
INSURANCE ________
  HOMEOWNERS ________
  RENTER'S ________
  AUTOMOBILE ________
  LIFE ________
  HOSPITALIZATION ________
  FLOATERS ________
  UMBRELLA ________
  DISABILITY ________
  OTHER ________
PROFESSIONAL DUES ________
CLUB DUES ________
BABYSITTERS ________
DOMESTICS ________
BURGLAR ALARM
  SERVICE ________
VOLUNTARY/COURT ORDERED
  SUPPORT ________

PAST-DUE INSTALLMENT
OBLIGATIONS
  CREDIT CARDS ________
  AUTO LOANS ________
  PERSONAL LOANS ________
  CHARGE ACCOUNTS ________
CREDIT CARD FEES ________
EDUCATION ________
ALLOWANCES ________
SPORTS & HOBBIES ________
DANCING LESSONS ________
MUSIC LESSONS ________
SPORT LESSONS ________
AUTO EXPENSES ________
  GAS ________
  MAINTENANCE ________
  COMMUTATION ________
  PARKING ________
  LIC. & REG. ________
  TRANSPORTATION ________
CAMP ________
HOUSEHOLD
  IMPROVEMENTS ________
HOUSEHOLD REPAIRS ________
APARTMENT
  MAINTENANCE ________
GARDEN MAINTENANCE ________
POOL MAINTENANCE ________
TERMITE/PEST SERVICE ________
TREE SERVICE ________
WATER SOFTENER ________
FURNITURE &
  APPLIANCES ________
FURNISHINGS ________
CONTRIBUTIONS ________
VACATIONS ________
CHRISTMAS TIPS ________
CHRISTMAS PRESENTS ________
CHANUKAH PRESENTS ________
OTHER PRESENTS ________
ENTERTAINMENT ________
MISC. SPENDING MONEY ________
EMERGENCIES ________
CABLE TV ________

DETAIL ALL OTHER EXPENSES BELOW:

____

____

____

____

____

____

____

____

____

____

TOTAL MONTHLY EXPENSES ______________

58. State whether anyone contributes to your support, income, and/or living expenses who has not been included in a previous interrogatory. If so, state:
    (a) Their names and addresses;
    (b) Their relationship to you;
    (c) The amount of support, income, and/or living expenses received by you during the last five (5) years and the frequency of said support, income, and/or living expenses;
    (d) The reason for said support;
    (e) The nature of said support.

LIABILITIES

59. Set forth a list of all credit card balances, stating:
    (a) The name of the obligor;
    (b) The total amount due at the present time and the amount due at the time of the service of the summons in this action;
    (c) The minimum monthly payment;
    (d) The name in which the card is listed, and the names of all persons entitled to use the card;
    (e) The exact nature of the charges for which the money is owed, if known;
    (f) Who incurred such obligation?
    Attach copies of all credit card statements for the past twelve (12) months.
60. Set forth, in detail, any outstanding obligations, including mortgages, conditional sales contracts, contract obligations, promissory notes, and/or government agency loans not included in your answers to any previous interrogatories, stating for each:
    (a) Whether the obligation is individual, joint, or joint and several;
    (b) The names and addresses of each creditor;
    (c) The form of the obligation;
    (d) The date that the obligation was incurred;
    (e) The consideration received for the obligation;
    (f) The description of any security given for the obligation;
    (g) The amount of the original obligation;
    (h) The date of interest on the obligation;
    (i) The present unpaid balance of the obligation;
    (j) The date and the amount of each installment repayment due;
    (k) Particularly itemize the disposition of the funds received for which the obligation was incurred.
61. List all judgments outstanding against you and/or your spouse not included in your answer to a previous interrogatory, and for each state:
    (a) The names of the parties and their respective attorneys;
    (b) The courts in which same were entered and the index or docket number assigned to each case;
    (c) The amount of each judgment.

62. If there is a wage execution, judgment, and/or order to pay out of income and earnings, state:
    (a) How much is taken from your earnings each week;
    (b) The obligor;
    (c) The balance due.
63. State the nature of any lien or security interest not indicated in your answer to a previous interrogatory to which any of the assets listed by you in previous interrogatories are subject, indicating for each:
    (a) The name and address of the holder thereof;
    (b) The holder's relationship to you;
    (c) The amount and frequency of the payments you make thereon;
    (d) The balance due.

EQUITABLE DISTRIBUTION

64. State the names and addresses of any and all expert witnesses you plan to have testify and the nature or areas of their expertise. Attach hereto copies of all written reports rendered to you by any such proposed expert witnesses. If the report is not written, supply a summary of any oral report rendered to you.
65. If any money, property and/or asset was acquired by you either before the marriage or after the service of the summons in this action, state for each with a value in excess of Two Hundred Fifty Dollars ($250) the following:
    (a) The nature of the property;
    (b) The date acquired;
    (c) The source of the acquisition;
    (d) Your interest therein;
    (e) The present market value.
66. If any other money, property, or assets described in the above interrogatory was sold, transferred, and/or disposed of, state for each:
    (a) The manner of disposition;
    (b) The date of disposition;
    (c) To whom sold, transferred, or disposed and their relationship to you;
    (d) The amount received.
67. List all gifts received by you from your spouse with a value in excess of One Hundred Dollars ($100), giving for each:
    (a) The date received;
    (b) The nature of the gift;
    (c) The market value of the gift.
68. List all gifts received by you from your family, your spouse's family, or any other party or entity, with a value in excess of One Hundred Dollars ($100), giving for each:
    (a) The name of the donee and the relationship of the donee to you;

(b) The date received;
(c) The nature of the gift;
(d) The market value of the gift.

MISCELLANEOUS

69. If you have prepared a financial statement of your assets and liabilities, either individually or for any business in which you have an interest within the past five (5) years, state:
(a) The dates of all such statements;
(b) The name and address of the person, firm, company, partnership, corporation, or entity for whom same were prepared;
(c) The name and address of all persons who worked on the preparation of such statements.
Attach copies of all said statements.

70. State what counsel fees you have paid and/or agreed to pay for services rendered in this action.

71. State whether you have made application for any loans with any lending institutions, individuals, companies, and/or corporations during the past five (5) years. If so, state for each:
(a) The name and address of the lending institution, individual, company, or corporation;
(b) The date of the application
(c) The amount of the loan
(d) Whether your application was approved or denied.
Attach a copy of all such loan applications.

72. List any contributions made by you in excess of Two Hundred Fifty Dollars ($250) within the past five (5) years. For each such gift or contribution, state:
(a) The name of the donee;
(b) The reason for the contribution;
(c) The amount of such contribution.

PLEASE TAKE NOTICE that a copy of such answers must be served upon the undersigned within twenty (20) days after the service of these interrogatories.

Dated: New York, New York
19 .

TO:

Depositions. If the use of interrogatories does not adequately meet your disclosure needs, all is not lost. You may request that depositions—commonly referred to as examinations before trial—be taken of your adversary and his witnesses. Depositions are simply the sworn testimony of a witness taken upon questioning not in open court which is subsequently reduced to written form and signed and sworn to by the witness.

Once you decide to take depositions you should send a notice to take such to your adversary and the witness or witnesses to be examined. You, as the attorney for your client, can personally sign the notice and you need not petition a court in order to take the deposition. The notice should state where and when the depositions will be taken. Also, it is important that you request the production at the deposition site of any documents which might be helpful to you. This would include data pertaining to savings accounts, income taxes, life insurance policies, pension plan, etc. A sample notice to take depositions follows.

SAMPLE NOTICE TO TAKE DEPOSITION

SUPREME COURT, STATE OF
NEW YORK: COUNTY OF

________________________________x

, :

Plaintiff, : *NOTICE TO TAKE DEPOSITION*

Index No.

-against- :

, :

Defendant. :

________________________________x

SIRS:

PLEASE TAKE NOTICE that the testimony of will be taken before , a person who is not an attorney, or employee of an attorney, or a party or prospective party in this action, and isn't a person who would be disqualified to act as a juror because of interest in the event or consanquinity or affinity to a party on , at , at , as to evidence necessary to prepare the (defense) (prosecution) of the instant action.

Such examined person will also produce the following at the examination:

1. All federal, state, and city income gift and estate tax returns and declarations prepared or filed by, or on behalf of, or affecting the plaintiff and for all businesses, trusts, partnerships, corporations, and ventures in which the plaintiff has or has had an interest, together with the IRS W-2 and 1099 forms, schedules, and worksheets thereof and all papers, documents, and records pertaining to any changes, audits, and amendments thereof, beginning January 1, 19 .

2. Records of all earnings, receipts of money, and income (tax reportable or not) in which the plaintiff has or has had an interest, including but not limited to salaries, wages, drawings, commissions, capital distributions, bonuses, sick pay, disability payments, pensions, retirement funds, reimbursed and reimbursable expenses, partnership and venture income, and distributions, beginning January 1, 19 .

3. All passbooks, certificates, statements, and records for all funds in which the plaintiff has or has had an interest and held by a financial savings and loan or banking institution, securities broker or investment house, irrespective of whether the same are current or closed, beginning January 1, 19 .

4. All checkbook stubs, cancelled checks, bank statements, duplicate deposit tickets for all accounts for which the plaintiff has or has had the power to sign checks (singly or with others) or in which the plaintiff has or has had an interest, irrespective of whether said accounts are current or closed, beginning January 1, 19 .

5. Stock certificates, bonds, notes, and other securities and statements and other records pertaining thereto (including but not limited to tax-exempt securities and foreign securities) purchased, sold, traded, or held by the plaintiff (singly or with others) or in which the plaintiff has or has had an interest, beginning January 1, 19 .

6. All current, past, and proposed employment contracts and agreements for providing services of the plaintiff to any businesses, partnership, corporation, or other entity, beginning January 1, 19 .

7. Deeds, contracts, closing statements, leases, agreements, and papers of all kinds pertaining to real property and interests in real property in which plaintiff has considered acquiring or has or has had a beneficial or legal interest, whether in the State of New York or elsewhere, beginning January 1, 19 .

8. Statements, agreements, tax returns, records, and papers relating to all retirement, profit sharing, pension and savings plans and tax shelters and any form of deferred income in which the plaintiff has or has had an interest, irrespective of whether the same are current or terminated.

9. All policies of insurance covering the plaintiff or in which the plaintiff has an interest, including but not limited to life, endowment, annuity, homeowner's, theft, floater, liability, and automobile policies, and all records showing payment of premiums and values thereof, irrespective of whether the same are current or expired.

10. Records and papers relating to all loans and obligations for which the plaintiff has or has had a direct or contingent liability, including but not limited to loan and credit applications and financial statements, disclosure statements, and payment records.

11. Records, vouchers, and statements for all charge accounts in plaintiff's name or for which the plaintiff has or has had charge privileges or any liability since January 1, 19 .

12. Records of family and personal living expenses of the plaintiff since January 1, 19 .

13. Records of the plaintiff's business expenses and other liabilities and obligations since January 1, 19 .

14. Copies of all balance sheets and operating statements of any corporation in which the plaintiff was or is an owner or holder of more than ten percent of the outstanding stock or was or is entitled to more than ten percent of the profits or revenues.

15. Copies of all balance sheets and operating statements of any partnership, venture, business, or syndicate in which the plaintiff was or is a partner or member of has or has had an interest.

16. With respect to such corporation, partnership, venture, business, or syndicate:

a) All agreements to which the plaintiff is a party;

b) All loan, personal expense, disbursement, and receipt accounts with respect to the plaintiff.

17. All records of membership in and contributions to any charity organization or association, including but not limited to private and professional clubs or associations, in which the plaintiff has or has had any interest or dealings.

18. Current and expired passports of the plaintiff.

19. All documentation to show the identification, the acquisition, and the cost, as well as the present values, of each item of marital and of separate property of the plaintiff.

20. Leases, bills, and any other records pertaining to any safe deposit box and other depositories in the name of the plaintiff, singly or with others, or for which the plaintiff has power of entry.

21. Personal and business diaries of the plaintiff and any business in which she has an interest.

Dated:

Yours, etc.

Attorney for

TO:

Once everyone is gathered for the taking of the deposition, an impartial person not a party to the action will be responsible for swearing the witness or witnesses and recording the testimony of the witnesses. Typically, the testimony is transcribed by a stenographer and is not written long handed. The impartial person mentioned above and the stenographer are selected by the party that desires the taking of the deposition.

Counsel for both sides will be permitted to examine the witness. The questions posed will be in the same vein as the questions asked in written interrogatories. (See sample written interrogatories supra in this chapter.)

After all questions have been asked of the witness, the questions and answers will be reduced to written form by the stenographer. Also, any exhibits referred to by the witness during the taking of the deposition will be attached to it. The witness will then swear to and sign the document before a notary public. Also, the impartial person before whom the deposition was taken shall certify on the deposition that the witness was sworn by him and that the deposition is a true record of the testimony given by the witness. Then this impartial person shall file the deposition in the court where the case in question is to be tried. Each party involved in the case is entitled to a copy of the deposition.

Discovery and Inspection of Documents. After you have conducted the deposition, and assuming that you have pursuant to questions posed during deposition ascertained the existence of other documents which you would like to review, you should request discovery and inspection of these documents. It is important that during the taking of the deposition you ask questions which will identify the documents you are seeking with particularity. When you draft your demand for production of documents you don't want an overly broad description which will result in your obtaining a truckload of documents to sift through. For example, if you want a particular written statement given by a witness to a particular individual you should be able to request that you be provided with Mr. X's statement to M or Y on Z date dealing with ABC material. You should never put yourself in a position where you have to ask for all statements given by Mr. X to obtain the statement that interests you.

Important. In attempting to obtain disclosure, you should not be afraid to use means outside the statutorily enumerated disclosure devices, e.g., interrogatories and depositions. For example, assume that you wish to see certain checking records and your adversary feels that they are not a proper subject for disclosure. Make a motion to the court requesting that the records be turned over to you. Courts are very liberal in allowing disclosure. This is particularly true if you can establish that disclosure will expedite the case. The court will only disallow disclosure if it is overly burdensome and unfair. A sample motion and order for records follows.

SAMPLE MOTION AND ORDER FOR RECORDS

SUPREME COURT OF THE STATE OF
NEW YORK: COUNTY OF

,	:	
		NOTICE OF MOTION
Plaintiff,	:	
		Index No.
-against-	:	
,	:	
Defendant.	:	

SIRS:

PLEASE TAKE NOTICE THAT, upon the annexed affidavit of , sworn to on , 19 , and upon all pleadings and proceedings heretofore had herein, the undersigned will move the Court on at , or as soon thereafter as counsel can be heard, for an order requiring that , furnish with .

Dated: , 19 .

Yours, etc.

Attorney for

SUPREME COURT OF THE STATE OF
NEW YORK: COUNTY OF

____________________________________x

, :

Plaintiff, :

-against- , :

, :

Defendant. :

____________________________________x

AFFIDAVIT IN SUPPORT

Index No.

State of ,

ss.:

County of ,

I, , being duly sworn, depose and state that:

1. I am the attorney for , in the instant action which was brought for , by service of a summons and complaint on , on .
2. I am familiar with all the facts and circumstances surrounding this action.
3. The following documents (list) are required because .
4. No request for the instant relief has been previously made.

WHEREFORE, your deponent respectfully requests that the court issue an order directing to furnish with the following documents (list)

____

PRESENT HON.____________

SUPREME COURT OF THE STATE OF
NEW YORK: COUNTY OF

,	:	*ORDER*
Plaintiff,	:	Index No.
-against-	:	
,	:	
Defendant.	:	

The by has moved this Court for an order to compel , to furnish with (list documents) because

NOW on motion of , attorneys for , it is:

ORDERED that the motion is granted and that furnish with .

E N T E R: ____________________

Bill of Particulars. A bill of particulars is a written demand for certain information. By a bill of particulars you can obtain additional data re your adversary's pleadings (i.e., the formal allegations of your adversary as to his or her claims). Generally, in a contested matrimonial action, you can only obtain by a bill of particulars information pertaining to the ground or basis for the divorce. Thus, if the ground for the divorce is adultery, you are only entitled to information pertaining to the adulterous acts. However, if for example your client is the husband and the wife is pursuing a claim for necessaries, your bill of particulars can request information pertinent to this claim.

A sample demand for a bill of particulars follows.

SAMPLE DEMAND FOR A BILL OF PARTICULARS

SUPREME COURT OF THE STATE OF
NEW YORK: COUNTY OF
_________________________________x

,	:	*Demand For A Bill of Particulars*
Plaintiff,	:	Index No.
-against-	:	
,	:	
Defendant.	:	

_________________________________x

SIRS:

PLEASE TAKE NOTICE THAT defendant, by his (her) attorney , demands that you serve such attorney within 10 days from this date a verified bill of particulars, pertaining to the allegations in the complaint filed in this action, as follows:

FIRST CAUSE OF ACTION

(List data you desire as to the first claim made by your adversary in his or her complaint. Do the same for second and third and other claims made by your adversary.)

Dated:

Yours, etc.

Attorney for Plaintiff

TO:

Attorney for Defendant.

Bill of particulars not technically a disclosure device. A bill of particulars is not technically one of the vehicles to be used to obtain the disclosure of information prior to a divorce trial. However, since certain information [such as that relevant to the grounds or basis for the divorce] cannot ordinarily be obtained prior to trial by the ordinary disclosure devices of interrogatories and depositions, but can be obtained by a bill of particulars, bill of particulars are frequently used to obtain the disclosure of information prior to the divorce trial. Ordinary disclosure devices can only be used to obtain information relating to the ground or grounds for the divorce if the court that has jurisdiction over the particular divorce action has allowed them to be used for such purposes. Such is rare.

Expert witnesses. Expert witnesses are a crucial part of any divorce proceeding. You may need several experts to value all the property in question and to adequately prepare Janet's case. For example, if Tony has his own business, you should have an accountant to value the business. Also, you should have one expert to place a value on real estate and another to value any pension plans.

It is imperative that you contact your experts immediately after you decide to commence a contested divorce proceeding. Crucially, you should have your experts in hand before you utilize any disclosure devices. You should permit the expert to guide you in the preparation of the case by informing you as to what he or she needs to help win the case. (Some examples of what the experts may need are Tony's tax returns; stocks, bonds, and certificate of deposit held by him; assets held by his business, income generated by the business and debts of the business; Tony's pension plans; and when the family home was bought, the price paid for it, any improvements made to the house, and the cost of the improvements.) Then, and only then, you should utilize the various disclosure devices available to seek the information desired by the expert.

Application for legal fees and expert witness fees. The court should be petitioned via motion for fees to be levied against your adversary if your client justifiably has difficulty in paying these fees. These fees may include your attorneys fees, accountant fees, actuary fees, etc.

Each individual from whom you receive a bill for fees should execute his or her own affidavit for fees. The affidavit should detail the area of expertise, the individual's experience, his or her fee schedule, the exact nature of the work that is to be done, the complexity of the work, the time to be expended, and the total fee requested.

SAMPLE MOTION FOR FEES

A sample motion for fees follows. This motion includes a sample affidavit by an attorney for legal fees.

SUPREME COURT OF THE STATE OF
NEW YORK: COUNTY OF

________________________________x

,	:	*Notice of Motion*
Plaintiff,	:	Index No.
-against-	:	
,	:	
Defendant.	:	

________________________________x

SIRS:

PLEASE TAKE NOTICE THAT upon the annexed affidavit of , sworn to on , and upon all pleadings and proceedings heretofore had herein, the undersigned will move this court, on behalf of , on at , or as soon thereafter as counsel can be heard for an order awarding interim attorney fees in the sum of $, with leave to apply for the sums that may be justified.

Dated:

Yours, etc.

Attorneys for

TO:

SUPREME COURT OF THE STATE OF
NEW YORK: COUNTY OF

,	:	*Affidavit*
Plaintiff,	:	Index No.
-against-	:	
,	:	
Defendant.	:	

State of)
ss.:
County of)

I, , being duly sworn, depose and state that:

1. I am the attorney for and write this affidavit to support motion for an interim award of attorney's fees.
2. The award should be based upon the nature and complexity of the case; the type of service to be rendered, the value of that service and the time to be spent for that service; and the respective ability to each party to pay for the counsel fees incurred during the litigation.
3. The nature of the case is
4. The services to be rendered are . The time to be spent on these services . The value of this time is because (state why). The fee arrangement that I have entered into with my client is .
5. My client is unable to pay any further sums for my counsel fees because . My client's spouse can pay all legal fees in this action because .

WHEREFORE, in view of the above, I respectfully request that this court issue an order mandating that be required to pay an interim award of counsel fees in the sum of $.

____

Subpoening witnesses. Subpoenas should be issued to every witness that you intend to call on Janet's behalf. This is true whether or not the witness in question is cooperative. By issuing a subpoena, you need not depend on the witness' good will for his or her appearance in Court.

You, as the attorney, can personally sign the subpoena sent to the witness. After you sign it, you should have someone over the age of eighteen (18) personally hand it to the witness. A sample subpoena and affidavit of personal service of subpoena follows. It should be noted that if the subpoena merely requires the production of the person subpoenaed, it is simply called a *Subpoena*. If in addition to the person subpoenaed certain documents are requested, it is called a *subpoena duces tecum*.

SAMPLE SUBPOENA AND AFFIDAVIT OF SERVICE

Court, County of
State of New York

,	:	*Subpoena Duces Tecum*
Plaintiff,	:	Index No.
-against-	:	
,	:	
Defendant.	:	

TO

GREETING:

YOU ARE commanded to appear before on , at , (P.M.) (A.M.) and at any recessed or adjourned date to testify as a witness, and bring with you at sucn time and place the following records.

Your failure to meet the requirements outlined in this subpoena shall subject you to contempt of court whereby you will be liable for a penalty up to $50 and all damages sustained to the person on whose behalf the subpoena was issued. WITNESS, Honorable ____________, a judge of ____________ Court, this ____________ day of ____________, 19 .

____
Attorney for

Court, County of
State of New York

,	:	*Affidavit of Service*
Plaintiff,	:	Index No.
-against-	:	
,	:	
Defendant.	:	

STATE OF NEW YORK)
) ss.:
COUNTY OF)

I, , being duly sworn, depose and state that:

1. I am not a party to the instant action and am over the age of eighteen (18) years.
2. I personally served a copy of the attached subpoena upon , (give description of person), on , at , by handing the subpoena to him.

____

Subscribed and sworn to
before me this day of .

____

It should be noted that in subpoening government agency records a subpoena issued by you may not suffice. A subpoena issued by a court may be required.

In obtaining a subpoena from a court a motion must be made for that subpoena and the court must sign an order that the subpoena be issued. Then, the court will sign the subpoena and you can have someone over eighteen (18) personally serve it.

A sample motion for a subpoena follows. Also a sample order is annexed which orders that a subpoena be issued. The subpoena itself can be in the form annexed above in this sub-section. The only difference would be that the court would sign the subpoena and not you, and the final clause in the subpoena would be "WITNESS, My hand, this day of , 19 " instead of "WITNESS, Honorable , a judge of Court, this day of , 19 ."

SAMPLE MOTION AND ORDER FOR ISSUANCE OF SUBPOENA

Court, County of
State of

---x

, : *Notice of Motion*

Plaintiff, : Index No.

-against- :

, :

Defendant. :

---x

SIRS:

PLEASE TAKE NOTICE THAT, upon the annexed affidavit of , sworn to on , 19 , and upon all pleadings and proceedings heretofore had herein, the undersigned will move this court on at , or as soon thereafter as counsel can be heard, for a subpoena which compels the production of

Dated: , 19

Yours, etc.

____

Attorney for

To:

Court, County of
State of

________________________________x

, : *Affidavit in Support*

Plaintiff, : Index No.

-against- :

, :

Defendant. :

________________________________x

STATE OF)
) ss.:
COUNTY OF)

I, , being duly sworn, depose and state that:

1. I am the attorney for in the instant action, which was brought for by service of a summons and complaint on (person served) on (date served).
2. I am familiar with all the facts and circumstances surrounding this action.
3. The following witnesses and documents are required. (detail individual or individuals required and documents). Such is true because (detail why individuals and documents required).
4. No request for the instant relief has been previously made.

WHEREFORE, your deponent respectfully requests that this court issue a subpoena directing to appear at the trial of the instant action and produce (list documents).

____

PRESENT HON.

Court of the State of

, County of

______________________________x

, : *Order*

Plaintiff, : Index No.

, :

Defendant. :

______________________________x

The by has moved this court for an order to compel production of (list witness) and (list documents) for the reason that (list grounds).

NOW, on motion of , attorney for , it is

ORDERED that the motion is granted and that a subpoena be issued by this court directing (person) to appear before , on , at , and at any recessed or adjourned date to satisfy as a witness and bring such time and place the following records.

ENTER:

____

Preparing witnesses for trial. Just as is true in the preparation of any trial, it is important that you thoroughly prepare the witness who will testify. This should include an in depth review of not only the testimony they plan to offer at trial, but any other statements or testimony they have given. A checklist on how to prepare your witness for trial follows.

CHECKLIST RE HOW TO PREPARE WITNESSES FOR TRIAL

1. Review in detail with witness testimony to be given by witness. Assure that no stone is left unturned.
2. Review with witness all statements given by him re case.
3. Ask witness to thoroughly explain any inconsistencies in statements given by the witness.
4. Instruct witness as to crucial issues in case and what place his testimony has.
5. Instruct witness on weak points in his testimony and that he should attempt to sidestep questions posed by your adversary to exploit these weaknesses.
6. Instruct witness as to strengths in his testimony and that he should attempt to inject this helpful testimony into answers to questions posed by your adversary.
7. Encourage witness not to discuss his testimony with anyone except you, and that he certainly should not on his own discuss his testimony with your adversary or other witnesses.

The Trial

Pre-trial memorandum. As you enter the trial phase of your case, you should prepare and submit to the court a pre-trial memorandum. This document outlines what you intend to prove in the case. It sets forth the facts of the case as urged by your client and applies the relevant law to these facts.

The pre-trial memorandum should be written the same way that you would write your appellate brief, i.e., the document that you would submit on appeal to an appellate court to attempt to show that the trial court improperly made a decision adverse to your client. The sample brief that appears infra in the "Appeal" section of this chapter will help you construct a pre-trial memorandum for your client.

Jury or nonjury. It is rare to have a jury involved in a matrimonial case. Indeed, in most jurisdictions [e.g., N.Y.] the Jury may only make findings re the case of action and all other findings will be made by the court.

Thus, unless your case presents the extraordinary situation where you feel that the jury will be more sympathetic than a court to your cause of action claims, you should conduct your entire case before a judge alone. Such an extraordinary situation will exist if your client's husband has on many occasions viciously beaten her, has abandoned her and the children for another woman, and your client is not only a perfect mother but the picture of sweetness, goodness, and innocence.

Opening statement. If you are appearing before a jury, the opening statement may be helpful to outline to them what you intend to prove. Otherwise, in the judge alone scenario, the opening statement is not important. This is true because the judge, with his experience and legal training, will quickly grasp what you intend to and are trying to prove.

Direct examination. Direct examination of your witness, particularly your client, is extremely important in a matrimonial action. In a matrimonial action, more than in any other action, credibility of your witnesses is the key to success.

This is true because judges and juries are aware that the emotional strain that bears on the parties in a matrimonial action and the personal interest that they have in the outcome of the action, may bear on their ability to tell the truth. If your client and/or other witnesses for your side give any indication that they are not credible, the court or jury may assume that emotional strain and/or personal interests has affected their ability to give truthful testimony. The court or jury may then discount their version of the fact and accept the version provided by the other side.

In view of the foregoing, you should take every step necessary to assure that the judge favors the version of the facts given by your client and your other witnesses. In this vein, you should be sure that while your witnesses are testifying their appearance, demeanor, and candor are beyond reproach. To insure this you should have them dress neatly and conservatively, and if a witness is a woman, have her avoid extravagant hair styles and too much makeup. Also, you should instruct your witness to sit up straight on the witness stand, avoid "wise-guy" remarks, look the attorney for the other side directly in the eye when he or she is asking questions, and treat the other attorney with respect. Finally, you should instruct your witness to review his/her testimony before testifying and testify as accurately and correctly as possible.

Important. Additionally, once your client's testimony is completed, your attempt to enhance his or her credibility does not end. You should make every effort to keep the client under control. At all costs you should prevent the client from expressing displeasure with the testimony given by your adversary's witnesses. To do this you should strongly instruct your client to sit quietly and make no facial expressions or verbal comments during anyone's testimony. You should tell the client to take notes as to what he or she finds objectionable in the testimony of the adversary's witnesses so that his or her tensions are directed toward the writing pad rather than the opposition witness.

Introduction of evidence. Matrimonial actions involve the introduction into evidence of literally hundreds of documents. These documents include checks, bank statements, profit and loss statements, inventory records, credit card receipts, insurance policies, premium plans, offering plans for co-ops, etc.

Matrimonial actions are largely paper cases with the introduction of a myriad of documents. Therefore, it is important that you pay close attention to the organization of your data and keep good track of the exhibits. This is particularly true since you will want to utilize the data gleaned from the exhibits in your post-trial memorandum.

To organize your data and keep track of your exhibits, you should construct an outline which lists precisely what you intend to prove with your documents and the evidence that you will use to prove it. You should also make a detailed list of the exhibits that you intend to use in the case and what each exhibit proves. Then, you should organize the exhibits in the sequence that you intend to offer them at trial. As certain exhibits are offered into evidence, place the exhibit number on your exhibit sheet and check off the point on the outline that it proves. Make sure to keep a copy of the exhibits offered into evidence for your future use.

Cross-examination. Cross-examination will be a primary tool that you will utilize to arrive at the truth as to the issues facing you in the divorce action. You should review the witnesses' testimony with them and force them to remember the details of events to which they testified during direct examination. Then, at a further point during the cross-examination, you should force the witnesses to again relate the details of a particular event. If the witness is not telling the truth, he or she might relate different details and you have adversely affected that witness' credibility. When a witness has not lived through a particular event and is fabricating it, it is difficult for that witness to explain the event the same way in detail on several occasions.

Further, in cross-examining a particular witness you should not review the story he has to say in chronological order. By skipping from different chronological points of the story, you might cause the witness to forget what he previously stated if he is not telling the truth. A witness who has not lived through a particular event and has fabricated it by attempting to memorize details as to it, will have difficulty in repeating the story if he cannot report it in chronological order.

Due to the fact that credibility is so crucial in the matrimonial action, it behooves you not to conduct too much cross-examination, or ask questions where you are not fairly sure of the answers you will receive. By conducting too much cross-examination through too many questions, or asking questions where you are not fairly sure of the witness' response, you may permit the witness to explain and harmonize certain contradictory testimony. Also, you might allow him to emphasize a certain point he has made during direct examination and which hurt your case. For example, if a witness has testified that your client is a bad mother, an extensive attempt by you to have the witness testify as to some of the good motherly qualities of your client may permit the witness to constantly harp on the witness' behalf that your client is a bad mother.

In cross-examining witnesses you should never ask open-ended questions such as "Why did you do that?", or "Could you explain your answer?" As is the case with asking too many questions, by doing the above you may permit the witness to harmonize his or her contradictory testimony or emphasize a point that hurt you during the witness' direct testimony. What you do not want to do is rehabilitate an opposition witness whose credibility has been compromised. Your questions should call for short and to the point replies or "Yes" or "No" replies.

Next, when it comes to the cross-examination of expert witnesses, you should be very circumspect. You will achieve this by only questioning the expert in areas where you are well versed and reasonably certain of what answer you will receive from the expert. Don't try to outsmart a witness in his own field unless you know that you can score a point. You can only score a point if you are extremely familiar with a particular area testified to by the expert and can force him to admit that his testimony is not entirely correct. For example, if an expert testifies that a particular piece of residential property is $100,000 and you have knowledge that similar properties near that residential property are valued between $100,000 and $200,000 where you want to show that the value of the property in question is worth more than $100,000, query the expert to establish the $100,000 to $200,000 value and thereby score a point for your side.

Closing statement. In the closing statement you should emphasize what you feel are the important issues in the case and why the fact finder should rule in your favor. For example, if custody of the children is a key issue, you should tell the Court why your client should have custody. Your client may be the perfect mother and your adversary (i.e., the husband) may have beaten them. You should emphasize the above to the court so as to have a custody ruling in your favor. Other key issues may be alimony or child support, share of marital property and right to reside in the marital residence. You should also emphasize what you feel are the crucial reasons for a favorable ruling for your client in these areas.

In addition, the closing statement might be an opportune time for you to advise the court what your client would like to have happen to certain property. In other words, after the court determines what share your client will receive of the marital property, you may want the court to include certain specific property in your client's marital share. In the vein you should inform the court what findings are important and what findings are not important re the actual distribution of the property. For example, your client may want certain dishes and a particular painting he or she loves and you should inform the court of these facts. Some courts will be interested in your narrative re the resolution of these property issues, while others will not be interested. This occurs because some courts are merely interested in satisfying as equitably as possible the parties' desires, as to what share of the marital property each party should receive, while other courts will take an interest in meeting the parties' desires as to what specific property should be included in a particular marital share.

Post-trial memorandum. After the case has been completed, you should submit a post-trial memorandum. Where your case has been complex, this document can be extremely important.

The post-trial memorandum allows you to marshall the evidence in the way which will be most beneficial to your client. You can amass the various exhibits in a way which will place your client in the best light.

You can apply the law to the facts in a manner which will benefit your client's cause. For example, if the law of your state is that the client's desires as to custody is a paramount concern in determining which parent shall obtain custody of the child, and the child in your case desires to reside with your client, argue that the child should remain with your client because the state law favors giving custody to the parent with whom the child desires to reside.

Also, in the post-trial memorandum, an attack can be made on the other side's credibility and the position taken by opposition expert witnesses.

Once you have discussed the evidence presented in the case, you should recommend the conclusions that you wish the Court to draw. For example, you should recommend that custody of the children be given to your client, (if that is what your client desires), that alimony and child support be provided in a certain amount, and that your client receive a certain percentage of the marital property. There are times when the conclusions are not very clear. This is your last opportunity to tie everything together and convince the Court that it should follow the conclusions you recommend.

Next, you should also incorporate in your post-trial memorandum a statement concerning what items of property should go to whom. For example, you might wish to recommend that certain rugs, jewelry, and furniture should be given to your client, and that a particular coin collection or painting be given to your adversary. Even if such a statement was prepared prior to trial, it is a good idea to reiterate your client's wishes so that the Court will order a just distribution of the property.

Warning. It should be emphasized that in advocating your client's position in the post-trial memorandum, you should not be overly zealous in arguing that position. For example, don't ask the court to rule in all respects for your client. By attempting to obtain too much, the court will view you as unreasonable. The court will be less likely to take cognizance of your arguments and your client may obtain less than he or she should obtain.

Important. It should also be noted that you must not expect to win your case with your post-trial memorandum. If you have not convinced the court prior to the post-trial memorandum that your client's cause is the more just, it is unlikely that you will convince the court of such in the post-trial memorandum.

SAMPLE POST-TRIAL MEMORANDUM

A sample post-trial memorandum follows. This sample will show you how a post-trial memorandum is organized and put together. From this sample you will be able to effectively create a post-trial memorandum for your client.

Court of the State of
; County of

——————————————————x

Rita Jones, :

Plaintiff, :

-against- :

Harvey Jones, :

Defendant. :

——————————————————x

Defendant's Post-Trial Memorandum

____
Attorney for Defendant

TABLE OF CONTENTS

Page No.

Court of the State of
; County of

---x

Rita Jones,		:
	Plaintiff,	:
-against-		:
Harvey Jones,		:
	Defendant.	:

---x

Factual Background

Rita and Harvey Jones were married on , fifteen years ago. They have no children.

On , Rita Jones commenced an action for divorce against Harvey Jones, by serving a summons upon him. Thereafter, a certified complaint was served on defendant, who in turn served a verified answer and counterclaim on plaintiff. On , plaintiff obtained an order for temporary maintenance directing defendant to pay the maintenance of $500 per week and awarding plaintiff's attorney $5,000 in interim counsel fees. (see Exhibits A-D.)

On , defendant sought and received from this court an order granting defendant reverse summary judgment in favor of plaintiff and bifurcating the financial aspects of this matter. The judgment of divorce was filed with the County Court on . (See Exhibit E.)

Defendant is the President of X, Y, Z corporation. He runs this company with his father. Defendant also separately owns X company. (See Minutes of Proceedings pp 50-100.)

Defendant contends that his ownership interest in X, Y, and Z company represents separate property and concedes that his interest in X company is marital property. (See Exhibits F, G.)

Defendant owns 50% of the shares in X, Y, and Z corporation. He received all of these shares on , prior to his marriage to plaintiff, as a gift from his father. (See Exhibits H-J, Minutes of Proceeding pp 162-212.)

SEPARATE VS. MARITAL PROPERTY

Statute X of our state defines separate property as "Property acquired by gift or before marriage."

Here, all of defendant's interest in X, Y, Z corporation was acquired not only by gift but prior to marriage. Thus, it should certainly be considered to be separate property.

Defendant created X corporation after his marriage to plaintiff. Thus, it is considered that his interest in this corporation constitutes marital property.

The next question involves what, if any, portion of the appreciation in the value of X, Y, Z corporation should be considered marital property. In *Kreb* v. *Kreb* 21 A.D.2d 34 (5th Dept. 1984), it was determined that if a wife participates in any significant fashion in a business owned by the husband prior to the marriage, the appreciation in the value of the business will be considered marital property.

Here, plaintiff testified that she worked 40 hours a week at the X, Y, Z corporation and that she brought much business to that corporation. (Minutes of Proceedings pp 341-382.) However, defendant and his father testified that the plaintiff never worked for the X, Y, Z corporation. Also, Mr. A, Mr. B, and Miss C, employees of the corporation, testified that plaintiff never worked at or for the corporation. (Minutes of proceeding pp 541-632.)

In view of the above, plaintiff's contention that she participated in a significant fashion in the X, Y, Z corporation, should be discounted. None of the increase in the value of the X, Y, Z corporation since plaintiff's marriage to defendant should be considered to be marital property.

Defendant concedes that the marital house and house furnishings are marital property and that all money in the joint savings accounts owned by defendant and plaintiff is marital property.

VALUATION OF ASSETS

Mr. S testified as an expert for plaintiff that defendant's interest in X, Y, Z corporation at the time of defendant's marriage to plaintiff was one million dollars and that the interest was worth two million dollars at the time of the commencement of the divorce action. Mr. S also testified that the value of X corporation at the time of the commencement of the divorce action was three million dollars. (Minutes of Proceeding pp 821-888.)

The primary method employed by Mr. S to arrive at these figures concerns the price earnings rate. In substance, the method requires that the earnings for each corporation be multiplied by a certain specific number, which in this case he determined to be 20 for the X, Y, Z corporation at marriage, 50 for the X, Y,

Z company at the time of the divorce action was commenced, and 25 for the X company at the time the divorce was commenced. He then multiplied the multiplier by the earnings of the company in question at the relevant point in time (Minutes of proceeding pp 831-842.)

Mr. T on the other hand, testified for defendant that the X, Y, Z corporation was worth $500,000 at the date of marriage of one million dollars at the time of the commencement of the divorce action, and that the value of the X corporation at the time of the commencement of the divorce action was two million dollars. Mr. T incorporated in depth and detailed analysis to arrive at his figures. The exact manner by which he arrived at his figures is shown in Exhibits K-S.

In sum, Mr. S based his evaluations on general and vague values while Mr. T based his evaluations on detailed analysis. Thus, the evaluation figures submitted by Mr. T should be accepted by this court.

Defendant and plaintiff have stipulated that the marital residence and house furnishings was worth one million dollars at the date of the commencement of the divorce action and that there was $500,000 in their joint savings account at the time of the commencement of the divorce action.

EQUITABLE DIVISION BETWEEN THE PARTIES

The criteria for the equitable distribution of property are detailed in X Statute at Section Y. In the instant case, plaintiff's entitlements to the marital property would be based on subdivision A of Section Y which involves plaintiff's contributions as a house maker and income earner.

Here, as previously discussed, plaintiff's contention that she worked in the X, Y, Z corporation should be discounted and a finding should be made that plaintiff brought no income to the marital unit.

Moreover, while defendant claims that she took care of all matters involving the running of the household, (Minutes of Proceeding pp 42-51), this claim should be discussed. Miss E testified that she worked for plaintiff and defendant since the date of their marriage. Miss E pointed out that she did everything as to running the household to include cooking the meals, doing the shopping, paying the bills, doing the cleaning, etc. (Minutes of the Proceeding, pp 814-981.)

In using the foregoing, plaintiff's contributions were indeed at best modest. She is only entitled to a distribution award amounting to 25% of all marital property. In this case, such a distributive award is $875,000.

MAINTENANCE PAYMENTS

Statute A declares that maintenance payments will be made by one of the parties in a divorce action to the other party only when that other party will experience a standard of living after divorce substantially below that experienced before divorce.

Here, the distributive award of $875,000 to plaintiff will allow her to live at a standard of living similar to that which she experienced before divorce. Considering that present interest rates are 12%, plaintiff can obtain for her distributive award a yearly income of approximately $100,000. Patently, plaintiff would not experience a standard of living substantially below that which she presently enjoys and thus, she should not be entitled to any maintenance payments.

SPECIFIC DISTRIBUTION OF PROPERTY

Defendant has spent much time and energy to create X corporation. Indeed, this corporation was his life's work. Thus, he asks that this court allow him to keep this asset and that plaintiff's distributive share be taken from the other assets.

COUNSEL FEES

Pursuant to an order of this court, plaintiff has received $5,000 in counsel fees from defendant with leave to plaintiff to seek further fees at trial, if warranted. Plaintiff has already received $100,000 in temporary maintenance payment and will receive a substantive distributive award. Under these circumstances, it is fair and equitable that each party pay his or her own counsel fees with no further contribution from the other.

CONCLUSION

Under all of the circumstances of this case, X, Y, Z corporation should be deemed to be separate property and plaintiff should have no claim to it or any claim to the appreciation in value of defendant's ownership interest in it. All of the marital property should be equitably divided with plaintiff recovering 25% of the values of such property. Plaintiff should receive no interest in X corporation and her distribution share should come from the other marital assets. Plaintiff, who has already received $100,000 in maintenance payments should receive no further such payments. Each party should pay his or her own legal and expert witness fees with no contribution by the other party.

Dated:

Respectfully submitted,

____

Attorney for Defendant.

Decision. The court's decision is a memorandum which directs counsel for each side to submit a proposed judgment. In any case which is complex, the court's decision is usually reserved. Once you have received the decision, you should read it carefully to assure that it reflects all the issues presented in the case. This should include distribution of property, alimony, child support, custody of children, counsel fees, expert fees, etc. Also, the decision should detail any methodology that must be utilized to effectuate the distribution of property and any other issues that might be outstanding. A sample decision is annexed at the end of the subdivision "How to Accomplish a Domestic Divorce."

Motion to amend decision. If you feel that a particular portion of the decision is unclear or unjust, you may wish to pursue a motion to clarify and/or modify the court's decision. Your request for an amendment should be narrow and specific. Don't ask the court to totally rewrite its decision. This will not happen.

For example, assume that the court has granted the divorce under the theory that you desired, has given your client custody of the children, has given child support and alimony almost to the extent that you desired, but has awarded your client 25% of the marital property rather than 50% that you expected and felt was reasonable. You should not move to amend the decision as to child support and alimony. You should limit your motion to contesting the distribution of marital property and you should request no more than 50% of such property, assuming of course that this 50% figures is indeed reasonable. The form of the motion should be the same as any other motion that you might make. (See Chapters 9, 13, and 14 for sample motions.)

Judgment. Once the court's decision is in its final form, you and your adversary will then submit a proposed judgment. The court will either choose the proposed judgment submitted by you or the one submitted by your adversary. Therefore, it is imperative that you submit an extremely reasonable proposed judgment so that your proposal will be selected over the proposal submitted by your adversary. For example if it is equitable for your client to receive 50% of the marital property, and receive $15,000 a year in alimony and child support, don't request 75% of the marital property and $50,000 a year in alimony and child support. Ask for 50% of the marital property and $15,000 a year in alimony and child support. A sample judgment is annexed at the end of the subdivision "How to Accomplish a Domestic Divorce."

Appeal. If your client is unsatisfied with the final decision rendered by the Court, he or she may still have recourse via an appeal. For example, your client may not have been awarded custody of the children although she was a perfect mother and her husband neglected and beat the children. Your client may rightfully desire to pursue an appeal to overturn the court's unfair awarding of custody to the husband.

You should quickly file a notice of appeal as there exists in all states a certain time period after the entry of the judgment beyond which a notice cannot be filed. For example, in New York, the notice of appeal must be filed within 30 days after the service of a judgment with notice of entry. A sample notice of appeal follows.

SAMPLE NOTICE OF APPEAL

Court: County of
State of

SUSAN DOE,	:	Notice of Appeal
Appellant,	:	Index No.
-against-	:	
JOHN DOE,	:	
Appellee.	:	

SIRS:

PLEASE TAKE NOTICE that SUSAN DOE hereby appeals to the Court from a judgment of the Court rendered , which (detail relief granted by judgment)

Dated:

Yours, etc.

TO: Clerk of Court

____
Attorney for Appellee

You should be aware that each state has detailed procedural requirements re the perfecting of an appeal. These requirements relate to ordering the record, filing the record, and filing the brief. It should behoove you to contact the clerk in the local appellate court to assure that you meet the necessary filing requirements. Also, appellate courts publish rules as to their procedural requirements relating to appeals. You should obtain a copy of these rules from the clerk of the appellate court that has jurisdiction over your action.

SAMPLE APPELLATE BRIEF

A sample Appellate brief which will guide you in filing a brief on Janet's behalf follows:

Argued by

____

____

N E W Y O R K S U P R E M E C O U R T

APPELLATE DIVISION SECOND DEPARTMENT

JANET JONES

Appellant,

against

TONY JONES,

Respondent.

____

____

Attorney for Appellant.

TABLE OF CONTENTS

NEW YORK SUPREME COURT

Appellate Division—Second Department

Janet Jones,

Appellant

-against-

Tony Jones,

Respondent.

APPELLANT'S BRIEF

Preliminary Statement

This is an appeal from a judgment of the Supreme Court, rendered June 7, 1983, which (state what court did in judgment.)

STATEMENT OF FACTS

(State the relevant facts addressed at the trial court [i.e., by way of exhibits and transcript testimony], as to custody issue.)

POINT I

Plaintiff Should Have Been Awarded Custody Of Her Children Monique and Barbara Jones

The trial court pursuant to a judgment of divorce awarded custody of Monique and Barbara Jones to Tony Jones, their father. The court should have awarded custody of the children to plaintiff Janet Jones, their mother.

(Analyze law relevant to child custody issue. In other words, state what the law is as to the child custody issue in your state with reference to applicable cases and statutes. For example, state "X State gives child custody to the parent who provides the best environment for the child. *Williams* v. *Williams*, .")

(Relate facts of your case to law and show why your client should have been awarded custody of the children. For example, state "Here Janet Jones helps the children with their school work, is always available to help them with their problems, and corrects their behavior by discussing with them what they should do to improve their behavior. On the other hand, Tony never desires to spend anytime with the children, leaves them with babysitters, and when they misbehave, his solution is to beat them. Thus, Janet would provide the best environment for the children and custody of them should have been awarded to her.")

CONCLUSION

Custody of the children should have been awarded to plaintiff.

Respectfully submitted,

____

Attorney for Plaintiff

Part 5

POST DIVORCE OR SEPARATION CONCERNS

CHAPTER 13

How to Enforce Divorce Decree or Separation Agreement or Decree

SITUATION

Jean and Doug Jones have been divorced for one year. Pursuant to the divorce decree Jean obtained custody of their two children and Doug received certain visitation rights. Part of Doug's visitation included the right to have the children live with him for three weeks during the summer vacation. Also, included in the divorce decree was a provision for weekly payments to Jean from Doug for alimony and child support.

During the first few months after the divorce was finalized, Doug timely made his support payments. However, during the last few months Doug has been late in paying many of the support payments. Indeed, Jean has not received a check from Doug for support for six weeks.

Additionally, the children are presently staying with Doug for their three week summer stay. Jean has obtained reliable information that Doug intends to depart with the children in five days for a 2 month visit to Europe. Such a trip would clearly be in violation of the custody and visitation provisions contained in the divorce decree.

Jean comes to you, her attorney, for help in enforcing Doug's support obligations. More urgently, she needs your immediate help to prevent Doug from leaving for Europe with the children.

HOW TO HANDLE NONCOMPLIANCE WITH SUPPORT OBLIGATIONS

First, addressing Jean's concern with Doug's failure to meet his support obligations, it should be pointed out that there are three vehicles by which she can seek to enforce this duty. They are garnishment, sequestration, and contempt. (Sample motions which incorporate requests for garnishment, sequestration, and contempt are included at the end of this section. You would bring this motion or motions in a state court which has jurisdiction over matrimonial actions. For example, in New York, you could bring this motion in the New York Supreme Court.)

Garnishment

Garnishment is the most popular of the three methods which can be utilized to enforce support obligations. By garnishment, a portion of Doug's salary would be paid directly to Jean to meet Doug's support obligations.

Many states have a limit on the amount that can be garnished for child support. For example, in New York, this limit is 65% of the employee's salary, if he has no dependants, and 50% if he has other dependants. There are, also, federal due process considerations under the 5th and 4th Amendments that may prevent garnishment above a certain percentage of the employee's salary. Certainly due process would permit the garnishment at or below 65% for child support.

Generally, in seeking garnishment, the aggrieved party must first show that a valid divorce decree or separation agreement or decree exists which entitles him or her to a certain fixed amount of support. Next, it must be established that the party obligated to pay support has been delinquent as to the payment of support, that due demand has been made for payment and that payment has still not been made. Finally, the fact that the delinquent party is employed by a particular employer, earns a particular salary, and is fully capable of making support payments, should be noted. (See the sample garnishment motion and order contained at the end of the instant "How to Handle Noncompliance With Support Obligations" section for an example of how you would establish Jean's right to garnishment of Doug's salary.)

In bringing a motion for garnishment, the court where you bring the motion may require you to serve not only the delinquent employee, but his employer. Even if you are not required to serve the employer, such is recommended. It is the employer who will ultimately pay Jean. Any problems that the employer might have in making these payment should be ascertained immediately and not when the court issues the payroll deduction order. By informing the employer of the garnishment proceeding you will more likely be made aware of any potential payment problems envisioned by that employer.

Once Jean has shown that she is entitled to and has not received certain support payments, the court has a *prima facie* duty to issue a payroll deduction order. (In some states, for example in New York pursuant to the procedures outlined under N.Y. Civil Practice Law and Rules Section 5241, payroll deductions can be extracted from Doug's salary without court intervention.) Doug is entitled to oppose the granting of this order and submit reasons why he has not met his support obligations. However, the fact that Doug has waited until he is in arrears to argue that he can not meet his support obligations, will cause his burden of proof to be extremely high. Courts are reluctant to grant relief to one who only complains that certain obligations can not be met, when attempts are made to enforce these obligations.

Sequestration

If Doug does not have a salary that can be garnished, or his salary is not readily susceptible to a payroll deduction order in some form, you should consider attempting to obtain from a court having jurisdiction over matrimonial matters (e.g., the Supreme Court in N.Y.) an order sequestering Doug's property. By sequestration, certain property can be obtained from Doug to satisfy his support obligation to Jean.

Any type of real or personal property can be sequestered. This would include, but not be limited to, bank accounts, a house, rents, and debts. Thus, there is virtually no limit to the assets, available to you in a sequestration proceeding for the payment of Doug's arrears.

In establishing your right to sequestration, you would establish the same basic preresquisites that are necessary to obtain garnishment. That is, you must establish that certain money is owed pursuant to a valid divorce decree or separation decree or agreement. And, you must show that arrears exist which have been demanded but not paid. In addition, you possibly will be required to show that garnishment is not a viable alternative. (See sample motion contained at the end of the instant "How to Handle Noncompliance With Support Obligations" section for an example of how you would establish your right to sequestration of Doug's property.)

In seeking sequestration of Doug's property, you should request that a receiver be appointed to handle all transactions necessary re the property. If the property is not a cash asset, you must also request that the court direct sale of the asset. Further, it is axiomatic that if the property value is less than or equal to the amount owed to Jean, payment of the total proceeds should be distributed to Jean. However, if the property value is greater than the amount owed to Jean, the amount owed should be paid and the remainder held in escrow. When support payments become due to Jean in the future, they can be satisfied by this escrow account.

Important. When bringing a motion for sequestration, you should assure that you serve not only Doug, but anyone who has an interest in the property held by Doug. To proceed otherwise might result in false expectations as to what you can collect pursuant to the sequestration proceeding. For example, assume that you discover that Doug holds an instrument evidencing that Mr. X owes him $1,000. However, Mr. X has paid $500.00 and only owes Doug $500.00. You don't want to obtain a court order directing Mr. X to pay you $1,000.00 only to subsequently discover that you can only collect $500.00 from him.

Contempt

If both garnishment and sequestration proceedings would prove futile, you should seek an order which would hold Doug in contempt of court for his failure to meet his support obligation. Pursuant to this devise, the court might imprison and/or fine Doug.

Contempt is a drastic remedy and is not obtainable except in extraordinary circumstances. Basically, to obtain an order of contempt, it is incumbent upon the moving party to establish that the other party has willfully refused to meet his or her support obligations and that no other method of enforcement is available. In other words, you must establish that a support obligation is owed and has not been met, that the failure to meet the support obligation is deliberate and that the support obligation can not be met by garnishment or sequestration. (See sample motion contained at the end of the instant "How to Handle Noncompliance With Support Obligations" section for an example of how you would establish your right to have Doug held in contempt of court.)

Even if you have met the above requirements, it would still be rare for a court to punish that wrongdoer by imprisoning him or her. However, a motion for an order of contempt is still a worthwhile weapon in the attorney's arsenal. This is particularly true since the mere bringing of such a motion might very well result in the defaulting party meeting his or her support obligation.

One final note re contempt orders should be made. It is important that on the face of the motion there is a warning that informs the defaulting party that the application in question may result in him or her being fined and/or imprisoned. Otherwise, you may not be deemed to have given such party sufficient notice for the imposition of these sanctions.

In order to help you prepare the documents necessary to force Doug to meet his support obligations, sample motions and orders follow which cover garnishment, sequestration, and contempt proceedings.

SAMPLE MOTION FOR AND ORDER OF GARNISHMENT

COURT OF THE STATE OF
COUNTY OF

---x

,	:	NOTICE OF MOTION
Plaintiff,	:	Index No.
-against-	:	
,	:	
Defendant.	:	

---x

PLEASE TAKE NOTICE that upon the annexed affidavit of , sworn to on , 19 , and the exhibits annexed thereto, and upon all the prior proceedings held herein the undersigned will move this Court at a Term, Part thereof, to be held at the Court of the State of , County of , located at on the- day of , 19 , at 9:30 o'clock in the forenoon of that day or as soon thereafter as counsel can be heard, for the following relief:

(a) A money judgment, pursuant to Domestic Relations Law Section , against the defendant in the sum of representing arrears in support the defendant was ordered to pay the plaintiff.

(b) A wage deduction and garnishment order and,

(c) Such other and further relief as the Court deems just and proper.

PLEASE TAKE FURTHER NOTICE that pursuant to answering affidavits, if any, must be served upon the undersigned at least ( ) days before the return date of this motion.

Dated:

Attorneys for

TO:

Attorneys for

COURT OF THE STATE OF
COUNTY OF

--x

,	:	*AFFIDAVIT IN SUPPORT OF MOTION*
Plaintiff,	:	Index No.
-against-	:	
,	:	
Defendant.	:	

--x

STATE OF)
) ss.:
COUNTY OF)

, being duly sworn, deposes and says:

1. I am the plaintiff in this matrimonial action and submit this affidavit in support of my motion for enforcement of the support award of this Court dated , 19 (, J.) (Exhibit "A"), which ordered my husband to pay $ a week maintenance and $ a week child support for our two children, effective , 19 . Retroactive sums were to be paid off at the rate of $ a week. Payments were to commence 10 days after service of a copy of the order with notice of entry. On , 19 , a copy of the order was so served on the office of , my husband's attorneys (Exhibit "B".)

2. Since the effective date of this order, my husband has made payments to me of $ a month, and thus, for the (#) weeks that have elapsed since the effective date of the order through , 19 , a total of $ was due and my husband has paid only $ leaving a balance due of $.

3. This money is urgently needed for the support of our two children, (name) and (name), who are and years old respectively, and live with me.

Although demand has been duly made for my husband to do so, he has failed to provide me with the money ordered by the Court. Because I had insufficient funds to support myself and our two growing children, numerous debts have been piling up. I have been threatened with the loss of telephone and electric service, and have received several foreclosure notices. (Exhibits "C" and "D".) Clearly, the monies my husband has been paying me have been insufficient to meet our needs.

4. As my husband has disregarded demands that payment be made under the order and in order to assure payment, I request that this Court, in addition to granting me a money judgment for the arrears due, issue a wage deduction and garnishment order in the sum of $ plus an additional $ a week until the arrears of $ are paid so that I can be assured of ongoing and continuing payments.

5. My husband has been employed by for years, earns yearly, and can continue to work for such employer as long as he desires. Thus, he is fully capable of meeting the above support obligations.

WHEREFORE, I respectfully request that the relief sought herein be granted in its entirety.

____

Sworn to before me this
day of , 19 .

____

PRESENT: HON. ______________________

COURT OF THE STATE OF
COUNTY OF

--x

,	:	WAGE DEDUCTION
Plaintiff,	:	AND
-against-	:	GARNISHMENT
,	:	ORDER
Defendant.	:	

--x

The plaintiff, , has requested that this Court issue an order granting plaintiff a wage deduction order, with respect to defendant's employment by , in order to enforce payment of alimony payments ordered under a final decree of divorce entered in the office of the Clerk of the County of , State of , on , 19 ;

NOW, on motion of , attorney for plaintiff, it is

ORDERED, ADJUDGED, and DECREED that , employer, will deduct form the amount payable to the defendant $ each week, which will be applied to ensure compliance with the order of support contained in the final decree of divorce between the parties, and $, which will be applied towards the arrears until $ shall be paid and to remit the deducted amount to plaintiff, , at , , within days of the date that defendant is paid; and it is further

ORDERED, ADJUDGED, and DECREED that , employer, will notify the plaintiff's attorneys promptly if , ceases to work for and will give if known, defendant's home and new employment address to plaintiff.

ENTER

____

SAMPLE MOTION FOR AND ORDERS OF CONTEMPT AND SEQUESTRATION

COURT OF THE STATE OF
COUNTY OF

---x

,	:	*NOTICE OF MOTION*
Plaintiff,	:	Index No.
-against-	:	
,	:	
Defendant.	:	

---x

Warning: THE PURPOSE OF THIS HEARING IS TO PUNISH , THE DEFENDANT HEREIN, FOR A CONTEMPT OF COURT, AND SUCH PUNISHMENT MAY CONSIST OF FINE OR IMPRISONMENT, OR BOTH, ACCORDING TO LAW.

Warning: YOUR FAILURE TO APPEAR IN COURT MAY RESULT IN YOUR IMMEDIATE ARREST AND IMPRISONMENT FOR CONTEMPT OF COURT.

PLEASE TAKE NOTICE that upon the annexed affidavit of , sworn to on , 19 , the Order of- Justice dated , 19 , and upon the exhibits annexed thereto and all the papers and proceedings heretofore had herein;

AND, it being alleged presumptively by the aforesaid affidavit, affirmation and the order directing the defendant-husband to pay to the plaintiff-wife *pendente lite, inter alia*, the mortgage payments, the premiums on the homeowner's insurance and the gas, electric, and water utility bills, as well as the medical and dental expenses of the children of the parties, and $ per week for the support of plaintiff and the children; and it being alleged that the defendant has deliberately and willfully failed and refused to comply with the said order, and that defendant is presently in default in *pendente lite* payments in the amounts enumerated in the annexed affidavit, and no security having been posted for the payment of arrears;

The Undersigned will move this Court, at a Term, Part , thereof, to be held at the Court,

County, , , on the day of , 19 , at A.M., or as soon thereafter as counsel can be heard, for the following relief:

1. For an order adjudging the defendant to be in contempt of Court pursuant to Domestic Relations Law, Section , for his failure and refusal to pay the Court ordered *pendente lite* sums awarded plaintiff and the children;
2. For an order granting plaintiff the right to docket a money judgment in the sum of $ against said defendant;
3. For an order pursuant to DRL, Section , causing defendant's personal property, including some or all of his dental office equipment, to be sequestered and sold to pay such sums as defendant has defaulted in paying;
4. Ordering defendant to pay plaintiff's additional legal fees and expenses incurred in connection with this proceeding, in the sum of $5,000;
5. For such other and further relief as to this Court may seem just and proper.

PLEASE TAKE FURTHER NOTICE that pursuant to answering affidavits, if any, must be served upon the undersigned at least ( ) days before the return date of this motion.

Dated: ,

, 19

, ESQS.

Attorneys for plaintiff

TO:

COURT OF THE STATE OF
COUNTY OF

---x

,	:	*AFFIDAVIT*
Plaintiff,	:	Index No.
-against-	:	
,	:	
Defendant.	:	

---x

STATE OF)
) ss.:
COUNTY OF)

, being duly sworn, deposes and says:

1. I am the plaintiff herein and make this affidavit in support of the relief requested in the annexed notice of motion, including holding defendant in contempt, and to enforce the order of Justice , dated , 19 directing defendant to pay certain expenses for the support and maintenance of myself and our two children.

DEFENDANT HAS WILLFULLY DISOBEYED THE ORDERS OF THIS COURT

2. It was defendant's unreliable and indifferent behavior with respect to payment of the necessary expenses for the two children and myself which led to my seeking and receiving an order of temporary maintenance and child support on , 19 (, J..) A true copy of Justice order is annexed hereto as Exhibit "A". Among other items, Justice ordered that defendant pay to me $ per week, *pendente lite*, for the support of myself and the children of the marriage. In addition, defendant was directed to pay, *pendente lite*, the mortgage payments, the premiums on the homeowners insurance, and the gas, electric, and water utility bills. Furthermore, defendant was ordered to pay the medical and dental expenses of the children, *pendente lite*. At that time I was also granted exclusive possession of the marital residence located at , , where

I reside with our two children, whom I was awarded custody of during the pendency of this action. Since the date of Justice order, defendant's payments of the above have been erratic and discretionary, and were often made only after numerous letters and telephone calls from my attorneys to his attorneys. For instance, defendant's payment of weekly support and maintenance for myself and the children is usually late, and each week I am unsure if he will even pay me at all.

3. It is because of defendant's refusal to comply with discovery requests that I do not possess any current financial statements and/or tax returns for defendant. In addition, upon information and belief, defendant earns in excess of $ per year. Annexed as Exhibit "B" is a copy of defendant's 19-- partnership return, of which defendant has a half interest, or approximately $, reported partnership income.

4. Annexed as Exhibit "G" is defendant's Net Worth Affidavit as of and sworn to on . I have set forth these documents, to show to this Court that defendant is well able to comply with the Supreme Court Order, and in fact, has made no motions to appeal this Court's decision.

5. I have absolutely no source of income or funds with which I can meet my expenses. I am living in a constant state of fear, with rising debts. I cannot live on the generosity and the patience of my friends and family, and the amount that I am able to borrow is not nearly enough to meet the minimum needs of my children and myself.

6. The following is a summary of the current outstanding bills which defendant was required by this Court to pay, but has not paid. As this Court will note, these include mortgage payments, doctor bills, and household utilities. I have already received several foreclosure notices from Bank, where our mortgage is held. Defendant is currently *four months* behind in mortgage payments, and we now stand to lose the house because of his wilful failure to comply with this Court's order. The various doctors and dentists which have treated my children are refusing further services unless their bills are brought up to date. Defendant has succeeded in placing me in a precarious and desperate situation, and I look to this Court for relief.

7. The total of the outstanding bills (Exhibit "D"), for which defendant remains in arrears and is solely responsible to pay, is $ ______________ . Defendant has the resources to pay these bills, which he has already been ordered to pay. Defendant's blatant disregard for this Court's orders and especially for the health and welfare of his children should be condemned by this Court, and an order of contempt should be granted. If defendant does not have the cash available to make these payments, then I request that his office equipment, valued in the net worth statement as worth at least $, be sequestered and sold to make these payments.

8. I respectfully state that defendant can well afford to comply with this Court's orders. His refusal to do so is contemptuous, arbitrary, and a harassment

of me and the children. In addition, I am faced with the constant threat of losing the house, having the water turned off, and being unable to obtain medical and dental services for the children.

9. I request that defendant be held in Contempt of Court, and that a money judgment in the amount of $ be awarded to me against defendant, and in addition, defendant's (enumerate property) be sequestered and sold to meet his obligations to myself and the children. Although I have requested a money judgment and sequestration as forms of relief, these remedies are basically ineffectual when it comes to paying the bills which are currently outstanding and long overdue. The threats of termination of utilities as well as the foreclosure of our home, are real and present, and the time it may take to enforce a money judgment or to sell defendant's dental equipment will merely prolong our suffering, aggravate the situation, and cause irreparable harm to the children and myself, while allowing defendant to openly defy the order of this Court.

10. The defendant's wilful purpose in unilaterally defaulting in the required payments, even after the Court has ordered him to do so, is to render it impossible for me to continue prosecuting this matrimonial action, and more importantly, to render it impossible for me and the children to live.

COUNSEL FEES

11. I respectfully request that this Court order defendant to pay me additional counsel fees and expenses which I have incurred solely as a result of his refusal to honor the order of this Court. I request that defendant pay me the sum of $ for the preparation of this motion. Inasmuch as defendant has engendered the bringing of this motion by his contempt of the Order of this Court, it is reasonable to direct him to pay the legal fees incident to said motion.

12. I urge the Court to act on this application in an expeditious manner and to punish the defendant for his callous indifference to the children and myself.

WHEREFORE, it is respectfully requested that the Court grant me the relief requested in the annexed notice of motion.

____

Sworn to before me this
day of , 19 .

____

PRESENT: HON. ____________________

Court of the State of
, County of

--x

,	:	Index No.
Plaintiff,	:	ORDER OF CONTEMPT
-against-	:	
,	:	
Defendant.	:	

--x

The plaintiff , has requested that this Court issue an order punishing defendant, , for his failure to make certain payments ordered under a judgment of this Court entered on .

NOW, on motion of , attorney for plaintiff, it is;

ORDERED, ADJUDGED, AND DECREED that defendant, , has committed the offenses charged and is guilty of contempt of court because he defaulted in his payment of money required to be paid by the judgment entered on , and his behavior was meant to and did defeat and prejuduce the rights of the plaintiff, and it is further;

ORDERED, ADJUDGED, AND DECREED

That a fine of $ be imposed on defendant for his behavior and that defendant pay plaintiff's attorney costs in this proceeding of $, and it is further

ORDERED, ADJUDGED, AND DECREED that defendant be committed to the County Jail and remain charged with contempt of Court until the above mentioned fine and attorney's fees shall be paid.

ENTER:

____

PRESENT:
HON. ______________________

Court of the State of
, County of
--x

, : Index No.

Plaintiff, : ORDER OF SEQUESTRATION AND APPOINTING RECEIVER

-against- :

, :

Defendant. :
--x

The plaintiff, , has requested that this Court issue an order which appoints a receiver of certain personal property and the rents and profits of certain real property of defendant in sequestration proceedings, in order to enforce alimony payments ordered under a fiscal decree of divorce entered in the office of the Clerk of the County of , State of , 19 .

Now, on motion of , attorney for plaintiff, it is;

ORDERED, ADJUDGED, AND DECREED that is appointed receiver of the personal property and the rents and profits of the real property of , is directed to take possession of such real and personal property and hold the same, will apply the personal property and rents and profits of the real property toward the amounts owes under a final decree of divorce entered in the office of the Clerk of the County of , on , and will deliver possession of his (her) personal and real property to the receiver.

ENTER:

____

VIOLATION OF CUSTODY AND VISITATION RIGHTS

Addressing last, but certainly not least, Jean's concern with Doug's contemplated violation of her custody and his visitation rights, Jean would be best advised to seek a writ of habeas corpus to solve this problem.

When a party is not under any time constraints re the enforcement of visitation and/or custody rights, it is more practical and appropriate to incorporate requests for relief in this area in the motion for enforcement of support. If support is being paid and the only violation by Doug is visitation and/or custody, you could utilize the same motion discussed earlier in the chapter re support without requesting any relief for support. In that motion, you might request an order of contempt for a particular party's wilful disregard for particular custody and/or visitation rights.

However—as is true in Jean's case—when a party requires immediate relief re a violation of custody and/or visitation rights, and the faulty party has physical possession of the children, seeking a writ of habeas corpus might be the only appropriate solution. While the relief that can be obtained pursuant to the writ is limited, i.e., obtaining the production or release of a particular person or persons, it can be a valuable tool in providing quick and effective solutions to custody and visitation problems. By the writ process, Doug can be forced to immediately bring the children before the court where an immediate decision will be rendered preventing him from taking them to Europe for two months.

The sample petition for a writ of habeas corpus included in Chapter 9 will enable you to prepare the documents necessary to quickly stop Doug's attempt to violate his visitation rights.

CHAPTER 14

How to Modify Divorce Decree or Separation Agreement or Decree

SITUATION

Anita Jones has been divorced from Gary Jones for two years. Before the divorce, Anita entered into a separation agreement with Gary. Considering that Anita intended to reside in the same town as Gary after their divorce, Gary was provided with weekly visitation of their 10 year old child in the separation agreement. Further, at the time Anita entered into the separation agreement, she had a job which paid very well. Indeed, Anita's high salary played a significant role in the determination of what support she would receive for herself and the child via the separation agreement. Moreover, once Anita divorced Gary, the rights and responsibilities of the parties outlined in the separation agreement became the rights and responsibilities of the parties after the divorce.

Recently Anita lost her job. She has been able to find other employment. However, the salary she will receive is much less than the salary she received at her old job. Additionally, this new job is located in another state at a 500 mile distance from her present residence.

DETERMINE WHAT CLIENT DESIRES

Anita has unsuccessfully attempted to negotiate with Gary for a modification of his visitation rights and support payments. She had hoped to change

Gary's visitation from once every week to several large blocks of time during the course of the year. Additionally, she had hoped to obtain more financial support from Gary in lieu of her changed financial circumstances. Indeed, Anita will have to substantially lower her standard of living if she does not receive additional support from Gary. Anita comes to you, her attorney, for help to obtain judicial modification of Gary's visitation rights and support obligations.

ANALYZE SEPARATION AGREEMENT

The first task that you must undertake is an analysis of the separation agreement. You must determine whether there was any overreaching on Gary's part when the separation agreement was entered into or whether the terms of the separation agreement are unconscionable. Specifically, you should (1) view Anita and Gary's financial and employment picture; and (2) evaluate Anita and Gary's custodial and visitation desires, at the time the separation agreement was formulated. Then, you should view the separation agreement to ascertain exactly what each obtained re custody and visitation, support, and division of assets. If Gary (1) gives support much below his ability to pay, and the needs of Anita and the children; (2) leaves Anita with few assets; and (3) receives custody and/or visitation rights which place tremendous burden on Anita and no burdens on him; you can safely assume that the separation agreement was unconscionable and that there was overreaching. (See Chapter 11 for a detailed discussion as to the procedures to follow to assure that your client obtains a fair separation agreement.) Further, you must determine whether any fraud or duress was employed by Gary in formulating the agreement. Specifically, you must talk to Anita and ask her what subtle pressures were employed by Gary to obtain the separation agreement; and what, if any, false claims or promises were utilized by Gary to obtain the separation agreement. If any of the above exists, the court will at the very least modify the terms of the agreement and may throw out the agreement in its entirety.

CHECK FOR ARBITRATION CLAUSE

Next, assuming for argument's sake that the separation agreement cannot be modified or invalidated pursuant to the above and that you have decided to commence a lawsuit to modify the terms of the agreement, you must check the agreement to determine if it contains an arbitration clause before commencing such a lawsuit. Courts have uniformly held that where the agreement contains such a clause, one must attempt to arbitrate any dispute before judicial relief can be obtained.

LUMP SUM BUYOUT

Assuming arguendo that the separation agreement cannot be invalidated, before you take any further action to modify Gary's support obligations for Anita and his child—whether by arbitration or judicial proceedings—you might want to consider negotiating with Gary's attorney for a lump sum payment which would satisfy Gary's future support obligations for Anita. You should not attempt a lump sum buyout as to Gary's child support obligations. For all intents and purposes, a lump sum buyout agreement is unenforceable as to Gary's child support obligations.

Advantages of Lump Sum Payment

The lump sum payment would be most advantageous for Anita if she anticipates that her financial status will improve considerably in the future, or that Gary's will decrease considerably. By the lump sum payment, (a) she would possess capital to overcome her present financial crises which should carry her until her financial conditions improve; (b) she would not have to pay income tax on the lump sum payment; [although she would have to pay income tax on any alimony received;] (c) she would be free to remarry without concerning herself as to the loss of alimony payments; and (d) she would cancel the need to concern herself with obtaining money due her for her support in the event Gary died or left for parts unknown.

The lump sum payment would also be beneficial for Gary. He would totally satisfy his support obligations for Anita. He would no longer be concerned with what effect an increase in his financial position, or a decrease in that of Anita's, would have on this obligation.

Calculating Lump Sum Payment

In working out the lump sum payment, actuarian tables pertaining to the life expectancy of the parties should be consulted. Usually, the life expectancy table pertaining to the wife will be utilized. This is true because the life expectancy of the wife would usually be longer than that of the husband. You should hire an actuary—who is an expert familiar with analyzing, preparing and reading actuarian tables—to determine what lump sum payment is warranted by a particular support obligation.

JUDICIAL MODIFICATION OF SUPPORT OBLIGATIONS

Alimony

In determining whether Anita might be entitled to a judicial modification of Gary's support obligations for her, it is crucial that you ascertain whether the separation agreement provided for merger into the divorce decree or whether the agreement survived that decree and was incorporated into it by reference. If the agreement merged into the divorce decree, you would be in the same situation that you would be in if there was no separation agreement and alimony had been awarded pursuant to a court decree entered after litigation. That is, you would only have to show that there was a change of circumstances in order to obtain relief. For example, if Gary's income greatly increased or decreased, or Anita's income or needs greatly increased or decreased since the separation agreement was consummated, the courts would probably determine that a change of circumstances has occurred which warrants judicial intervention.

On the other hand, if the separation agreement survived the divorce decree, then Anita would only be entitled to an increase in support if she can show that there has been an incredible change in circumstances which will produce severe financial hardship. She would have to be on the verge of being placed on welfare to be entitled to relief. Likewise, if Gary was attempting to modify an agreement which survived the divorce decree, he would have to establish that he was utterly financially unable to meet the support obligations imposed on him by the agreement.

In Anita's instant situation, her drastic drop in income would probably entitle her to relief if the separation agreement had been merged into the divorce decree.However, considering that Anita is not destitute, she would probably not be entitled to any relief if the argreement survived and was merely incorporated by reference into the divorce decree.

Important. It is important to note at this juncture that in drafting a separation agreement, you should assure that it survives the divorce decree if you wish finality as to support obligations. Only the rarest of circumstances will enable a court to modify the support obligations contained in a separation agreement that has survived the decree. If you desire that support obligations change with changing circumstances, you should provide for merger of the separation agreement into the decree. Most attorneys opt for a survival provision and finality. Otherwise, they may find themselves in court every other week litigating whether there has been a new change in circumstances.

Note. It should also be noted that even if a divorce decree is amicably obtained,(i.e., without litigation); if it is obtained without the benefit of a separation agreement, any provision relating to support will be automatically merged into the decree. Thus, the alimony arrangements obtained pursuant to a divorce which does not have the benefit of a separation agreement may undergo constant revision. Whenever one party feels that circumstances have changed as to entitle that party to a more favorable support provision, the court will be petitioned for a modification of support obligations.

Child Support

In the recent past, the general rule was that child support and spousal support would be viewed in the same light. That is, a determination as to whether a separation agreement merged into or survived the divorce decree was crucial. Today, the general rule has changed. In regard to child support, all that need be shown today, to obtain a modification of the support obligations, is that something arose in regard to the support obligation that was unforeseen when the separation agreement was written. Thus, today, basically any change will justify review of the child support obligation and this is true whether the separation agreement has merged into or survived the divorce decree.

In Anita's case, she would have no trouble obtaining an increase in child support. The fact that she lost her job and had to settle for a new job whose salary was considerably less than the old job, is not a circumstance that can be said to have been foreseen when the separation agreement was constructed.

JUDICIAL MODIFICATION OF CUSTODY AND/OR VISITATION

Doctrine of Merger and Survival Inapplicable

In determining whether there should be a change in custody and/or visitation, the doctrine of merger and survival is inapplicable. No matter how the existing arrangements came about, the courts will grant relief if there has been an unforeseen change in circumstances. The paramount issues involve an analysis as to what is in the child's best interests.

Change in Custody

As to a change in custody, the court will be concerned with whether there has been a change in regard to which parent can provide the best financial and emotional climate for the child. For example, one parent may now be much better able to absorb certain education expenses of the child than the other parent. Also, the custodial parent may be encountering disciplinary problems re the child that the other parent would not encounter. Additionally, one of the parents may now have a drug problem or be involved in a homosexual or heterosexual relationship that might not be emotionally healthy for the child. Further, aside from the question of which parent can now provide the best financial and emotional climate for the child, the custodial parent might affect his or her right to sole custody by moving to a location which deprives the other parent of visitation rights. For example, assume that both parents reside in New York at the time of divorce and the divorce decree or separation agreement provides for visitation by the noncustodial parent every other weekend. If the custodial parent moves to Alaska, the noncustodial parent will be effectively deprived of his or her visitation rights. In this posture, the court might very well determine that some sort of joint or shared custody arrangement might be appropriate.

Change in Visitation

As to a change in visitation, the courts will view the stability of the parent entitled to visitation. If that parent, for example, has become an alcoholic, he or she may no longer be entitled to overnight visitation and may be restricted to daytime visitation. The same result may ensue if the parent entitled to visitation is having tremendous conflicts with the child or children. Additionally, if one parent is moving a considerable distance from the other parent so that frequent visitation is no longer practical, the parent entitled to visitation may receive less often but longer periods of visitation. For example, instead of having visitation every other week, the visiting parent may have the child or children during the entier summer vacation and the winter and spring recesses.

In Anita's case, considering the great distance she is moving from Gary, she should be able to obtain a modification of Gary's visitation rights. She should be able to force Gary to accept several large blocks of visitation during the course of the year. However, she should at this time be extremely careful not to commit any act or take any course of conduct which might affect her custodial rights. Gary may attempt to utilize her move and financial instability to obtain permanent custody of the child.

HOW TO INITIATE ACTION FOR MODIFICATION OF DIVORCE DECREE OR SEPARATION AGREEMENT OR DECREE

In order to permit you to file the necessary documents on Anita's behalf, a sample motion and order for modification of support and visitation follows. If Anita did not have custody of the children and was seeking a change in custody in addition to a change in support and visitation, she would merely add a change in custody to the items requested in the motion and order and could insert reasons justifying her custody request in her supporting affidavit. This motion should be filed in the court in your state which has jurisdiction over domestic relations. For example, if Anita resided in New York, she could file her motion in the Supreme Court in her county of residence.

SAMPLE MOTION AND ORDER FOR MODIFICATION OF SUPPORT AND VISITATION

At a Special Term, of the State of New York, held in and for the County of , at the , New York, on the day of

PRESENT:

HON. ______________________
Justice

---x

,	:	Index No.
Plaintiff,	:	*ORDER TO SHOW CAUSE*
-against-	:	
,	:	
Defendant.	:	

---x

Upon reading and filing the affidavit of , sworn to on , and upon all papers and proceedings herein,

LET, , the , show cause before at a Special Term of this Court, to be held at , County, on the day of at (time) , or as soon thereafter as counsel can be heard, why this Court should not issue an order which:

1) Modifies the divorce decree and the Separation Agreement between the parties, dated , 19 .
2) Reduces plaintiff's obligation to pay maintenance and child support in the sum of per month to per month on the grounds of a substantial change in financial circumstances.
3) Modifies the periods of visitation on the ground that plaintiff is required to move and will be denied visitation under the existing visitation schedule.
4) Awards plaintiff such other and further relief as this Court may deem just and proper.

SUFFICIENT reason appearing, let personal service of a copy of this order and the papers upon which it was granted, on or before the day of , be deemed sufficient.

ENTER:

____

AFFIDAVIT

Court of the State of
: County of

, Plaintiff,	:	Index No.
	:	AFFIDAVIT
-against-	:	
,	:	
Defendant.	:	

STATE OF)
) ss.:
COUNTY OF)

, being duly sworn, deposes and says:

1. I am the plaintiff in the above entitled action and make this affidavit in support of my motion to modify the divorce decree entered on , 19 , and the Separation Agreement between defendant and myself, dated , 19 , (which was incorporated but not merged in the divorce decree) reducing my required payments to defendant of maintenance and child support, and modifying the periods of visitation due to the substantial changes in circumstances.
2. Defendant and I entered into a Separation Agreement on
We were divorced on

3. Under paragraph of the Separation Agreement, I was required to pay to defendant for her support and maintenance and the support and maintenance of our children. Under paragraph of the Separation Agreement, my visitation was .
4. On I lost my job. I have found a new job whose salary is less than my previous job. Also, the new job is in the state of , miles from where my children and wife reside.
5. WHEREFORE, based on the foregoing substantial change in circumstances, I respectfully request that this Court issue an order modifying the Separation Agreement and reducing my obligation for maintenance and child support to , and changing my schedule of visitation to .

____

Sworn to before me this
day of , 19 .

ORDER OF MODIFICATION

____

PRESENT: HON. _______________

Court of the State of
: County of

---x

, : Index No.

Plaintiff, : *ORDER OF MODIFICATION*

-against- :

, :

Defendant. :

---x

The plaintiff , has moved this court for an order modifying the divorce decree entered in and the separation agreement executed , by plaintiff and defendant.

NOW, on motion of , attorney for , it is:

ORDERED AND ADJUDGED, AND DECREED:

That the said divorce decree and separation agreement are modified in accordance with the dictates of this order, and it is further;

ORDERED, ADJUDGED, AND DECREED

That the plaintiff pay to the defendant on Monday of each week, commencing on , to the defendant at the following address, or at any other place defendant may designate pursuant to a written communication to plaintiff, the sum of $, per week, for the weekly support and maintenance of defendant and the children of the parties, and it is further;

ORDERED, ADJUDGED, AND DECREED that plaintiff shall have visitation with the parties' two children on the following days and at the following times, and it is further;

ORDERED that any relief requested by the parties other than that addressed above, is denied.

ENTER

____

Part 6

HOW TO BILL YOUR CLIENT

CHAPTER 15

Legal Fees and Retainer Agreements

SITUATION

Karen Jones has decided to retain you to handle her impending divorce. You have not discussed with her what and how she should pay you to handle her case. Indeed, you are in a quandary as to what remuneration should be requested and when it should be paid.

You know that there exist three basic fee arrangements i.e., contingency fees,flat fees, and hourly rates. But, you are not certain as to what fee mechanism you should utilize. You know that retainer agreements are commonly entered into with clients. But, you do not know what sum of money you should immediately request from Karen as the *quid pro quo* for commencing work on her action.

DETERMINING WHICH FEE MECHANISM TO UTILIZE

Contingency Fees

Contingency fee arrangements (i.e., receipt of a certain fee if you successfully advance your client's cause or a percentage of the property and/or alimony received by your client) are not appropriate in actions involving domestic relations. Indeed, almost every state has determined that contingency fee arrangements in the domestic relations arena are unethical.

Thus, even if your state permits such a fee, it should be incumbent on you not to attempt to utilize such a fee arrangement to obtain renumeration for your services to Karen because the contingency arrangement may cause your client at the time of settlement to believe you possess a conflict of interest.

Flat Fees

With the advent of our modern, complicated society and resultant more complicated legal process, the popularity of flat fees has greatly diminished. Indeed, it is only in the rare case, e.g., a simple uncontested divorce action, that a flat fee should be utilized. To make use of this fee arrangement in most situations would prevent you from accurately charging your client for the actual time you have invested in the client's case, since contingencies would inevitably arise that would significantly increase the estimated time.

Some attorneys have attempted to retain the use of the flat fee by charging a flat fee and adding to it if the attorney determines that the case has consumed more time than anticipated. The problem with this approach is that increases in fees are not based on any concrete basis and the client is left with the feeling that the attorney is taking advantage of him or her.

Thus, you would be best advised to avoid using any variation of flat fee arrangements in billing Karen unless, of course, time spent on her cause can be precisely determined.

Hourly Rates

By far the most prevalent method for remuneration in the domestic relations action is the hourly rate. By this method you can not only accurately bill Karen, but she will know exactly what she is receiving for the money she dispenses.

In determining what to charge, a different rate should apply when a senior partner, a junior partner, and/or an associate works on the case. Also, a different rate could be applied for time spent for negotiations as opposed to litigation. Time spent for litigation would be assessed at a higher rate.

In computing the time consumed by negotiations, time spent on the telephone should be included. Also, the travel time spent to reach the place where negotiations are held should also be added to the negotiation time. Likewise, the travel time spent to reach the court where a particular litigation is taking place, should be added to the litigation time.

Many attorneys add a bonus arrangement to their retainer agreement to compensate them for extraordinary results in the client's behalf.

In order to help you ascertain what hourly rate you should charge Karen, the hourly rate in 1986 for attorneys in major metropolitan areas such as New York, Boston, Los Angeles, and Houston varied from $175 to $350 per hour. The 1986 hourly rate for cities where population is approximately 100,000, varied from $150 to $200 per hour. The 1986 hourly rate for rural communities varied from $100 to $125 per hour.

In addition to the hourly rate billings that will be given to Karen, she should also be responsible for the payment of certain out-of-pocket disbursements. These should include, but not to be limited to, court fees, expenses for expert witnesses and other witness fees, charges by consultants, accountants, actuaries, appraisers, travel expenses, court reporter expenses, photocopy fees, and long distance telephone call expenses.

DRAFTING RETAINER AGREEMENTS

After you have determined which approach you will use to charge Karen, you should draft a retainer agreement which will be signed by Karen and yourself and returned to you. This agreement should outline exactly how you intend to bill her. Also, assuming that you intend to bill Karen by an hourly rate, the agreement should outline the fact that in addition to the hourly rate, Karen will be responsible for certain out-of-pocket expenses. Moreover, in this agreement you should require that Karen make a prompt payment (i.e., the retainer) of a certain amount. In 1986 in New York City, the typical retainer ranged from approximately $2,500 to $10,000. The $10,000 retainer was reserved for the complex matrimonial action which involved the distribution of millions of dollars in property and assets.

In order to enable you to draft a professional retainer agreement for Karen, the following sample retainer agreement letter has been attached.

SAMPLE RETAINER AGREEMENT LETTER

Dear :

This letter will serve to confirm the fact that you have retained my firm to represent you in the captioned matter from this date on. You have agreed to pay us promptly a retainer of $, and in this regard we are enclosing a copy of our bill. Your retainer will cover our time up to an approximate total of hours based upon our time records commencing with the initial interview on 19 .

If the time exceeds the initial time period you will be liable for an additional fee based upon our time rate of $ per hour for each additional hour.

If you should decide to discontinue our services for you in this matter prior to its resolution or in the event of a reconciliation, then you shall only be responsible for time computed at the above rate of $ per hour.

This retainer does not include any work in appellate courts, any other actions or proceedings or out-of-pocket disbursements. Out-of-pocket disbursements include but are not limited to, costs of filing papers, court fees, expert witnesses, consultants, accountants, actuaries, appraisers, postage, calendar service, process servers, witness fees, court reporters, long distance telephone calls, travel, parking, and photocopies normally made by us or requested by you, which disbursements shall be paid for or reimbursed to us upon our request.

You have been advised that under the New York Equitable Distribution Statute there is a possibility that title to any part of or all of the Marital Assets may be transferred to you or to your husband and that there may be a question in defining what is a Marital Asset, subject to transfer, and Separate Property, which is not. Because it is presently unknown what transfers may occur or be deferred, it is impossible to place a value upon the results. Our time rate does not contemplate the results achieved with regard to obtaining or deferring the transfer of assets or any other aspects of the outcome of this matter. You may, therefore, be liable for an additional fee which cannot presently be ascertained, and which is in addition to that part of our fee based upon time. This will be left to our further discussions after the results are reviewed and our future agreement of what is fair and reasonable based upon those results. We shall, of course, endeavor to collect from your husband all or part of the legal fees chargeable to you.

Please sign one copy of this letter and return same to me with your retainer check.

Sincerely yours,

I have read and I understand
the above letter, having received
a copy of same, and I accept all
of its terms.

____

Index

D

E

O

P

Q

R

S

W

[illegible] 95 1295/-